D1285429

The American Woman
in Colonial and Revolutionary Times,
1565–1800

A SYLLABUS WITH BIBLIOGRAPHY

The American Woman in Colonial and Revolutionary Times, 1565–1800

A SYLLABUS WITH BIBLIOGRAPHY

Eugenie Andruss Leonard
Sophie Hutchinson Drinker
Miriam Young Holden

GREENWOOD PRESS, PUBLISHERS
WESTPORT, CONNECTICUT

Library of Congress Cataloging in Publication Data

Leonard, Eugenie Andruss, 1888-
  The American woman in colonial and Revolutionary
times, 1565-1800.

  Reprint of the ed. published by the University of
Pennsylvania Press, Philadelphia.
    1. Women--United States--Bibliography. 2. United
States--Social life and customs--Colonial period,
ca. 1600-1775--Bibliography. I. Drinker, Sophie
Lewis Hutchinson, joint author. II. Holden, Miriam
Young, joint author. III. Title.
[Z7964.U49L4 1975]   016.30141'2'0973   74-27221
ISBN 0-8371-7883-5

Originally published in 1962 by the University of Pennsylvania Press,
Philadelphia

© 1962 by the Trustees of the University of Pennsylvania

Reprinted with the permission of the University of
Pennsylvania Press

Reprinted in 1975 by Greenwood Press
A division of Congressional Information Service
88 Post Road West, Westport, Connecticut 06881

Library of Congress Catalog Card Number 74-27221

ISBN 0-8371-7883-5

Printed in the United States of America

10 9 8 7 6 5 4 3

Contents

Introduction

As AMERICAN WOMEN we owe, in large part, whatever rights and privileges we now enjoy to our colonial forebears. It was the pioneer women who, through their fortitude and industry, gave us the unique position we hold at present. The problems concerning our functions in society that we now face have the roots of their answers in the beliefs and actions of the pioneer women. These cannot be understood fully without a knowledge of their beginnings in the primitive colonial settlements.

Nearly 3,000 years ago, a Hebrew philosopher raised the question, "Who can find a virtuous woman, for her price is above rubies?" (Proverbs 31;10) He answered his own question by listing the perennial duties of the homemaker. It is amazing how well he described the woman of colonial America and, in essential elements, the woman of today.

But seeking information regarding women of bygone days is like looking for a needle in the proverbial haystack of historical writings. For the present study, over 1,200 sources on life in America from 1500 to 1800 were consulted for data on women. The present *Bibliography* contains 765 books, 309 magazine articles, and 8 pictorial publications. In the collection of this data, I have been assisted by Sophie Hutchinson Drinker, who is chiefly responsible for the addition of the magazine articles, and Miriam Young Holden, both of whom have suggested sources and made helpful suggestions regarding the compilation of the *Syllabus*.

The *Syllabus* has been organized to give the student an inclusive picture of the colonial woman in all aspects of her life and work. A number of references have been included under each topic, not only for breadth of information but also because some of the references may not be readily available.

5

To facilitate the study of the individual women of note, a *List of 104 Outstanding Women* has been compiled by Sophie Hutchinson Drinker, with references on each.

It is hoped that *The Syllabus with Bibliography* will prove useful as an outline for the study of the colonial women and as a ready reference for writers and others interested in the life of the period.

Eugenie Andruss Leonard
August 15, 1960

Key To Use

The *American Woman in Colonial and Revolutionary Times* contains three parts that are closely interrelated. They consist of:

1. The SYLLABUS, in which the references are grouped under specific headings and sub-headings. In order to save space, only the initials of the authors are given, the titles of books (including pamphlets) and magazine articles are contracted, and the names of magazines are abbreviated. Commas are used in the titles of books and magazine articles to indicate the omission of words. The abbreviations of the names of the magazines with the full name of each are given below.

2. The LIST OF 104 OUTSTANDING WOMEN has the references grouped under the name of each woman. These are indicated by item numbers of the references to be found in the BIBLIOGRAPHY. The item numbers of the references are followed by page numbers where needed. Thus, to look up Mrs. Charlotte Browne, page 113, one would turn to the two item numbers under her name, e.g., item no. 149 in the BIBLIOGRAPHY, Calder, Isabel M., Colonial Captures etc., pp. 169-198, and item no. 793, Browne, Charlotte, "Mrs. Browne's Diary" etc., V. M. H. B. 32:305-320 (1924).

A few of the 104 women are included specifically in the SYLLABUS because they made a significant contribution in the particular field of endeavor.

3. The BIBLIOGRAPHY consists of three parts, e.g., books (including pamphlets), magazine articles, and pictorial publications. All items in the BIBLIOGRAPHY are alphabetically numbered from 1 to 1082. Under Books and Pictorial Publications are given the full name of the author, the full name of the book, the place of

publication, the name of the publisher, and the date of publication of the edition used.

Under Magazine Articles are given the full name of the author, the full title of the article, the abbreviation of the name of the magazine, and the volume number, page numbers, and years of publication.

Abbreviations

American Colonial Tracts	Amer. Col. Tracts
American Philosophical Society. Proceedings	Amer. Phil. Soc. Proc.
American Repository for Useful Information	Amer. Repository
Antiquarian	Antiqu.
Antiques	Antiques
Bibliographical Society. Papers	Biblio. Soc. Papers
Bibliographical Society. Proceedings	Biblio. Soc. Proc.
Bostonian Society. Publications	Boston Soc. Publ.
Boston Public Library Quarterly	Boston Libr. Quart.
Camden County Historical Society Magazine	Camden Co. H.S.M.
Connecticut Magazine	Conn. Mag.
Connecticut Quarterly	Conn. Quart.
Dedham Historical Register	Dedham H.R.
Delaware History	Del. Hist.
Essex Antiquarian	Essex Antiq.
Essex Institute Historical Collections	Essex Inst. H. Colls.
Florida Historical Quarterly Review	Fla. H.Q. Rev.
The Friend	The Friend
Friends Historical Association Bulletin	Friends H.A. Bull.
Friends Historical Society Journal	Friends H.S. Journ.
Friends Intelligencer	Friends Intell.
Georgia Historical Quarterly	Ga. H. Quart.
Georgia Review	Ga. Rev.
Granite State Magazine	Granite State Mag.
Granite Monthly	Granite Monthly
Half Moon Series	Half Moon Series
Huguenot Society of South Carolina. Transactions	Huguenot S.S.C. Trans.
International Studio	Internat. Studio

Ipswich Historical Publications	Ipswich H. Publ.
Johns Hopkins University Studies	Johns Hopkins Univ. Studies
Lancaster County (Pa.) Historical Society Journal	Lancaster Co. H.S. Journ.
Long Island Historical Society Quarterly	Long Island H.S. Quart.
Lower Norfolk County (Va.) Antiquary	Lower Norfolk Co. Antiq.
Maryland Historical Magazine	Md. H. Mag.
Massachusetts Historical Society Collections	Mass. H.S. Colls.
Massachusetts Historical Society Proceedings	Mass. H.S. Proc.
Medical Review of Reviews	Medical Rev. Rev.
Moravian Historical Society Transactions	Moravian H.S. Trans.
Nantucket Historical Association Proceedings	Nantucket H.A. Proc.
New England Magazine	New Engl. Mag.
New England Quarterly	New Engl. Quart.
New Haven Colony Historical Society Collections	New Haven Col. H.S. Colls.
New Jersey Historical Society Collections	N.J.H.S. Colls.
New Jersey Historical Society Proceedings	N.J.H.S. Proc.
New Music Review	New Music Rev.
Newport Historical Society Bulletin	Newport H.S. Bull.
New York Historical Society Collections	N.Y.H.S. Colls.
New York Historical Society Proceedings	N.Y.H.S. Proc.
New York Historical Society Publication Fund	N.Y.H.S. Publ. Fund
New York State Historical Association. Proceedings	N.Y. State H.A. Proc.
New York State Historical Association Quarterly Journal	N.Y. State Quart. Journ:
North Carolina Historical Review	N.C.H. Rev.
North Carolina Law Review	N.C.L. Rev.

Pennsylvania Historical Magazine	Pa. H. Mag.
Pennsylvania Magazine of History and Biography	P.M.H.B.
Smith College Studies	Smith College Studies
South Carolina Historical and Genealogical Magazine	S.C.H.G. Mag.
South Carolina Historical Association Collections	S.C.H.A. Colls.
South Carolina Historical Association Proceedings	S.C.H.A. Proc.
South Carolina Historical Association Publications	S.C.H.A. Publs.
Southern Historical Society Publications	Southern H.S. Publs.
Tyler's Quarterly of History and Genealogy Magazine	Tyler's Quart.
University of Maine Bulletins	Univ. Maine Bulls.
University of Texas Bulletins	Univ. Texas Bulls.
Virginia Magazine of History and Biography	V.M.H.B.
William & Mary Quarterly	W.M. Quart.
Worcester Society of Antiquity Bulletins	Worcester S.A. Bulls.
Worcester Society of Antiquity Collections	Worcester S.A. Colls.
Wyoming Historical and Genealogical Magazine	Wyoming H.G. Mag.

The American Woman
in Colonial and Revolutionary Times,
1565–1800

A SYLLABUS WITH BIBLIOGRAPHY

Syllabus

I

GENERAL REFERENCES FOR THE PERIOD

Whoever would understand women in the American Colonial and Revolutionary periods must first review the general setting of their life and work. At their husbands' side or alone, they played a dynamic part in the struggle, first for continued existence in the new world and later for the creation of a nation.

The following references were selected chiefly because of their emphasis on family and productive life in which women made their major contributions.

Allen, W. Amer. Biog. Dict.
Andrews, C. M. Colonial Background.
Beard, C. and M. Hist. U. S.
Boorstin, D. The Americans.
Calhoun, A. W. Soc. Hist., Amer. Family, Vol. 1.
Carman, H. J. Amer. Husbandry, Vols. 1 & 2.
Channing, E. Hist. U. S. Vols. 1 & 2.
Coman, K. Indust. Hist. U. S.
Commons, J. R. Hist. Labor U. S. Vol. 1.
Hale (Mrs.) S. J. Distinguished Women.
Johnson, A. Dict. Amer. Biog. Vols. 1 - 20.
Malone, D. Dict. Amer. Biog.
Schlesinger, A. M. New Viewpoints in Amer. Hist.
Sutherland, S. Population Distribution of Colonial Amer.
Wertenbaker, T. J. First Americans.
Wilson, J. G., & Fiske, J. Cyclopaedia Amer. Biog.
Wright, L. B. Cultural Life Amer. Colonies.

II

ENGLISH AND EUROPEAN BACKGROUNDS OF THE WOMEN WHO EMIGRATED TO THE NEW WORLD

The women who emigrated from England and the European continent during the sixteenth to eighteenth century brought with them the knowledge, skills, and cultural heritage of their homelands. These included ability in a wide variety of home industries, merchandising enterprises, professional services, educational endeavors, and religious leadership. Most of these abilities are discussed in the research studies listed below.

Anderson, J. Memorable Women, Puritan Times, 2 Vols.
Benson, M. S. Women, 18th Cent. Amer., pp. 1 - 99.
Calhoun, A. W. Soc. Hist., Amer. Family. Vol. 1, chaps. i, ii.
Clark, A. Working Life, Women, 17th Cent.

Clark, D. L. Brockden Brown and the Rights of Women.
Gardiner, D. English Girlhood at School, pp. 194-393.
Meyer, G. B. The Scientific Lady in England.
Pinchbeck, I. Women Workers and Indust. Revolution (English).
Putnam, E. The Lady, pp. 211-281.
Reynolds, M. The Learned Lady, England.
Riley, H. T. Liber Albus.
Seybolt, R. F. Apprenticeship and Apprenticeship Educ., pp. 1-21.
Smith, F. M. Mary Astell.
Stenton, D. M. The English Woman, Hist.
Stopes, C. C. British Freewomen.
Van Rensselaer (Mrs.), J. K. Mana-ha-ta, pp. 1-17.
Wallas, A. Before the Blue Stockings.
Wheeler, E. R. Famous Blue Stockings.
Woody, T. Hist. Educ. Women. Vol. 1, chaps. i, ii.
Wright, L. B. Atlantic Frontier, pp. 3-49.

III

WOMEN IN THE EARLIEST SETTLEMENTS OF THE FUTURE UNITED STATES

On most of the exploratory trips to the New World, women were not included in the ship's companies. When permanent settlements were considered, women emigrated as members of families or as individuals.

1. General Statements

In the first century of immigration to the New World, many national groups were represented. Also, many different motives sent the wanderers adrift from their homes. Some sought the unknown for sheer adventure. Some came from religious motives, either to Christianize the natives or to gain freedom of religious thought for themselves. Others dreamed of financial gain. Some came from fear of political oppression or vengeance. Some, white and negro, men and women, came in chains and found no freedom.

Beard M. Through Women's Eyes, pp. 10-53.
Eggleston, E. Beginners of a Nation.
Moller, H. "Sex Composition, Colonial Amer." W. M. Quart. Ser.
     3, Vol. 2: 113-153.

2. From Spain and Portugal

Women and children were among the earliest settlers in Florida. Francisca Hinestrosa, wife of a Spanish soldier in Fernando De Soto's expedition, is known to have been with the expedition on March 4, 1541, when she was killed in a fire set by the Chickasaw Indians. Other women from Spain and Portugal came with the colonization expeditions of Don Luis de Velasco (1550) and Pedro de Aviles Menendez

(1565, 1573) and became a part of the first permanent colony in the New World.

Onate's expedition from Mexico established the first Spanish settlement in New Mexico (1598) with 400 soldiers, of which 130 were members of families. From New Mexico they emigrated west to Arizona, north to Colorado, and east to Texas.

Anza's first expedition from Mexico to California (1774) included a few women who were part Indian. In his second expedition (1775-1776), twenty-nine wives of soldiers were included and became part of the first permanent Spanish settlement in California.

Bancroft, H. H. Works. Vol. 18 (Hist. of Càlif. Vol. 1) : 387-393, 732-744.

Bancroft, H. H. Hist., Ariz., & N. M., pp. 145 ff.

Blackman, L. W. Women, Fla., pp. 21-29.

Bolton, H. E. Anza's California Expedition. Vol. 1 & 2.

Bolton, H. E. Spanish Exploration, Southwest, p. 211 ff.

Bolton, H. E. Rim of Christendom, pp. 8-11, 502-510.

Chapman, C. E. Founding, Spanish Calif., pp. 120, 127, 218, 347-350, 462.

Chapman, E. E. Hist., Calif., pp. 221-222, 299, 303-305, 398-400.

Chavez, Fray A. Origins, N.M. Families. Intro., p. 19 ff.

Fairbanks, G. F. Spaniards, Fla.

Hamilton, P. J. Hist., N. Amer. Vol. 3: 10-18, 24.

Hammond, G. P. Onate and Founding, N.M., pp. 69-70, 89.

Hittell, T. H. Hist., Calif. Vol. 1: 509, 518-531.

Hodge, F. W. et al. Revised Memorial Benevides.

James, G. W. In and Out, Old Missions, pp. 1-43.

Jones, W. H. Hist., Catholic Educ., Colo., pp. 3-9.

Robertson, J. A. De Soto's Discovery of Fla. Vol. 2: 149, 368.

Robinson, W. W. Ranchos Become Cities.

Sargent, D. Our Land and Our Lady, pp. 1-64.

Shea, J. G. Hist., Catholic Church, U.S. Vol. 1: 100-215.

Shipp, B. Hist., De Soto and Fla., p. 398.

Smith, B. De Soto's Conquest. Fla. Vol. 1: 105; Vol. 2: 133-134.

Teggart, F. J. Anza's Expedition. Vol. 3, no. 1, 25 ff.

Twitchell, R. E. Spanish Arch., N.M. Vol. 1, see index under women's names.

Twitchell, R. E. Facts, N.M. Hist. Vol. 1: 310 ff.

U.S. De Soto Expedition Committee. Final report, pp. 83, 226.

Varner, J. G. & J. J. Fla. of the Inca, p. 403.

3. From the British Isles

Women comprised a part of each of the English colonizing expeditions. Seventeen suffered from an unknown fate of the lost colony on Roanoke Island in 1587. In spite of repeated disasters, the women continued to come to the new, rough-hewn settlements along the Atlantic coast from Maine to Georgia.

A. Jamestown and Other Southern Settlements

The first permanent English settlement in the New World was made at Jamestown in 1607 by the London Company. Mistress Forrest and Ann Burras joined the colony in 1608 and other women soon followed to help in building the colony.

In 1633, a group of dissenters in the colony moved south and formed the first English settlements in the Carolinas.

Leonard Calvert and his 200 colonists, 52 of whom were women, landed in Maryland in 1634 and established a thriving colony along the Chesapeake Bay.

In 1733, Theophilus Oglethorpe left England with 130 persons (35 families) and established the first permanent settlement at Savannah.

Andrews, M. P. Founding, Md. Vol. 1: 59-60, 85, 199-200.
Beverly, R. Hist., Va., pp. 24-89, 231-232.
Bozman, J. L. Hist., Md. Vol. 2: 30.
Brewer, J. M. List, Early Md. Settlers.
Browne, W. H. Md., Hist., Palatinate.
Coulter, E. M. "First Ga. Settlers," Ga. Hist. Quart. Vol. 31: 282-288.
Early, R. H. By Ways, Va. Hist., pp. 152-153.
Eggleston, E. Beginners of a Nation, pp. 71-72.
Fiske, J. Old Va. and Neighbors. Vol. 1: 156-318.
Green, H. C. & M. W. Pioneer Mothers. Vol. 1: 8-9, 221-223, 299-311.
Hall, C. C. Narratives, Early Md., see index, women's names.
Hamilton, P. J. Hist., No. Amer. Vol. 3: 50-382.
Hotten, J. C. Original list, Persons, pp. 35-145, 149-155, 169-195, 265.
Jester, A. L., & Hiden, M. M. Adventurers, Purse and Person.
Logan, M. S. Part Taken by Women, pp. 30-37
Neill, E. D. Va. Carolorum, pp. 328-330.
Newsome, A. R. "Records of Emigrants," No. Car. Hist. Rev.
    Vol. 11: 39-54, 129-142.
Nugent, N. M. Cavaliers and Pioneers.
Rogers, L. Tar Heel Women, pp. 1-8.
Sargent, D. Our Land and Our Lady, pp. 119-167.
Shea, J. G. Hist. Catholic Church, U.S. Vol. 1: 40-86, 93-94, 371 ff.
Sioussat, A. M. Colonial Women, Md., pp. 11-17.
Spruill, J. C. Women's Life and Work, pp. 3-11, 14.
Spruill, J. C. "Women Founding Southern Colonies," No. Car. Hist.
    Rev. Vol. 13: 202-218.
Stanard, M. M. Colonial Va., pp. 15-54.
Va. Mag. Hist. & Biog. "London Order." Vol. 6: 232.
Woody, T. Hist., Educ., Women. Vol. 1: 239-240.
Wright, L. B. Atlantic Frontier, pp. 50-160, 258-301.

B. New England Settlements

In 1620, the Mayflower passengers from London and Leyden landed at Plymouth, Massachusetts. Among the 102 colonists were 24 women who had survived the tortuous journey. By the end of the first year there remained only 15 women in the colony. Undeterred, other women followed them into the wilderness with each new colonizing group.

Massachusetts Bay Colony was established in 1629. New Hampshire was colonized in 1623 by David Thomson and a small band of pioneers who settled at Rye. Connecticut had a permanent settlement by 1634, and Roger Williams brought a group of religious zealots from Massachusetts Bay Colony to form a new colony in Rhode Island in 1636. Sir Fernando Gorges set up a colony in Maine in 1635 and Vermont had a permanent English settlement at Brattleboro by 1724.

Ames, A. Mayflower Log, pp. 58, 65, 145, 154, 169, 184, 278.
Andrews, C. M. The Colonial Period. Vol. 1: 60-64, 100-113, 134-139, 500-502.
Andrews, H. F. Listing, Freemen, Mass. Bay Colony, 1630-1691.
Beedy, H. C. Mothers, Maine, pp. 34-36.
Bolton, C. K. Scotch-Irish Pioneers.
Bradford, W. Hist., Plymouth, pp. 106-400.
Earle, A. M. Colonial Dames, pp. 49-52.
Flint, M. B. Early Long Island, pp. 104-115.
Fowler, W. W. Women, Amer., Frontier, pp. 20-21.
Green, H. C., & M. W. Pioneer Mothers. Vol. 1: 221-223.
Hinchman, L. S. Early Settlers, Nantucket.
Holman, M. C. "Story, Amer. Womanhood: Lady Fenwick," Conn. Mag. Vol. 11: 251-254.
Hotten, J. C. Lists of Persons.
Hudson, A. S. Hist., Sudbury, Mass., pp. 27-29.
James, B. B. Hist., No. Amer. Vol. 5: 26-60.
Lewis, A. Hist., Mass., pp. 74-75.
Marble, A. R. Women, Mayflower.
Noyes, E. J. Women, Mayflower and Plymouth.
Pew, W. A. "Lady Arabella," Essex Inst. Hist. Coll. Vol. 66: 395-410.
Weeden, W. B. Hist., New Engl. Vol. 1: 193.
Willison, G. P. Saints and Strangers, pp. 156-157.
Winsor, J. Mem. Hist., Boston. Vol. 4: 332-333.
Wright, L. B. Atlantic Frontier, pp. 98-160.

C. Settlements in New York, New Jersey, and Penna.

The English settlers in the middle Atlantic colonies were few in number before 1664, when Richard Nicholls established English sovereignty in what is now New York and New Jersey. William Penn established his colony in Pennsylvania in 1682. Women's names appear in each of the lists of colonizers.

Best, M. A. Rebel Saints, pp. 296-312.
Clement, J. M. Settlers, Newton, N.J., pp. 109-125.
Fiske, J. Dutch and Quaker Colonies. Vol. 2.
Mickle, I. Reminiscences, Gloucester, N.J., p. 49.
O'Callaghan, E. B. Hist. New Netherlands. Vol. 1: 258-287.
Overton, J. Long Island Story, pp. 41-43, 53-54.
Stewart, F. H. Notes, Gloucester, N.J., pp. 293-302.
Thompson, B. Hist., Long Island, pp. 83-84, 438-443.
Va. Mag. Hist. & Biog. "Order to Send 100 Children." Vol. 6: 232.
Whitehead, W. Arch. New Jersey. Ser. 1, Vol. 1: 414, 490.

4. From Holland, Belgium, and Germany

The Dutch settled in Manhattan between 1615 and 1623. The Belgians (or Walloons) came to the New Netherlands in 1624 and moved north to settle near Albany, New York. Pastorius and his German Mennonite group settled in Germantown, Pennsylvania, in 1682. Another group of Germans settled at Salzburg, Georgia, in 1751.

> Bayer, H. G. The Belgians.
> Bernheim, C. D. Hist., German Settlements, pp. 56-190.
> Bittinger, L . F. Germans, Colonial Times.
> Calhoun, A. W. Soc. Hist., Amer. Family. Vol. l: 48-49, 252.
> Colton, J. Annals, Manhattan.
> De Brahm, J. G. Hist., Three Provinces: So. Car., Ga., East Fla.,
>   p. 20 ff.
> Faust, A. B. German Element, U.S. Vol. 1, chaps. i-xi.
> Fernow, B. Docs., Colonial N.Y. Vol. 14: 325-326.
> Fiske, J. Dutch and Quaker Colonies in Amer. Vols. 1 & 2.
> Green, H. C. & M. W. Pioneer Mothers. Vol. l: 155-158, 397-410.
> Hamilton, P. J. Hist., No. Amer. Vol. 3: 306, 381.
> James, B. B., & Jameson, J. F. Journ., Jasper Dankaerts, p. 236.
> James, J. F. Narratives, New Netherlands, p. 75.
> Jones, F. R. Hist., No. Amer. Vol. 4: 180-208.
> Van Rensselaer (Mrs.), J. K. Mana-ha-ta, pp. 1-53.
> Wright, L. B. Atlantic Frontier, pp. 161-257.

5. From Africa and the West Indies

In 1619, some Dutch ship masters sold their first cargo of Negro slaves to the planters at Jamestown, Virginia. Other ship masters followed their example; some traded directly from Africa and others by way of the West Indies.

> Green, H. C. & M. W. Pioneer Mothers. Vol. l: 14.
> Greene, L. J. The Negro, Colonial New Engl., pp. 15-48, 337-347.
> Hamilton, P. J. Hist., No. Amer. Vol. 3: 83.
> Smith, G. G. Story Ga., pp. 33-34, 48-50, 67.

6. From Sweden and Finland

The Swedish colonists settled in Delaware in 1638, and in 1643 began settlements in Pennsylvania.

> Acrelius, I. Hist., New Sweden, pp. 23-43.
> Benson, A. B., & Hedin, N. Swedes in Amer., pp. 6-86.
> Biddle, G. B., & Lowrie, S. D. Notable Women, Pa., pp. 2-4.
> Clay, J. C. Annals, Swedes, Del.
> Johnson, A. Swedes, Del., pp. 144-151.
> Stockton, F. R. New Jersey, pp. 51-56.

. From Jewish Settlements in Europe

Small groups of Jewish people joined other refugee colonists and settled in
ach of the colonies. They came to New Amsterdam in 1684 and to Georgia in
733. The first land (100,000 acres) purchased for a Jewish settlement was bought
y Joseph Salvador near Fort Ninety-six in South Carolina in 1755.

  Elzas, B. Jews, So. Car.
  Fiske, J. Dutch and Quaker Colonies. Vol. 2: 333-336.
  Hirsh, M. B. "Jewish Colony, Lancaster Co., Pa.," Lancaster Co.
    Hist. Soc. Papers. Vol. 5: 91-105.
  Lebeson, A. B. Jewish Pioneers, Amer., pp. 1-95.
  Lee, F. D., & Agnew, J. L. Hist., Savannah, p. 8.
  Marcus, J. R. Early Amer. Jewry. Vol. 1: 24, 58-72.
  Pool, D. S. Portraits Etched in Stone, see index women's names.
  Weeden, W. B. Hist., New Engl. Vol. 1: 161.

. From France

Women were among the French Huguenots who came to South Carolina in 1562
nd to Florida in 1564. Both settlements were destroyed, and the women and chil-
ren killed or taken prisoners by the Spanish and English. The first permanent
'rench colony was established in New Orleans, Louisiana, in 1699. However,
housands of French Protestant refugees joined colonizing groups in England and
olland and settled in each of the colonies along the Atlantic seaboard. In 1755,
hen the British expelled the French Acadians from Nova Scotia, several thou-
ands of French women were forced to emigrate to New England, South Carolina
nd other southern settlements.

  Baird, C. W. Hist., Huguenot Emigration. Vol. 2: 112-114, 182-183,
    396-397.
  Bayer, H. G. The Belgians, p. 149.
  Cable, G. W. Stories, La., pp. 25-38.
  De Forest, E. J. A Walloon Family, Amer. Vol. 1: 92-101, 205-208.
  Fairbanks, G. R. Spaniards, Fla., pp. 13-23.
  Fosdick, L. J. French Blood, Amer., pp. 125-362.
  Green, H. C. & M. W. Pioneer Mothers. Vol. 1: 410-420.
  Hamilton, P. J. Hist., No. Amer. Vol. 3: 33-36, 144, 196-269, 381.
  Jones, F. R. Hist., No. Amer. Vol. 4: 179-185.
  King, G. E. New Orleans, pp. 52-54.
  Lord, R. H. et al. Hist., Arch Diocese, Boston, pp. 203-209.
  McCrady, E. Hist., So. Car. Proprietary Govt., pp. 319-323.
  Rightor, H. Hist., New Orleans, p. 8 ff.
  Smith, H. E. Colonial Days and Ways, pp. 125-166.
  Webber, M. L. "Journ., Ann Manigault," So. Car. Mag. 20, 21; see index.
  Winsor, J. Mem. Hist., Boston. Vol. 2: 249-268.
  Woody, T. Hist., Educ., Women. Vol. 1: 240.

. From Mediterranean Countries

21

Florida became an English colony in 1763. In 1769, Dr. Andrew Turnbull interested 1,500 people from Greece, Italy, and the Minorcas to emigrate to Florida and establish "New Smyrna" and to cultivate indigo and tropical fruits.

Blackman, L. W. Women, Fla., p. 49.
Dogget, C. Smyrna Colony, pp. 17-18.
Panagopoulos, E. P. "Greek Settlers in New Smyrna Colony," Fla. Hist. Quart. Vol. 35: 95-115.

IV

HEROIC AND PATRIOTIC ACTIVITIES OF COLONIAL WOMEN

All of the early settlements from Maine to Florida had certain hardships in common. Indians had to be placated or fought for the occupation of land. The land itself had to be cleared for crops and houses built with timber felled with tools that were crude and scarce. Local governments had to be worked out for the common welfare. Women shared the hazards of pioneer life with the men. Battles with the Indians were fought in their own back yards. Many of the women followed their husbands in the struggle for independence. Others guarded their homes and children. No colony was without a long list of such heroines who fought and died for freedom.

Andrews, M. P. Va., pp. 105-106
Baker, J. W. Hist., Hart. Co., Ga., pp. 25-30.
Barber, J. W., & Howe, H. Hist. Colls., N.J., pp. 101,212, 259, 343, 365.
Bartlett, H. R. 18th Cent. Ga. Women, pp. 79-88.
Biddle, G. B., & Lowrie, S.D. Notable Women, Pa., pp. 16-17, 21-23, 36-38, 52-54, 59-60, 67-68, 71-73.
Blackman, L. W. Women, Fla., pp. 42-48.
Blumenthal, W. H. Women Camp Followers.
Boorstin, D. Amer., pp. 349-350.
Boudinot, J. J. Life, Elias Boudinot. Vol. 1: 28.
Bradley, A. M. "Hannah Bradley," Granite Mon. Vol. 43: 315-317.
Brown, A. et al. Three Heroines, pp. 15-134.
Bunce, O. B. Romance, Revolution, pp. 110-117, 147-150, 162-165, 236-252, 273-275, 323-326.
Butler, C. Hist., Groton, Mass., pp. 336-337.
Butts, S. H. Mothers, Ga., pp. 139-140.
Calhoun, A. Soc. Hist., Amer. Family. Vol. 1: 278-283.
Campbell, A. D. "Some Men of Revolution," Quart. N.Y. State Hist., Assoc. Vol. 3: 155-168.
Chapman, J. A. School Hist., So. Car., pp. 135-138.
Clement, J. Noble Deeds, Penna. Women, pp. 80-84, 95-96, 108-110, 125.
Cometti, E. "Women, Amer. Revolution," New Engl. Quart. Vol. 20: 329-346.

Coulter, E. M. Hist., Ga., pp. 132-134.
Coulter, E. M. "Nancy Hart, " Ga. Hist. Quart. Vol. 39: 118-151.
Crawford, M. C. Little Journeys, pp. 37-58, 130-146, 170-189.
Darrach, H. "Lydia Darragh," P.M.H.B. Vol. 23: 86-91.
Desmond, M. E. "Hannah Dustin" Granite Monthly. Vol. 31: 287-293.
Dexter, E. A. Colonial Women, pp. 74-77.
Earle, A. M. Colonial Dames, pp. 246, 258-275.
Egle, W. H. Some Penna. Women, see Index.
Ellet, E. F. Women, Amer. Revolution. Vols. 1, 2, & 3: see index.
Ellet, E. F. Domestic Hist., Amer. Revolution, pp. 61, 100.
Fowler, W. W. Women, Amer. Frontier, pp. 22-23, 34-67, 81-83, 90-
121, 125-149.
Freeze, J. G. Hist., Columbia Co., Penna., pp. 196-205.
Garden, A. Anecdotes, Revolutionary War. Vol. 2: 213-420; Vol. 3:
10-201.
Green, H. C. & M. W. Pioneer Mothers. Vol. 1: 241-279, 375-383,
425-442. Vol. 2: 4-7, 31-452; Vol. 3: 1-526.
Griffin, A. Journ., pp. 135-143.
Hall, E. H. Margaret Corbin.
Hanaford, P. A. Daughters, Amer., pp. 33-64.
Harriman, W. "Mary Woodwell" Granite Monthly. Vol. 4: 233-239.
Hart, A. B. Com. Hist., Mass. Vol. 3: 306-334, 338.
Hazard, S. Register, Penna. Vol. 1: 48; Vol. 8: 24-27.
Heard, J. John Wheelwright, pp. 128-136.
Holden, J. A. "Jane McCrea," N.Y. State Hist. Assoc. Proc. Vol. 12:
249-294.
Holliday, C. Women's Life, pp. 116-124, 301-312.
Hulton, A. Letters of a Loyalist Lady.
Humphrey, G. Women, Amer. Hist., pp. 30-54.
Hurd, I. H. Hist., Essex Co., Mass. Vol. 1: 704.

Iconophiles, Soc. of. Washington's Reception, Trenton, N.J.

Jackson, F. Hist., Newton, Mass., pp. 191-192.
Jones, F. R. Hist., No. Amer. Vol. 4: 203.

Kercheval, S. Hist., Valley, Va., pp. 96-108, 370-371.
Knight, L. L. Ga.'s Landmarks. Vol. 2: 1040-1042.

Lamson, D. F. Hist., Manchester, Mass., pp. 325-326.
Lebeson, A. B. Jewish Pioneers, pp. 231-239.
Lee, F. B. N.J., Colony & State. Vol. 2: 259-262.
Lee, F. B. Arch., N.J. Ser. 2, Vol. 2: 102, 195-196, 270, 343-344.
Logan, M. S. Part Taken by Women, pp. 18-204.
Lord, R. H. et al. Hist., Arch Diocese, Boston. Vol. 1: 39, 44-47.
Lyman, S. E. "Three N.Y. Women," N.Y. Hist. Soc. Quart. Bull.
No. 29: 77-82.
McArthur (Mrs.), J. L. "Women of the Revolution," N.Y. State Hist.
Assoc. Proc. Vol. 5: 153-163.
McCrady, E. Hist., So. Car. Proprietary Govt., pp. 196-197.
McLean (Mrs.) D. "Baroness de Riedesel," N.Y. State Hist. Assoc.
Proc. Vol. 3: 39-44.
Mann, H. Female Review.
Marcus, J. R. Early Amer. Jewry. Vol. 2: 96-99, 104-107.

Marvin, A. P. Hist., Lancaster, Mass., pp. 10, 95, 98-114.
Meloon, E. S. "N.H. Heroines," Granite Monthly. Vol. 60: 22-25
Merrill, J. Hist., Amesbury & Merrimack, p. 283.
Messler, A. Hist., Somerset Co., N.J., pp. 121-125.
Mills, E. L. "How Molly Saved the Fort." Granite Monthly. Vol. 14: 276-281.
Mills, W. J. Hist. Houses, N.J., pp. 108-114, 227.
Moschzisker, A. von. Emergency Aid.
Nelson, W. Arch., N.J. Ser. 1, Vol. 27: 657; Ser. 2, Vol. 4: 167, 188-189, 235-236, 486-488, 502-505, 552, 640-642.
Norton, M.L. "A Mistery Solved," Conn. Quart. Vol. 2: 59-65.
Nourse, H. S. Records, Lancaster, Mass., pp. 98-106, 131-137, 323-326.
Parker, A. C. "Baroness Riedesel," N.Y. State Hist. Assoc. Proc. Vol. 26: 109-119.
Parry, E. S. Betsy Ross.
P.M.H.B. Narratives, Indian Captives, P.M.H.B. Vol. 29: 407-420.
Perley, S. "Moll Pitcher" Essex Antiq. Vol. 3: 33-35.
Phillips, J. D. Salem, 18th Cent., pp. 13-17.
Post, L. M. Diary, Grace Barclay.
Powers, G. "Frontier Heroine" Granite Monthly. Vol. 6: 55-56.
Powers, G. Hist., Coos Co., N.H., pp. 148-151.
Quynn, D. M. "Flora MacDonald" No. Car. Hist. Rev. Vol. 18: 236-258.
Raum, J. O. Hist., N.J. Vol. 1: 76-78; Vol. 2: 19, 70-71.
Rawle, A. "Loyalist's account," P.M.H.B. Vol. 16: 103-107.
Reed, W. B. Life of Esther de Berdt Reed.
Reed, W. B. Life and Correspondence, pp. 253-269.
Ricord, F., & Nelson, W. Arch., N.J. Ser. 1, Vol. 9: 226-228; Ser. 1, Vol. 10: 547-548, 614-615.
Riley, A. J. Catholicism, New Engl., pp. 280-296.
Rochefoucault-Liancourt, F. Travels. Vol. 1: 373-375.
Rogers, L. Tar Heel Women, pp. 9-22.
Ross, P. Hist., Long Island. Vol. 1: 235-236.
Salley, A. S. "Col. M. Bruton," S.C.H.S. Mag. Vol. 2: 148-151.
Scharf, J. T., & Westcott. T. Hist., Phila. Vol. 2: 1689-1691.
Scheer, G. F., & Rankin, H.F. Rebels and Redcoats, see index.
Scudder, H. E. Men and Manners, pp. 22-23.
Sellards, E. H. "Captivity, Jennie Wiley," Tyler's Quart. Vol 31: 256-262.
Sickler, J. Hist., Salem Co., N.J., p. 174.
Sinnickson, L. "Baroness Riedesel," P.M.H.B. Vol. 30: 385-408.
S.C.H.G. Mag. "Emily Geiger," S.C.H.G. Mag. Vol. 2: 90-91.
Stafford, S. S. "Flag of 'Bon Homme Richard,'" N.J.H.S. Proc. Ser. 2, Vol. 2: 193-194.
Stockton, F. Hist., N.J., pp. 59-68, 130-140.
Stone, E. M. Hist., Beverly, Mass., pp. 83-84.
Stone, W. L. Letters and Journal, Mrs. Riedesel.
Stryker, W. S. Battles of Trenton and Princeton, p. 122, note.
Stryker, W. S. Arch., N.J. Ser. 2, Vol. 1: 280-281, 418-420.

Symmes, F. R. Hist., Old Tennent Church, pp. 102-103, 106-107.

Taylor, E. W. "Hannah Dustin" Granite Monthly. Vol. 43: 177-183; Vol. 46: 207-214.

Temple, J., & Sheldon, G. Hist., Northfield, Mass., see index under Mrs. Rowlandson.

Terry, R. "Minister's Wife, Revolution" Conn. Mag. Vol. 11: 523-532.

Trumbull, J. R. Hist., Northampton, Mass. Vol. 1: 299-314, 349-356, 488-491, 508-540.

Tyler, L. G. "Lady Virginia Murray," W. M. Quart. Ser. 1, Vol. 24: 85-101.

Vinton, J. A. Life of Deborah Sampson.

Virginia Gazette, 1769. "Ladies of the Association," W. M. Quart. Ser. 1, Vol. 8: 36.

Waters, T. F. Ipswich, Mass. Vol. 2: 298-300.

White, G. Hist. Colls., Ga., pp. 441-443.

Whiton, J. M. Hist., N.H., pp. 28-29, 50-53, 62, 100-101.

Whitton, M. O. These Were the Women, pp. 1-27.

W. M. Quart. "Heroines of Virginia," W. M. Quart. Ser. 1, Vol. 15: 39-41.

Winsor, J. Mem. Hist., Boston. Vol. 3: 150; Vol. 4: 341.

Wister, C. J., & Irwin, A. Worthy Women, pp. 9-42, 71-111, 113-127, 229-257, 259-328.

Worcester Soc. Antiq. "Heroines." Bull. No. Vol. 16: 396-397.

Worthington, E. "Widow Draper," Dedham Hist. Soc. Reg. Vol. 7: 1-6.

V

THE STATUS AND RIGHTS OF COLONIAL WOMEN

In American colonial life, the rights and privileges accorded women varied from approximate equality with men to the negation of all equal rights. Laws in most cases protected their property rights and their rights of inheritance. Their rights in marriage were limited by laws, but pioneer conditions often voided the laws. Their right to participate in the governing bodies and to hold office in the community was limited except where necessity forced the issue. As productive units in society, they were essential; and it is in these areas that the customs and courts protected the rights of both the free women and those in bondage, in spite of laws to the contrary.

1. The Free Woman

There is no sharp line of demarcation between the free woman and the woman in bondage during the colonial period. "Free woman" is used to indicate all those women who, whether married or not, were accorded rights to their person and were given some property and inheritance rights.

A.   The Attitudes Toward Women

a.   Men's Opinions

Men's attitudes toward women in the colonial period fall into
four general categories. Burnaby, Byrd, Franklin, Winthrop, and
others wrote of women as very limited in mental capacity. Stearns,
John Adams, Branagan, Neal, and many others stressed their amiabil-
ity and moral strength. The Dutch in New Amsterdam, the Quakers, and
the Moravians educated the women along with the men, but gave them no
political rights. Thomas Paine and Brockden Brown wrote vigorously
in defense of the equal rights of women in home and community life.

Adams, J. Sketches, Hist., Fair Sex.
Bassett, J. S. Writings, Wm. Byrd, p. 361.
Benson, M. S. Women, 18th Cent. Amer., pp. 104-135.
Bowne, E. S. Girl's Life 80 Years Ago, pp. 60-61.
Branagan, Excellency, Female Character.
Burnaby, A. Travels, No. Amer., pp. 1-107.
Calhoun, A. Soc. Hist., Amer. Family. Vol. 1: 92, 274-275.
Clapp, T. "Womanhood, Early Amer.," Conn. Mag. Vol. 12:
    233-239.
Clark, D. L. Brockden Brown, Rights of Women, pp. 37-48.
Conway, M. D. Life, Thomas Paine. Vol. 1: 45-47.
Hammond, G. P. Onate and the Founding, N.M., pp. 69,89,etc.
Holliday, C. Women's Life, pp. 132-133.
Morison, S. E. Builders, Bay Colony, pp. 234, 239-240.
Neal, J. A. Essay, Female Sex.
Smyth, A. H. Writings, Benjamin Franklin. Vol. 2: 87.
Spruill, J. C. Women's Life and Work, pp. 11, 164.
Stearns, C. Ladies' Philosophy of Love.
Stifler, J. M. My Dear Girl.
Wertenbaker, T. J. Patrician and Plebian, pp. 82-90.
Winsor, J. Mem. Hist., Boston. Vol. 3: 169.
Woody, T. Hist., Educ., Women. Vol. 1: 89, 177-179, 183, 239-
    240, 244, 246-247.

b.   Women's Opinions

Women's opinions regarding their status in the colonies is found in
their actions rather than in their writings. Only Mercy Warren chal-
lenged in her published writings the limited rights of women in the community. However, as early as 1637, Ann Hutchinson demanded the right
to speak in religious meetings. Among the Quakers and the Moravians,
women took an active part in the churches as preachers and religious
leaders. In the productive life, women took their full share of responsibility and leadership. In political life, their opinions were less clearly
defined. In 1648, Margaret Brent made the only recorded demand for
the right of a woman to vote in a colonial governing body. But the annals of local governments record the votes of women property owners

along with those of the men in most of the New England and Middle
Atlantic colonies.

Earle, A.M. Colonial Dames, pp. 45-48.
Ellis, G. E. Puritan Age, pp. 300-362.
Green, H. C. Pioneer Mothers. Vol. 1: 299-311.
Holliday, C. Women's Life, pp. 104-105, 144-145.
Meyer, A. N. Women's Work, p. 260.
P.M.H.B. "Sentiments, Amer. Women," P.M.H.B. Vol. 18:
361-366.
Smith, T. M. "Feminism, Phila.," P.M.H.B. Vol. 68: 243-268.
Van Rensselaer, (Mrs.) J.K. Mana-ha-ta, pp. 25-28.
Willison, G. P. Saints and Strangers, p. 418.

B.   The Rights of Free Women in the Colonies

While the legal status of most women in the colonial period was that
of dependence and limited rights, the force of circumstance set aside many
of the restrictive measures. Widows had to be recognized as heads of families. Women who produced cloth or bread had to be paid. There were not
enough male workers to meet the needs of the colonies so that women worked
in many fields and gained permanent status from their ability to meet the
needs of the growing settlements.

Adams, J. T. Provincial Society, pp. 80-82.
Ames, S. M. Studies, Va., pp. 175-196.
Ames, S. M. "Law in Action," W. M. Quart. Ser 3, Vol. 4:
177-191.
Baber, R. E. Marriage and the Family, pp. 26-27, 39-43.
Benson, M. S. Women, 18th Cent. Amer., pp. 223-241, 244-249.
Blake, F. E. Hist., Princeton, Mass. Vol. 1: 85-87, 137, 141.
Blake, J. W. Hist., Warwick, Mass., pp. 35-37.
Boorstin, D. The Americans, pp. 186-187.
Bridenbaugh, C. Cities, Wilderness, pp. 387-388.
Buck S. J. & E. H. Western Penna., p. 330.
Calhoun, A. Soc. Hist., Amer. Family, Vol. 1: 101, 138, 192, 238,
277-278.
Clement, J. M. Settlers, Newton, N.J., p. 318.
Cobbledick, M. R. Status, Women, New Engl.
Dall, C. A. College, Market, Court., pp. 356-360.
Dexter, E. A. Colonial Women, pp. 18,100,138,139,180-188.
Dole, E. P. "Rights, Married Women, N.H.," Granite Monthly.
Vol. 3: 264-268.
Duxbury, Mass. Records, pp. 241, 247, 250, 264, 272, 278.
Earle, A. M. Curious Punishments.
Fernow, B. Docs., Colonial N.Y. Vol. 14: 496, 510, 522, 736-740.
Fleet, B. Va. Colonial Abstracts. Vol. 12: 92-93.
Fowler, S. P. "Records, Overseer, Poor," Essex Inst. H. Colls.
Vol. 2: 85-92.
Goodell, A. C. "Court Records, Essex," Essex Inst. H. Colls.
Vol. 7: 129.

Gray, F. C. "Early laws, Mass," Mass. H.S. Colls. Ser. 3, Vol. 8.

Greene, E., & Harrington, V. Amer. Population.

Hart, A. B. Commonwealth Hist., Mass. Vol. 3: pp. 334-347.

Hening, W. W. Statutes at Large, Va. Vol. 3: 140; Vol. 11: 11,161.

Hill, D. G. Hist., Dedham, Mass. Vol. 4, see index under Mary Judson and others.

Holliday, C. Women's Life, pp. 291-313.

Jackson, F. Hist., Newton, Mass., pp. 50-51, 126.

Johnson, R. G. Hist., Account, Salem, West Jersey, p. 111.

Judd, S. Hist., Hadley, Mass., pp. 11-12, 203-204.

Mason, G. C. Reminiscences, Newport, pp. 144-148.

Morison, S. E. Builders, Bay Colony, pp. 217, 230-234.

Morris, R. B. Hist., Amer. Law, pp. 128, 197.

Nelson, W. Arch. N.J. Ser. 1, Vol. 11: 414-415, 426-428; Vol. 24: 432; Vol. 27: 86, 648; Vol. 28: 214; Vol. 29: 479; Ser. 2, Vol. 4: 389.

Nourse, H. S. Records, Lancaster, Mass., pp. 17-19, 46-47, 267-268, 320.

Pennypacker, S. W. Penna. Colonial Cases, p. 54.

Peterson, A. E. 18th Cent., N.Y.C. Part I, 182-199.

Ricord, F. W., & Nelson, W. Arch., N.J. Ser. 1, Vol. 9: 226-228.

Ross, P. Hist., Long Is. Vol. 1: 116.

Stanard, M. M. Colonial Va., pp. 349-350.

Twitchell, R. E. Spanish Archives, New Mexico, see index under women's names.

Van Winkle, D. Old Bergen, p. 49.

Watertown. Records. Vol. 2: 69, 74.

Wenham Hist. Soc. Town Records, pp. 66, 96, 165-181, 193-194.

Wertenbaker, T. J. Patrician and Plebian, pp. 82, 87-88, 126.

Wharton, A. H. Colonial Days, pp. 125-152.

Whitehead, W. A., ed. Arch., N.J. Ser. 1, Vol. 2: 326.

Winthrop, J. Hist., New Engl. Vol. 2: 161-163.

Wise, J. C. Kingdome, Accawmacke, pp. 43-47.

Woody, T. Hist., Educ., Women. Vol. 1: 168-170, 175, 180-189, 239-269.

C. Rights of Free Women in Marriages

Due to religious beliefs and the economic and social conditions in the colonies, married women acquired definite rights and privileges that had not been theirs in England or on the continent.

a. Purchase Brides

The position of the wife in the home and community was affected by the fact that groups of women were shipped to most of the colonies and purchased by the men on landing. Some men paid only the passage money for their brides; others paid the market price, whatever it was.

Baudier, R. Catholic Church, La., p. 49.
Beverly, R. Hist., Va., pp. 231-232.
Calhoun, A. Soc., Hist., Amer., Family. Vol. l: 216, 251-254.
Cook (Mrs.), H. L. "Maids for Wives," V.M.H.B. Vol. 50: 300-
    332; Vol. 51: 71-86.
Earle, A. M. Colonial Dames, pp. 26-29.
Early, R. H. By-Ways, Va. Hist., pp. 152-153.
Fiske, J. Old Va. Vol. l: 188-189.
Green, H. C. & M. W. Pioneer Mothers. Vol. l: 10-11.
Gregory, G. C. "N. & J. Martian," V.H.M.B. Vol. 42: 145-148.
Phillips, U. P. Plantation and Frontier. Vol. l: 355.
Sioussat, A. M. Colonial Women, Md., pp. 11-12.
Spruill, J. C. Women's Life, p. 9.
Stanard, M. M. Va.'s First Cent., pp. 135-137.
Wharton, A. H. Colonial Days, p. 79.

b.   Rights as a Wife

According to the laws in most of the colonies, married women
had very few inherent rights except where they had been defined in a
pre-nuptial agreement. Women could inherit and own property, both
personal and real, but could not alienate it. They were not responsible
for their personal actions and had almost no right of divorce, regard-
less of cause. Pioneer conditions and the endeavors of the women
tended to nullify the stringency of the laws.

Baber, R. E. Marriage and Family, pp. 26-27, 39-43.
Bartlett, H. R. 18th Cent. Ga. Women, pp. 41-52, 63-65.
Calhoun, A. Soc., Hist., Amer. Family. Vol. l: 147, 192, 238-
    239, 276-279.
Dexter, F. B. "Correspondence, Jared Ingersoll," New Haven
    Col. H.S. Colls. Vol. 9: 202-203.
Essex Inst. "Marriage Contract," Essex Inst. H. Colls. Vol. 81:
    385-387.
Hart, A. B. Commonwealth Hist., Mass. Vol. 2: 355-417;Vol. 3:
    334-335.
Mass. Bay Colony. Record, Court Assistants. Vol. 1, see index
    under Divorce.
Morison, S. E. Builders, Bay Colony, pp. 217, 230-234.
Morris, R. Hist., Amer. Law, pp. 126, 128, 139-143, 162, 185-200.
Neill, E. D. Va. Carolorum, pp. 294-406.
Nelson, W. Arch., N.J. Ser. 1, Vol. 27: 10-11, 17-20, 30-34;
    Vol. 28: 31-32; Vol. 29: 166, 177; Ser. 2, Vol. 3: 192-193,
    203, 275-276; Vol. 4: 116, 150.
Reeve, T. Law, Baron & Femme.
Ricord, F., & Nelson, W. Arch., N.J. Ser. 1, Vol. 13: 190.
Sewall, S. E. Legal Condition, Women, Mass.
Spalletta, M. "Divorce in Colonial N.Y.," N.Y.H.S. Quart Bull.
    Vol. 39: 422-440.
Spruill, J. C. Women's Life and Work, p. 169.

Stryker, W. Arch., N.J. Ser. 2, Vol. 1: 134.
V.M.H.B. "Marriage Agreement," V.M.H.B. Vol. 4: 64-66.
Winsor, J. Mem. Hist., Boston. Vol. 4: 343.
Woodruff, M. R. "Marriage Contract," Conn. Mag. Vol. 1: 110.

D.   Property Rights of Free Women

In most of the colonial settlements, single women and widows were given equal land grants with the men as heads of families. In Maryland, wives were given grants equal to that of their husbands. In the first settlements in Georgia no grants of land were given women, but this proved so impractical that the law was soon revised. Women also had the right to own and operate business ventures, and in most cases, the legal right to all their earnings.

Abbott, E. Women, Indust., pp. 12, 33.
Adams, H. B. "Allotments of Land, Salem," Essex Inst. H. Colls. Vol. 19: 167-175.
Allen, M. C. Hist., Wenham, pp. 51-52.
Ames, S. M. Studies, Va., pp. 18-56, 73, 134.
Ames, S. M. Va. County Records, see index women's names.
Andrews, C. M. River Towns, pp. 47, 56-57.
Andrews, M. P. Founding, Md. Vol. 1: 59-60, 85, 199-200.
Andrews, M. P. Hist., Md. Vol. 1: 267.
Arnold, J. N. Records, Narragansett, see index under women's names.
Bancroft, H. H. Works of H. H. Bancroft. Vol. 34: 306.
Barker, C. "The Gulph Mill," P.M.H.B. Vol. 53: 168-174.
Barlett, H. R. 18th Cent. Ga. Women, pp. 1-9.
Biddle, G., & Lowrie, S. Notable Women, Pa., pp. 2-4, 17-19, 26-28.
Blake, F. E. Hist., Princeton, Mass. Vol. 1: 88-89.
Bland, S. "Petition," Tyler's Quart. Vol. 1: 40-41.
Brandon, E. G. Records, Cambridge, pp. 5-19.
Brett, C. "Letter, N.Y.H.S. Colls. Vol. 6: 190-192.
Bruce, P.A. Econ. Hist., Va. Vol. 2: 249.
Cadbury, H.J. "Hannah Penn," P.M.H.B. Vol. 81: 76-82.
Calhoun, A. Soc. Hist., Amer. Family. Vol. 1: 68, 95, 247, 276.
Calvert, C. Papers. First Selection. Vol. 1: 165.
Carteret, E. "Petition," N.Y.H.S. Proc. Ser. 2, Vol. 1: 33-36.
Chavez, A. Origins, N.M. Families, p. 19 ff, see index under women's names.
Cogswell, E. C. Hist., Nottingham, N.H., pp. 84-85, 92-93, 102-105.
Corey, D. P. Hist., Malden, Mass., pp. 59-61, 376-377, 497-498.
Corry, J. P. "Bosomworth Claims," Ga. H. Quart. Vol. 25: 196-224.
Cotton, J. B. "Early Records, Md.," Md. H. Mag. Vol. 16: 279, 298, 369-385; Vol. 17: 60-74, 292-308.
Coulter, E. M. "Mary Musgrove," Ga. H. Quart. Vol. 9: 1-30.
Custis, J. & F. "Marriage Agreement," V.M.H.B. Vol. 4: 64.

Dexter, E. A. Colonial Women, pp. 98-106.
Dow, G. F. Records, Salem, Mass., pp. 14-57, 107-119.
Drake, F. S. Town, Roxbury, Mass., pp. 49-50.
Drummond, S. "Petition, Land," V.M.H.B. Vol. 22: 234-235.
Duxbury, Mass. Old Records, pp. 20, 193, 195, 236.
Earle, A.M. Colonial Dames, pp. 45-52, 85.
East, R. A. Business Enterprise, p. 21.
Ellis, F., & Evans, S. Hist., Lancaster Co., Pa., 20-21, 748, 926.
Elzas, B. A. Jews, So. Car., pp. 112-113.
Essex Antiq. Norfolk County Records, Essex Antiq. Vol. 1: 19-24.
Essex Inst. Wills. Essex Inst. H. Colls. Vol. 1: 3-4.
Essex Inst. Grants of Land. Essex Inst. H. Colls. Vol. 4: 95-96.
Fernow, B. Docs., Colonial N.Y. Vol. 14: 346-347.
Flint, M. B. Early Long Is., pp. 104-115.
Gray, F. C. "Early Laws, Mass.," Mass. H.S. Colls. Ser. 3, Vol. 8: 191-237.
Green, H. C. & M. W. Pioneer Mothers. Vol. 1: 221-223, 299-311, 397-410, 455-485.
Hart, A. B. Commonwealth Hist., Mass. Vol. 3: 334-337.
Hazard, S. Annals, Pa., pp. 637-642.
Hazen, H. A. Hist., Bellerica, Mass., pp. 5, 13.
Hening, W. H. Statutes At Large, Va. Vol. 3: 172, 238; Vol. 7: 519-520.
Hill, D. G. Records, Dedham, Mass. Vol. 3, see index under women's names; Vol. 4, see index, Mary Judson & other women.
Holliday, C. Women's Life, pp. 297-300.
Honeyman, A. V. Arch, N.J. Ser. 1, Vol. 30: see index under women's names.
Hudson, A. S. Annals, Sudbury, Wayland, Maynard, see index under women's names.
Hudson, A. S. Hist., Sudbury, pp. 26-56, 62-68, 110-123.
Jackson, F. Hist., Newton, Mass., pp. 223-230.
James, B. B., & Jameson, J. F. Journ., Jasper Dankaerts, pp. 101-103.
Jones, F. R. Hist., No. Amer. Vol. 4: 203-204.
Judd, S. Hist., Hadley, Mass., pp. 31, 191, 275, 278, 283.
Lamb, M. J. Hist., N.Y.C. Vol. 1: 114-115, 123.
Lamson, D. F. Hist., Manchester, Mass., p. 20.
Lee, F. D., & Agnew, J. L. Hist. Record, Savannah, pp. 4, 20-25.
Logan, J. A. Part Taken by Women, pp. 43-49.
McCrady, E. So. Car. Proprietary Govt., see index under women's names.
Manchester. Town Records, pp. 12, 29, 87.
Md. Hist. Mag. "First Grants," Md. H. Mag. Vol. 3: 158-169.
Md. Hist. Mag. "Land Office Records." Vol. 5: 166-167, 170, 172-173, 263-264, 369.

Morris, R. B. Hist., Amer. Law, pp. 130-131, 144-155.
Nelson, W. Arch., N.J. Ser. 1, Vol. 21, see index under women's
    names. Ser. 2, Vol. 3: 203-227, 271.
New York, Hist. Soc. "Tax List," N.Y.H.S. Colls. Ser. 2, Vol.
    1: 387-388.
Nicklin, J. B. "Benj. Strother and his wives," Tyler's Quart.
    Vol. 19: 224-225.
Nugent, N. M. Cavaliers and Pioneers. Vol. 1, see index, wo-
    men's names.
Oliver, F. E. Pychon's Diary, p. 131.
Paige, L. R. Hist., Cambridge, pp. 443-444, 446.
Putnam, E. "Danvers tax list," Essex Inst. H. Colls. Vol. 29:
    181-183.
Ramey, M. E. Margaret Brent.
Rawle, W. B. "First tax list, Phila.," P.M.H.B. Vol. 8: 82-105.
Ricord, R., & Nelson, W. Arch. N.J. Ser. 1, Vol. 10: 547-548,
    614-615; Vol. 13: 87-90, 190, see index, Elizabeth Carteret;
    Vol. 14: 284, 385, 398, 471, 478, 483, 509-513, 523.
Sheldon, G. Hist., Deerfield, Mass. Vol. 1: 304-305, 506-507, 595
    606.
Sioussat, A. "Colonial Women, Md.," Md. H. Mag. Vol. 2: 214-
    226.
Smith, H. A. "Charleston," S.C.H.G. Mag. Vol. 9: 12-27, 85-
    101, 152-160.
Spruill, J. C. Women's Life, pp. 9, 11, 14, 17.
Sweeney, W. M. "Pre-nuptial agreement," Tyler's Quart. Vol.
    22: 139-141.
Temple, J., & Sheldon, G. Hist., Northfield, Mass., pp. 139,
    282, 319.
Tilden, W. S. Hist., Medfield, Mass., pp. 48, 56, 76-78, 93, 112.
Tilton, C. H., & Bliss, L. Hist., Rehoboth, pp. 22, 23, 29, 33, 57,
    93-95.
Torrence, C. "Lady of Quality," V.M.H.B. Vol. 56: 42-56.
Twitchell, R. E. Spanish Arch., N.M. Vol. 1: 27-28, 33, 40, 43,
    45.
Valentine, D. T. Manual, Corp, N.Y.C., p. 594.
Van Rensselaer (Mrs.), J. K. Mana-ha-ta, pp. 268-269.
Van Wyck, F. Keskachauge, pp. 216-217, 219-222, 738-740.
Vermont Colonial Dames. Ann Story.
Wainwright, N.B. "Plan of Phila.," Pa. Mag. Vol. 80: 164-176.
Watertown, Records. Vol. 1: 187-189, 191-197.
Wharton, A. H. Colonial Days, pp. 75-76.
White, G. Hist., Colls., Ga., pp. 21-31
Whitehead, W. Arch., N.J. Ser. 1, Vol. 1: 408-414.
W. M. Quart. "Census Tithables," W. M. Quart. Ser. 1, Vol. 8:
    161-164.
Willison, G. F. Saints and Strangers, p. 162.
Wise, J. C. Accawmacke, pp. 36-39, 94, 327, 348-350.
Woody, T. Hist., Educ. Women. Vol. 1: 253.
Worcester Soc., Antiq. Colls. Vols. 2 & 3, see index under wo-
    men's names.

E.   Inheritance Rights of Free Women

A woman's rights of inheritance varied little in the different colonies. As a widow, she inherited one-third of the family estate. She could be willed an entire estate and could make disposition of her own property by will. She was frequently named as executrix or administratrix of an estate and handled the legal aspects of the inheritance.

Brigham, W. Compact, New Plymouth, pp. 281, 299-300.
Calhoun, A. Soc., Hist., Amer. Family. Vol. 1: 95, 96, 176, 227.
Felt, J. Annals, Salem, p. 258.
Grimes, J. B. No. Car. Wills and Inventories, see index, women's names.
Hamilton, P. J. Hist., No. Amer. Vol. 3: 245.
Hening, W. W. Statutes at Large, Va. Vol. 3: 335, 371, 372, 374; Vol. 12: 139, 145-146, 220.
Holliday, C. Women's Life, p. 298.
Martyn, B. Am Account, Ga., pp. 275-278, 281, 282.
Morris, R. B. Hist., Amer. Law, pp. 134, 155-162, 166-173.
Opdike, C.W. OpDyck Geneology, pp. 79-80, 91, 189, 211, 228.
Paige, L. R. Hist., Cambridge, Mass., pp. 175-176.
Reeve, T. Baron & Femme, pp. 37-59.
Ricord, F., & Nelson, W. Arch., N.J. Ser. 1, Vol. 13, see index under Elizabeth Carteret; Vol. 14: 284, 513.
Salley, A. Narratives, Early Car., pp. 250-252.
Sioussat, A. M. Colonial Women, Md., pp. 17-18.
Spruill, J. C. Women's Life, pp. 14-17.
Streeter, S. F. Early Hist., Md., pp. 280-283.
Twitchell, R. E. Spanish Arch., N.M. Vol. 1: 4 ff.
Van Rensselaer (Mrs.), J. K. Mana-ha-ta, pp. 268-269.
Weeden, W. B. Hist., New Engl. Vol. 1: 189, 217; Vol. 2: 543-544.
Withington, L. "Va. gleanings," V.M.H.B. Vol. 18: 83.
Woody, T. Hist., Educ. Women. Vol. 1: 168, 253.

F.   Rights of Free Women in Community Life

The laws that the English colonists brought with them did not restrict the voting privilege to the men; so widows and spinsters voted in many of the early settlements as property owners. Women held the power of attorney in court cases, both as representatives for their husbands' interests and in behalf of others. They acted as jurors in special cases involving women and held such public offices as official interpreter, tax-treasurer, state printer, and postmistress.

a.   Right to Vote

The right to vote on community issues was based on property rights, which included women as heads of households owning property. In New Jersey, women voted until 1807.

Andrews, C. M. Beginnings, Conn., pp. 43, 54-55.
Andrews, C. M. River Towns, pp. 66, 89.
Andrews, M. P. Hist., Md. Vol. l: 267-268.
Barnes, E. Women, Modern Society, p. 174.
Bates, S. A. Braintree Records, pp. 381, 509.
Bishop, C. F. Hist., Elections, pp. 65-66.
Blake, F. E. Hist., Princeton, Mass. Vol. l: 137, 141.
Boatwright, E. M. "Political and Civil Status, Women," Ga. H.
    Quart. Vol. 25: 301-305.

Brandon, E. J. Records, Cambridge, p. 291.
Brent, C. H. Descendents, Giles Brent, pp. 42-50.
Brigham, W. Compact, New Plymouth, pp. 33, 156.
Bronner, E. B. "Political Action, Women," Friends H.A.
    Bull. Vol. 43: 29-32.

Browne, W., & Hall, C. Arch., Md. Vol. l: 215.
Calhoun, A. W. Soc., Hist., Amer. Family. Vol. l: 188, 277-
    278; Vol. 2: 79-80.

Cambridge, Mass. Records, Cambridge, p. 291.
Chapin, H. Address, Unitarian Church.
Clement, J. M. Settlers, Newton, N.J., p. 318.
Coffin, A. The Coffin Family, pp. 56-57.
Cogswell, L. W. Hist., Henniker, N.H., p. 107.
Davis, W. A. Records, Fitchburg. Vol. l: 39, 115, 124, 214, 280.
Dexter, E. A. Colonial Women, p. 100.
Earle, A. M. Colonial Dames, p. 45.
Edwards, G. W. N.Y., 18th Cent., Part II, pp. 43-44, 85-86.
Elmer, L. Q. "Constitution, N.J.," N.J.H.S. Colls. Vol. 7:
    3, 47-49.

Fernow, B. Records, New Amsterdam. Vol. 5: 221-225 and see
    index; Vol. 7: 149-153, and see index.

Green, H. C. & M. W. Pioneer Mothers. Vol. l: 299-311.
Hart, A. B. Commonwealth Hist., Mass. Vol. 3: 334-338.
Hening, W. H. Statutes at Large, Va., Vol. 3: 172, 238: Vol.
    8: 307.

Hinchman, L. S. Early Nantucket, pp. 122, 126.
Hudson, A. S. Hist., Sudbury, pp. 118-122.
Lapham, A. G. Planters, Beverly, Mass., pp. 68-69.
Lovell, A. A. Worcester, Rev., p. 118.
McCormick, R. P. Hist., Voting, N.J., pp. 78, 93, 98-100.
McKinley, A. E. The Suffrage Franchise, pp. 192-193, 270, 472.
Meyer, A. N. Woman's Work, p. 260.
Moller, H. "Sex Composition in Colonial Amer.," W. M. Quart.
    Ser. 3, Vol. 2: 153.

Morris, R. Hist., Amer. Law, pp. 133-135.
N.J. Hist. Soc. "Minute Book, Nottingham," N.J.H.S. Proc.
    Vol. 58: 24, 129, 189-190.
Philbrook, M. "Woman's Suffrage," N.J.H.S. Proc. Vol. 57:
    87-98.
Porter, K. H. Hist., Suffrage, U.S., p. 8.
Rawle, W. B. "Phila. Co. Tax List," P.M.H.B. Vol. 8: 82-105.

Shinn, H. C. "Early Poll List," P.M.H.B. Vol. 44: 77-81.
Starbuck, A. Hist., Nantucket, pp. 21, 133, 518-531.
Turner, E. R. Women's Suffrage, N.J., pp. 165-187.
Van Rensselaer, M. G. Hist., N.Y.C. Vol. 1: 423.
Weston, Mass. Tax List, p. 2 ff.
Whitehead, W. A. East Jersey, p. 134.
Whitehead, W. A. "Suffrage, N.J.," N.J.H.S. Proc. Ser. 1,
    Vol. 8: 101-105.
Willison, G. F. Saints and Strangers, pp. 143, 335, 385.
Woody, T. Hist. Educ. Women, Vol. 1: 175
Worcester Soc., Antiq. Colls. Vol. 2: 9, 37; Vol. 3: 312.
Worcester Soc., Antiq. "Listings" Bull. Vol. 16: 373-388,
    451-452.

b. Right to Hold Office in the Community

Generally speaking, a woman's right to hold office in the community was based on her unusual abilities, as in the case of the official
interpreters who negotiated treaties with the Indians, and the women
who acted as jurors in adultery and infanticide cases. In some instances, widows, inheritors of their husbands' businesses or positions,
were given the responsibility of carrying on the work, as in the case
of several state printers and a tax-treasurer.

Ames, S. M. Studies, Va., p. 178.
Andrews, C. M. Beginnings, Conn., pp. 54-55.
Andrews, M. P. Hist., Md. Vol. 1: 268.
Andrews, M. P. Founding, Md., pp. 201-202.
Bartlett, H. R. 18th Cent. Ga. Women, pp. 10-40.
Biddle, G. B., & Lowrie, S. D. Notable Women, Pa., pp. 16-17,
    41-42, 148-149.
Bridenbaugh, C. Cities in the Wilderness, p. 387.
Cometti, E. "Women, Amer. Revolution," New Engl. Quart.
    Vol. 20: 333.
Corry, J. P. "Bosomworth Claims," Ga. H. Quart. Vol. 25:
    196-224.
Coulter, E. M. Hist., Ga., pp. 1-30, 132.
Coulter, E. M. "Mary Musgrove," Ga. H. Quart. Vol. 9: 1-30.
Davis, W. A. Records, Fitchburg, p. 181.
Dexter, E. A. Colonial Women, pp. 172, 174-176, 213.
Earle, E. A. Colonial Dames, p. 60.
Egle, W. H. Penna. Women, pp. 87-89.
Fernow, B. N.Y. Colonial Docs. Vol. 14: 540.
Flint, M. B. Early Long Is., pp. 104-115.
Freeze, J. G. "Madame Montour," P.M.H.B. Vol. 3: 79-87.
Hillhouse, M. P. Hist. and Gen. Colls., pp. 144-146.
Hurd, D. H. Hist., Essex Co., Mass. Vol. 1: 699.
Johnson, R. G. Hist., Salem, West Jersey, p. 111.
Jordan, F. Life, William Henry, pp. 19-28, 52-53.
Knight, L. L. Ga. Landmarks. Vol. 1: 379.

Lamb, M. J. Hist., N.Y.C. Vol. 1: 207.
Lee, F. D., & Agnew, J. L. Hist., Savannah, pp. 4, 20-25.
Lovell, A. A. Worcester, Revolution, p. 117.
Meyer, A. N. Woman's Work, pp. 220-221.
Nourse, H. S. Records, Lancaster, Mass., pp. 153-154.
Pennypacker, S. W. Penna. Colonial Cases, p. 53.
Peterson, A. A. N.Y., 18th Cent., Part. I, p. 190.
Richardson, H. D. Side Lights, Md. Hist. Vol. 1: 148-150.
Seybolt, R. F. Town Officials, pp. 49, 77, 102, 128, 191, 237.
Sickler, J. Hist., Salem Co., N.J., pp. 90-91.
Smith, G. G. Story of Ga., pp. 31-32.
Spruill, J. C. Women's Life, p. 304.
Stewart, F. H. Notes, Old Gloucester, p. 95.
Van Rensselaer, M. G. Hist., N.Y.C. Vol. 1: 479.
Van Wyck, F. Keskachauge, p. 740.
White, G. Hist., Colls. Ga., pp. 21-31.
Woody, T. Hist., Educ., Women. Vol. 1: 248-249, 262.
Worcester Soc. Antiq. Colls. Vol. 4: 324, 325, 335, 375-376, 396, 449.

c.   Right to Carry on Productive Enterprises

By the law of "couverte de Baron" of 1419, English women had the right to carry on productive enterprises as "Feme Sole." This right was evident in all the English colonies. The women from Holland had long had similar rights: German and French women had comparable opportunities; so women are found in occupational life in all of the colonies.

Abbott, E. Woman, Industry, pp. 32-33.
Ames, S. M. Studies, Va., pp. 117-125.
Calhoun, A. W. Soc., Hist., Amer. Family. Vol. 1: 48-49, 167-168.
Edwards, G. W. 18th Cent. N.Y., Part II, pp. 43-44, 51-53, 85-86.
Fernow, B. Records, New Amsterdam. Vol. 5: 221-225; Vol. 7: 149-153.
Morris, R. B. Hist., Amer. Law, pp. 128, 164, 171-184.
N.Y. Hist. Soc. Publ. Funds. Colls. Vol. 18: 19, 54-106, 457.
Oberholtzer, E. P. Hist., Phila. Vol. 1: 102.
Riley, H. T. Liber Albus, pp. 181-182.
Scharf, J. T., & Westcott, T. Hist., Phila. Vol. 1: 194.
Spaulding, M. C. Hist. Handbook, N.J., p. 95.
Spruill, J. C. Women's Life, p. 169.
Twitchell, R. E. Arch., N.M., see index.
Van Rensselaer, M. G. Hist., N.Y.C. Vol. 1: 423.
Woody, T. Hist., Educ., Women. Vol. 1: 164-168.

Women in Economic Servitude in the Colonies

The economic servitude of white women, like that of white men, ranged from ract agreements between free individuals to conditions bordering on virtual ery. Some colonies offered grants of land after ten years of servitude to white ιen servants from Europe.
Other white women were shanghied and sold into bondage. The Negro women ə almost universally sold into bondage. Some women servants, both Negro and ιe, were given apprenticeship education.

Adams, S. W., & Stiles, H. R. Hist., Wethersfield, Conn. Vol. 1: 689-695.

Ames, S. M. Studies, Va., pp. 72-76, 79-81, 83-87, 89-100, 102-103, 105, 107, 187-191.

Andrews, C. M. Colonial Folkways, pp. 186-190.

Ballagh, J. C. White Servitude, Va.

Beverly, R. Hist., Va., pp. 219-222.

Booghers, W. F. Amer. Repository, pp. 56-57, 166.

Bruce, P. A. Econ. Hist., Va. Vol. 1: 572, 601, 604, 605, 612-614; Vol. 2: 2-4, 11, 15, 51, 408.

Bruce, P. A. Inst. Hist., Va. Vol. 1: 311-312, 613-614.

Buck, S. & E. Western Pa., p. 279.

Calder, I. M. Colonial Captivities, pp. 151-152.

Calhoun, A. Soc., Hist., Amer. Family. Vol. 1: 77, 119-125, 171-172, 229, 250-251, 313-329.

Camden Co. Hist. Soc. "Manumission of Slaves by Friends," Camden Co. H.S.M. Vol. 1, No. 6: 5-6.

Clews, E. W. Educ. Legislation, pp. 93, 350, 355-357.

Dexter, F. B. "Correspondence of Jared Ingersoll," New Haven Col. H.S. Colls. Vol. 9: 208-211.

Dow, G. F. Arts and Crafts, New Engl., pp. 185-196.

Fleet, B. Va. Colonial Abstracts. Vol. 12: 42.

Gloucester Co. Hist. Soc. Minutes, Gloucester Co. Court, 1686-1687, pp. 9, 21, 31.

Gottesman, R. S. Arts and Crafts, N.Y., 1726-1776, pp. 335-343.

Greene, L. J. The Negro in Colonial New Engl., pp. 167-168, 177-187, 292-294.

Hall, C. C. Narratives, Early Md., pp. 354-361.

Hamer, M. B. "Cent. Before Manumission," N.C.H. Rev. Vol. 17: 232-236.

Hamilton, P. J. Hist., No. Amer. Vol. 3: 111.

Hening, W. W. Statutes at Large, Va. Vol. 1: 257, 336-337, 441-444; Vol. 3: 87, 453; Vol. 8: 135-136, 358-360, 393, 529; Vol. 11: 362-363.

Herrick, C. A. White Servitude, Pa.

Jackson, F. Hist., Newton, Mass., pp. 87-97.

Jervey, T. H. "White Indentured Servant," S.C.H.G. Mag. Vol. 12: 163-171.

Jernegan, M. W. Laboring and Dependent Classes, pp. 3-56.

Leonard, E. A. Origins, Personnel·Services, p. 10.

McCormac, E. I. White Servitude in Md., pp. 27-106.
McCrady, E. So. Car. Proprietary Govt., pp. 196-197.
Mass. Bay Colony, Record Court Assistants. Vol. 1: 25-33, 198.
Morris, R. B. Hist., Amer. Law, p. 237.
Morton, L. Robert Carter, pp. 90-117, 251.
Nelson, W. (ed.) Arch., N.J. Ser. 1, Vols. 11, 12, 24, 25, 27, 29, Ser. 2; Vols. 3, 4, see index under apprentice, servant runaway, and negro.
Neible, G. W. "Servants and Apprentices," P.M.H.B. Vols. 30, 31, 32, see index.
Phillips, U. P. Plantation and Frontier. Vol. 1: 341.
Rochefoucault-Liancourt, F. Travels. Vol. 2: 409-410, 440.
Ross, P. Hist., Long Is. Vol. 1: 120.
Rush, B. German Inhabitants, Pa., pp. 7, 8.
Salmon, L. M. Domestic Service, pp. 16-73.
Seybolt, R. F. Apprenticeship and Apprenticeship Educ., pp. 15, 22-103, 196.
Smith, A. E. Colonists in Bondage, pp. 104, 108, 122, 126, 366.
Stryker, W. Arch., N.J. Ser. 2, Vol. 1, see index under runaway, negro, apprentice and servant.
Van Rensselaer (Mrs.), J. K. Mana-ha-ta, pp. 16-17, 109.
Virginia Hist. Soc. "Trapanned Maiden," V.M.H.B. Vol. 4: 218-220.
Wallace, D. D. Hist., So. Car. Vol. 1: 378-381.
Waters, T. F. Ipswich, Mass. Vol. 2: 391-392.
Weeden, A. Hist., New Engl. Vol. 1: 85-86, 103, 148-149, 193-194, 202-203, 273; Vol. 2: 695-696.
Wertenbaker, T. J. Partrician and Plebian, pp. 157-166, 184-185, 205-211.
Woody, T. Hist., Educ., Women. Vol. 1: 190-192, 264-268.

VI

WOMEN IN THE RELIGIOUS LIFE OF THE COLONIES

1. General Statement

Women made significant contributions to the religious life of the Colonies. In a few cases women were the foundresses of new schools of religious thought; in others, they were the initiators of the organization of a church. In some instances they were effective preachers and missionaries, and in others they contributed their teaching ability or their handiwork to further the cause of their faith. The predominant faiths of the period have been grouped for study and convenience.

Bridenbaugh, C. Cities, Wilderness, pp. 100-107, 257-265, 418-425.
Crawford, M. C. New Engl. Churches.
Earle, A. M. The Sabbath, New Engl.
Ellis, G. Puritan Age.

Fiske, J. Beginnings, New Engl.
Holliday, C. Women's Life, pp. 3-69.
Meyer, A. N. Women's Work, pp. 206-209.
Moller, H. "Sex Composition of Colonial Amer.," W. M. Quart. Ser.
  3, Vol. 2: 145-153.
Winsor, J. Mem. Hist., Boston. Vol. 3: 401-420.

Women in Catholic Settlements

In the French colony at New Orleans, a group of Ursuline nuns started the
'st school for girls in the United States, in 1727, as well as a hospital and or-
anage. In Florida, New Mexico, and Maryland, outstanding Catholic women
ntributed to the stability and growth of their churches and colonies.

Bolton, H. E. Rim, Christendom, p. 418.
Brent, C. H. Descendants, Giles Brent, pp. 42-50.
Heard, J. John Wheelwright, pp. 128-136.
Keidel, George C. "Catonsville, Biog." Md. H. Mag. Vol. 17: 74-88.
King, G. E. New Orleans, pp. 51-74.
Lathrop, G. P. & R. H. Story of Courage, pp. 146-177.
Logan, M. S. Part Taken by Women, pp. 43-49.
Lord, R. H. et al. Hist., Archdiocese, Boston, pp. 203-209.
Ramey, M. E. Margaret Brent.
Riley, A. J. Catholicism, New Engl., pp. 280-296.
Shea, J. G. Hist., Catholic Church, U.S. Vol. 1: 197-198, 568-582,
  592.
Sioussat, A. M. Old Manors, Md., pp. 30-32.
Spruill, J. C. "Margaret Brent," Md. H. Mag. Vol. 29: 259-268.
Thomas, J. W. Chronicles, Md., pp. 26, 44-45, 351.

Women in the Puritan (Congregational) Church

Women in the Puritan churches were greatly restricted under a narrow in-
rpretation of the Pauline statements regarding women.

A.   Position of Women

While women in the Puritan church theoretically had no voice in the
affairs of the church, actually they signed church covenants, contributed
funds, and voted on church issues.

Adams, C. F. "Church discipline, New Engl.," Mass. H.S.
  Proc. Ser. 2, Vol. 6: 477-516.
Blake, F. E. Princeton, Mass. Vol. 1: 137, 141.
Cogswell, L. W. Hist., Henniker, p. 107.
Corey, D. P. Hist., Malden, Mass., p. 146.
Dexter, E. A. Colonial Women, p. 209.
Fisher, S. G. Men, Women, and Manners. Vol. 1: 139.
Lapham, A. G. Old Planters, Beverly, Mass. pp. 68-69.
Merrill, J. Hist., Amesbury & Merrimac, p. 185.

Metcalf, J. G. Annals, Mendon, Mass., pp. 98, 126-128.
Smith, P. Hist., Modern Culture. Vol. 2: 604.
Stone, E. M. Hist., Beverly, Mass., p. 258.
Trumbull, J. R. Hist., Northampton, Mass. Vol. 1: 106-107.
Winslow, O. E. Meetinghouse, pp. 144-145, 192-196, 230-236.
Winsor, J. Mem. Hist., Boston. Vol. 3: 401-420.
Winthrop, J. Hist., New Engl. Vol. 1: 338-340; Vol. 2: 338.
Woody, T. Hist., Educ., Women. Vol. 1: 171-172.
Worcester Soc., Antiq. Colls. Vol. 4: 175.
Worcester Soc., Antiq. Bull No. 16, pp. 7-8, 15-16.

B.   Witchcraft

The religious hysteria of witch-hunts centered on women and serious-
ly affected their position, not only in Salem, Massachusetts, but to some
extent in all the colonies.

Adams, S. W., & Stiles, H. R. Hist., Wethersfield, Conn. Vol. 1:
    681-686.
Bruce, P. A. Inst. Hist., Va. Vol. 1: 278-289.
Calhoun, A. Soc. Hist., Amer. Family. Vol. 1: 274.
Chever, G. F. "Prosecution, Ann Pudiator, Witch," Essex
    Inst. H. Colls. Vol. 4: 37-42, 49-54.
Chever, G. F. "Prosecution of Philip English & Wife," Essex
    Inst. H. Colls. Vol. 1: 157-181; Vol. 2, see index; Vol. 3:
    17-29, 67-79, 111-120.
Child, F. S. Colonial Witch.
Crawford, M. C. Little Journeys, pp. 225-240.
Drake, S. G. Annals, Witchcraft.
Drake, S. G. More Wonders, Invisible World.
Felt, J. Annals, Salem, pp. 303-319.
Fiske, J. New France and New Engl., pp. 133-196.
Folsom, J. F. "Witches, N.J.," N.J.H.S. Proc. New Ser., Vol.
    7: 293-305.
Gould, E. P. "Rebecca Nurse," Essex Antiq. Vol. 4: 135-137.
Green, H. C. & M. W. Pioneer Mothers. Vol. 1: 223-238.
Greene, J. L. The Negro in Colonial New Engl., pp. 153-154.
Green, S. A. "Trial of Ann Hibbens," Mass. H.S. Proc. Ser. 2,
    Vol. 4: 313-316.
Hanscom, E. D. Heart, Puritan, pp. 227-247.
Harris, R. B. "Philip and Mary English," Essex Inst. H. Colls.
    Vol. 66: 282-284.
Hart, A. B., & Curtis, J. G. Amer., Hist. Vol. 2: 35-48.
Hoadly, C. J. "Witchcraft, Hartford," Conn. Mag. Vol. 5:
    557-561.
Jackson, S. Witchcraft, Salem.
James, B. B. Hist., No. Amer. Vol. 5: 313-326.
James, E. W. "Witchcraft in Va.," W. M. Quart. Ser. 1, Vol. 1:
    127-129; Vol. 2: 58-60.
James, E. "Grace Sherwood, Witch," W. M. Quart. Ser. 1, Vol.

3: 96-101, 163-164, 190-192, 242-245; Vol. 4: 18-23.
Judd, S. Hist., Hadley, Mass., pp. 225-233.
Kittredge, G. L. Witchcraft.
Lower Norfolk Co. Antiq. "Witchcraft." Vol. 1: 20-21, 56.
Lower Norfolk Co. Antiq. "Va. Witch." Vol. 3: 34-38, 52-57.
Mather, C. "Diary," Mass. H.S. Colls. Ser. 7, Vol. 7: 142, 160-161, 178.
Nelson, W. Arch., N.J. Ser. 1, Vol. 11: 220-222.
Nevins, W. S. Witchcraft, Salem.
Parke, F. N. "Witchcraft, Md.," Md. H. Mag. Vol. 31: 271-298.
Pennypacker, S. W. Pa. Colonial Cases, pp. 35-36.
Reynard, E. The Narrow Land, pp. 151-175.
Richardson, H. D. Sidelights, Md. Hist. Vol. 1: 141-143.
Robbins, F. G. "Witchcraft," Essex Inst. H. Colls. Vol. 65: 209-239.
Ross, P. Hist., Long Is. Vol. 1: 173-174.
Sheahan, H. B. Amer. Memory, pp. 73-74.
Smith, E. Hist., Newburyport, pp. 28-37.
Trumbull, J. R. Hist., Northampton. Vol. 1: 42-52, 237.
Van Rensselaer (Mrs.), J. K. Mana-ha-ta, pp. 171-173.
Wells, M. B. "N.H. Witches," Granite State Mag. Vol. 5: 293-296.
Wendell, B. "Salem Witches," Essex Inst. H. Colls. Vol. 29: 129-147.
Winsor, J. Mem. Hist., Boston. Vol. 2: 131-172.
Winthrop, J. Hist., New Engl. Vol. 2: 323, 345-346.
Worthen, S. E. "Witches, N.J.," N.J.H.S. Proc. new Ser., Vol. 8: 139-143.

Women Among the Baptists, Anabaptists and Mennonites

Women in these groups had considerable voice in the affairs of their churches because of the emphasis that each group placed on the right of individuals to deter-mine by conscience their beliefs and morality.

A. The Women of the Ephrata Cloister

The Mennonites had a cloister for the women as well as the men at Ephrata, Pennsylvania, where many religious and other rights were held equally by the members of the two sexes.

Acrelius, I. Hist., New Sweden, pp. 373-384.
Langdon, W. C. Everyday Things, 1607-1706, pp. 77-86.
Sachse, J. F. German Pietists, pp. 80, 303-307.
Sachse, J. F. Ephrata Community, P.M.H.B. Vol. 14: 394-402.
Tyler, A. F. Freedom's Ferment, pp. 111-115.

B.   Ann Hutchinson

Ann Hutchinson disagreed with the ministers in the Massachusetts
Bay Colony and was forced to leave the colony. She settled in Rhode Island
and continued to be a dynamic influence in the church. See also List of 104
Outstanding Women.

Abramowitz, I. First Great Prisoners, pp. 307-340.
Adams, C. F. Antinomanism.
Adams, C. F. Three Episodes. Vol. 1: 371-532.
Augur, H. Amer. Jezebel.
Briggs, L. V. Hist., Gen., Cabot Family. Vol. 1: 220-225.
Brooks, G. Dames and Daughters, pp. 1-30.
Crawford, M. C. Little Journeys, New England, pp. 210-224.
Curtis, E. Ann Hutchinson.
Dexter, E. A. Colonial Women, pp. 142-146.
Dexter, F. B. "Trial, Ann Hutchinson," Mass. H.S. Proc.
      Ser. 2, Vol. 4: 158-192.
Eggleston, E. Beginners, Nation, pp. 327-342.
Ellis, G. E. Puritan Age, pp. 300-362.
Ellis, G. E. Ann Hutchinson.
Felt, J. B. Annals, Salem, pp. 87, 99, 101, 108, 110, 134.
Fisher, S. G. Men, Women and Manners. Vol. 1: 152-158.
Green, H. C. & M. W. Pioneer Mothers. Vol. 1: 201-221.
Hadaway, W. S. Anne Hutchinson.
Hart, A. B., & Curtis, J. G. Amer., Hist. Vol. 1: 382-386.
Holliday, C. Women's Life, pp. 39-40.
Humphrey, G. Women, Amer. Hist., pp. 18-29.
Logan, J. A. Part Taken by Women, pp. 37-42.
McVicker, E. R. "Anne Hutchinson," N.Y. State H.A. Proc.
      Vol. 9: 256-266.
Miller, P. The New Engl. Mind, see index, Ann Hutchinson.
Morgan, E. S. Puritan Dilemma, pp. 134-140, 147-154.
Morgan, E. S. "Ann Hutchinson," New Engl. Quart. Vol. 10:
      635-649.
Rugg, W. K. Anne Hutchinson.
Westchester Co. Hist., Soc. Anne Hutchinson and Other
      Papers.
Winsor, J. Mem. Hist., Boston. Vol. 4: 333-335.
Winthrop, J. Hist., New Engl. Vol. 1: see index; Vol. 2:
      39, 138.

C.   Lady Moody of Long Island

Deborah Moody also disagreed with the Puritans in the Massachusetts
Bay Colony. She moved to Long Island, where she established a settlement
in which complete religious liberty was observed. See also List of 104 Outstanding Women.

Dexter, E. A. Colonial Women, pp. 188-189.
Edwards (Mrs.), H. M. "Deborah Moody," Essex Inst. H.
Colls. Vol. 31: 96-102.
Ellis, G. E. Puritan Age, pp. 381-386.
Felt, J. B. Annals, Salem, pp. 160,239, 530-531.
Fernow, B. N.Y. Colonial Docs. Vol. 14: 51, 290, 299-300,
327-329.
Flick, A. C. "Lady Deborah Moody," Long Island H.S.
Quart. Vol. 1: 69-75.
Holliday, C. Women's Life, p. 288.
Lewis, A. Hist., Lynn, Mass., pp. 74-75.
Ross, P. Hist., Long Is. Vol. 1: 22, 355-364.
Thompson, B. Hist., Long Is., pp. 83-84, 438-443.
Van Rensselaer (Mrs.), J. K. Mana-ha-ta, pp. 109-110.
Van Wyck, F. Kesachauge, pp. 98, 100, 565.
Winthrop, J. Hist., New Engl. Vol. 2: 148-150, 164, 339-340,
430.

Women in the Church of England (Episcopalian)

While women in the Church of England had very few rights, they contributed
ᴧe churches and donated their services in many necessary duties.

Bean (Mrs.), R. B. "Colonial Church, Va.," V.M.H.B. Vol. 55: 78-84.
Dalcho, F. Acct., Church, So. Car., pp. 15, 34-35.
Davidson, E. H. Establishment, English Church, pp. 11-78.
McCrady, E. So. Car. Proprietary Govt., pp. 333-334.
Tyler, L. G. Narratives, Va., p. 339.
Van Rensselaer (Mrs.), J. K. Mana-ha-ta, p. 272.
Winsor, J. Mem. Hist., Boston. Vol. 3: 447-466.

Women in the Lutheran, Dutch Reform, and Moravian Churches

Women in this group of churches had more freedom than in the Puritan
ches but less than in the more radical branches of the Protestant faiths.
ᴦ believed in equal elementary education for both sexes and in advanced edu-
ᴐn for women in the Moravian Church.

Acrelius, I. Hist., New Sweden, pp. 404-408, 422-426.
Fernow, Berthold, ed. Records, New Amsterdam. Vol. 2: 154.
Fries, A. L. Records, Moravians. Vol. 1: 119-151, 213, 216-223.
Fries, A. L. Road, Salem.
Henry, J. Moravian Life, pp. 73, 82, 93, 110, 125, 129-132.
Holder, E. M. "Social Life, Moravians," N.C.H. Rev. Vol. 11: 167-
184.
Innes, J. H. New Amsterdam, pp. 78-79.
Maurer, M. "Moravians, N.C., " W.M. Quart. Ser. 3, Vol. 8: 214-
227.
Myers, E. L. Moravian Sisters, pp. 15-71, 141-160, 165-192.
Reichel, L. T. Hist., Church, United Brethern, pp. 85-86.
Sachse, J. Wayside Inns, pp. 60-62.

Woody, T. Hist., Educ., Women. Vol. 1: 179-185.

7. Women in the Organization of the Methodist and Presbyterian Churches

The Methodist Church in the United States was started in New York in 1766, largely by the efforts of Barbara Heck, who was an ardent follower of the Wesleyan faith. John Melish, traveling through Georgia, reported hearing the gifted Dorothy Ripley, a Negro Methodist preacher. Among the Presbyterians many women made noteworthy contributions.

> Buckley, J. M. Hist., Methodism. Vol. 1: 1, 17, 119, 126.
> Buoy, C. W. Women, Methodism, pp. 243-333.
> Clement, J. Noble Deeds, pp. 213-217.
> Coles, G. Heroines, Methodism, pp. 128-187.
> Dexter, E. A. Colonial Women, pp. 148-150.
> Melish, J. Travels. Vol. 1: 37.
> Stevens, A. Women, Methodism, pp. 175-256.
> Symmes, F. R. Hist., Old Tennent Church, pp. 178-181.
> Wakely, J. B. Early Hist., Methodism, pp. 35-36.
> Winsor, J. Mem., Hist., Boston. Vol. 3: 433-446.

8. Women Among the Friends (Quakers)

A. Position of Women

The Society of Friends recognized the equality of women's religious rights more fully than any other religious group. Women became outstanding preachers, teachers, and leaders in the periodic meeting of the Friends. They were also missionaries, and many suffered persecution for their faith.

> Biddle, G.B., & Lowrie, S.D. Notable Women, Pa., pp. 11-12.
> Clement, J. "Elizabeth Estaugh," N.J.H.S. Proc. Ser. 3,
> Vol. 7: 103-105.
> Drinker, S.H. Hannah Penn.
> Hopkins, S. Susanna Anthony.
> Jones, R.M. Quakers, Amer., pp. 249-305, 313-314.
> Jones, R.M. Later Quakerism. Vol. 1: 115-117, 277, 299-306.
> Vaux, G. Early Settlers, Merion, Pa., P.M.H.B. Vol. 13: 296.

B. Quaker Women as Preachers and Missionaries

Quaker women missionaries came from England to preach in the colonies and to form churches. They trudged up and down the colonies, preaching wherever they could gather a group to listen. They were persecuted in every colony but Rhode Island. Some suffered martyrdom, but nothing stayed them from their religious work.

> Adams, J. T. Founding, New Engl., pp. 264-273.
> Ames, S. M. Studies, Va., pp. 235-238.
> Anderson, J. Memorable Women. Vol. 1: 221-242.
> Benson, M. S. Women, 18th Cent. Amer., p. 267.

Best, M. A. Rebel Saints, pp. 106-116, 215-257.
Biddle, G. B., & Lowrie, D. S. Notable Women, Pa., pp. 4-5, 11-12, 88-89.
Bliss, W. R. Sidelights, Meeting House, pp. 111-116.
Brailsford, M. R. Quaker Women, see index.
Bruce, R. Inst., Hist., Va. Vol. 1: 225-237.
Carroll, K. L. "Md. Quakers," Md. H. Mag. Vol. 47: 297-312.
Coffin, C. C. Old Times, Colonies, pp. 109, 219-223.
Cresson, C. Diary, pp. 8, 189.
Dexter, E. A. Colonial Women, pp. 146-148, 209-210.
Ellis, G. E. Puritan Age, pp. 441-470.
Evans, W. & T. Friends Library. Vol. 1: 460-481; Vol. 2: 68-83, 184-212; Vol. 4: 10-59, 171-214, 450-468; Vol. 5: 1-23; Vol. 6: 478-480; Vol. 7: 430-478; Vol. 10: 441-480; Vol. 11: 72-119, 188-287, 449-473; Vol. 12: 1-145, 254-367, 413-480; Vol. 13: 50-93, 163-173, 179-201; Vol. 14: 278-380.

Friends. Memorials, Deceased Friends, pp. 39-41, 52-57, 80-82, 176-179.

Green, J. J. "Letter, Hannah Penn.," Friend's H.S. Journal. Vol. 4: 133-139.

Gummere, A.M. "Hannah Penn," The Friend. Vol. 100: 362, 379-380.

Hallowell, R. P. The Quaker Invasion, pp. 34-60, and appendix.
Hart, A. B., & Curtis, J. G. Amer. Hist. Vol. 1: 479-481.
Hopkins, S. Susanna Anthony.
Hubbs, R. Memoirs, Rebecca Hubbs.
Hudson, D. Jemima Wilkinson
James, B. B. Hist., No. Amer. Vol. 5: 161-168.
Jones, R. Quakers, Amer., see index, women's names.
Jones, R. Later Quakerism. Vol. 1: 107-121, 277, 299-307.

Klain, Z. Educational Activities, Quakers, pp. 1-5.

Nelson, W. Arch., N.J. Ser. 1, Vol. 26: 322-323.
Paige, L. R. Hist., Cambridge, Mass., pp. 344-364.
Parsons, J. L. Diary, J. Hiltzheimer, pp. 65-66, 145.
Perley, S. "Persecution, Quakers," Essex Antiq. Vol. 1: 135-140.

Pomfret, J. E. West N.J., pp. 121-122, 287.
Rochefoucault-Liancourt, F. Travels. Vol. 1: 210-215.
Ross, P. Hist., Long Is. Vol. 1: 163-169.
Rubincam, M. "Lydia Wright," N.J.H.S. Proc. Vol. 58: 103-118.

St. John, R. P. "Jemima Wilkinson," N.Y. State H.A. Quart. Vol. 11: 158-175.

Scharf, J. T., & Wescott, T. Hist., Phila. Vol. 2: 1685-1695.
Seaver, J. E. Mary Jemison.
Sewel, W. Hist., Quakers. Vol. 1: 203, 204, 217, 218, 243, 246, 249.

S.C.H.G. Mag. "Mary Fisher Crosse," S.C.H.G. Mag. Vol. 12: 106-108.
Starbuck, A. Hist., Nantucket, pp. 21, 133, 518-531.
Thomas, A. L. Journ., Nancy Lloyd.
Tyler, A. F. Freedom's Ferment, pp. 115-121.
Van Rensselaer (Mrs.), J. K. Mana-ha-ta, pp. 110-111.
Updike, W. Hist., Episcopal Church, Narragansett, pp. 233-236.
Watson, J. F. Annals, Phila. Vol. 1: 47-49, 531-533.
Webber, M. L. "Records, Quakers," S.C.H.G. Mag. Vol. 28: 24, 98, 105, 178.
Weeden, W. Hist., New Engl. Vol. 2: 544, 808-809.
Wisbey, H. A. "Jemima Wilkinson," N.Y. State H.A. Quart. Vol. 38: 387-396.

9.   Ann Lee, Foundress of the Shakers

Ann Lee was the foundress of the Millenial Church of the Shakers in the United States. She arrived with six men and two women in New York in 1774 and settled her religious colony near Albany. Her religious tenents included a belief in celibacy and communal life. See also List of 104 Outstanding Women.

Andrews, E. D. The Gift to be Simple.
Andrews, E. D. People Called Shakers, pp. 1-69.
Bentley, W. Diary. Vol. 2: 144-155, 173.
Brainard, J. M. "Mother Ann's Children," Conn. Mag. Vol. 3: 461-474.
Dexter, E. A. Colonial Women, pp. 150-153.
Evans, F. W. Ann Lee, Founder, Shakers.
Green, C., & Wells, S. Y. Millennial Church.
Melcher, M. F. The Shaker Adventure, pp. 15-119.
Rochefoucault-Liancourt, F. Travels. Vol. 2: 93-96.
Rourke, C. Roots, Amer. Culture, pp. 195-237.
Sears, C. E. Old Shaker Journs.
Shaker, E. Mother Ann Lee.
Tyler, A. F. Freedom's Ferment, pp. 140-165.

10.   Women in the Synagogues

Jewish women contributed to the support and care of their churches, often under extremely difficult situations and at great sacrifice to themselves.

Lebeson, A. L. Jewish Pioneers, pp. 111-126.
Logan, M. S. Part Taken by Women, p. 631.
Pool, D. Portraits Etched in Stone, see index, women's names.

VII

THE EDUCATION OF COLONIAL WOMEN

1. Attitudes Regarding the Education of Girls and Women by Areas

A. In New England

The attitude of men concerning the education of the girls in New England beyond home duties was that of grudging consent under pressure. The authorities permitted the use of public funds and facilities only when the boys were otherwise occupied. Parents generally educated their daughters only to the extent that the girls themselves demanded. Thus, a few were very well educated, but many could not sign their own names. However, a woman gave the first plot of ground for a free school in Massachusetts, and in all the settlements they sought to gain admission to the public schools.

> Adams, C. F. Familiar Letters, p. 339.
> Basset, J. S. Writings, Colonel Wm. Byrd, p. 361.
> Bliss, W. R. Sidelights, Meeting House, pp. 53-56.
> Bowne, E. S. A Girl's Life, pp. 56-59, 60-61.
> Brown, A. Mercy Warren, pp. 23-24.
> Calhoun, A. Soc. Hist., Amer. Family. Vol. 1: 82-86.
> Dexter, E. A. Colonial Women, pp. 21, 82.
> Dexter, F. B. Removal of Yale College, New Haven Col. H.S.
> Colls. Vol. 9: 80.
> Earle, A. M. Child Life, p. 93.
> Holliday, C. Women's Life, pp. 70-75, 90-91, 142-145.
> Mather, C. Diary, Mass. H.S. Colls. Ser. 7, Vol. 7: 534-537.
> Meyer, A. N. Woman's Work, pp. 19, 27.
> Morgan, E. S. The Puritan Family, pp. 28-29.
> Morison, S. E. Intellectual Life, pp. 83-84.
> Updegraff, H. Origin, Moving School, p. 115.
> Willison, G. F. Saints & Strangers, pp. 385-387.
> Winthrop, J. Hist., New Engl., p. 225.
> Woody, T. Hist. Educ. Women. Vol. 1: 124-130, 142.

B. In the Middle Atlantic Colonies

The attitude of men in the Middle Atlantic Colonies concerning the education of women was less grudging than in New England. From the first, girls were given elementary education along with the boys. Later, the religious tenets of the Quakers and Moravians particularly tended to encourage the further education of women. It was in New York and Pennsylvania that Bennett, Rush, Neal and others made the strongest pleas for the advanced education of women toward the close of the period.

Bennett, J. Strictures, Female Education.
Calhoun, A. Soc. Hist., Amer. Family. Vol. 1: 188.
Good, H. G. Benjamin Rush, pp. 226-234.
Holliday, C. Woman's Life, pp. 70-71.
Kilpatrick, W. H. Dutch Schools, New Netherlands, p. 229.
Neal, J. A. Essay, Female Sex.
Pennypacker, S. W. Settlement, Germantown, p. 189.
Rush, B. Essays, pp. 19-20, 75-92.
Wharton, A. H. Colonial Days, pp. 125-6, 178, 186, 197-199.
Woody, T. Hist. Educ. Women. Vol. 1: 179, 301-305, 328.

C.   In the Southern Colonies and the Southwest

The attitude concerning the education of women in the Southern colonies was that of almost complete indifference. Only approximately a fourth of the women could sign their own names by 1700. A few brilliant women were privately educated, but the public facilities for the education of girls were very limited throughout the south and southwest areas.

Andrews, M. P. Virginia, p. 363.
Bruce, A. P. Inst. Hist., Va. Vol. 1: 452-457.
Calhoun, A. Soc. Hist., Amer. Family. Vol. 1: 297.
Holliday, C. Woman's Life, pp. 70-75.
James, E. Notes on Illiteracy, W.M. Quart. Ser. 1, Vol. 3: 98.
McCrady, E. So. Car., Royal Govt., pp. 485-486.
Wharton, A. H. Colonial Days, p. 94.
Woody, T. Hist. Educ. Women. Vol. 1: 246-248.
(see also schools of religious groups)

2.   Educational Practices in Colonial Days Concerned with Women

A.   General Statements

The education of women during the Colonial and early Federal periods was carried on through (1) dame schools (public and private), (2) publicly supported schools, (3) private schools including charity schools and the later seminaries, and (4) private tutoring. Women were the teachers in the dame schools and in some of the publicly supported schools. Women taught in many of the private schools as owners, helpers, or assistants to their husbands, who usually taught the boys. Private tutoring appears to have been almost exclusively done by men.

Benson, M. S. Women, 18th Cent. Amer., pp. 136-187.
Dexter, E. A. Colonial Women, pp. 78-79, 97.
Earle, A. M. Child Life, pp. 63-89, 90-116.
Hart, A. B. Commonwealth Hist., Mass. Vol. 2: 355-385.
Holliday, C. Woman's Life, pp. 70-94.
Hurd, I. H. Hist., Essex Co., Mass. Vol. 1: 131-132.
Woody, T. Hist. Educ. Women. Vol. 1: 460.
(See also schools of religious groups)

B. Schools in the New England Colonies

The first compulsory education law passed in the colonies was the Massachusetts Bay Court Order of 1642, which required all parents and masters to educate their children and apprentices to read, write, and do some elementary arithmetic. Not all parents or masters could comply with the law; so schools were started in most of the settlements. The law of 1647 required every town of fifty families in the colony to establish a school. The schools ranged from the early dame schools to the later private seminaries and charity schools.

a. Dame Schools in New England

Dame Schools were started by 1635 and were taught by women in their homes. Some were partially or wholly supported by the town. Others were private ventures. Reading, writing, and simple arithmetic were the subjects generally taught; but sewing, embroidery, and music were sometimes included in the curriculum.

Adams, S.W., & Stiles, H. R. Hist., Wethersfield, Mass. Vol. 1: 383-384.
Bentley, W. Diary. Vol. 2: 31, 173, 215, 291, 315, 358, 360, 364, 441.
Brooks, C. History, Medford, Mass., p. 283.
Calder, I. M. New Haven Colony, p. 131.
Dexter, E. A. Colonial Women, pp. 78-87, 97.
Dexter, E. G. Hist., Educ., pp. 424-425.
Drake, F. S. Roxbury, Mass., p. 86.
Earle, A. M. Child Life, p. 98.
Hart, A. B. Colonial Children, pp. 201-233.
Holliday, C. Women's Life, pp. 71-72
Hudson, C. Hist., Lexington, Mass. Vol. 1: 379-380.
Johnson, C. Schools and Books, pp. 1-28, 44-45.
Phillips, J. D. Salem, Mass., 18th Cent., p. 345.
Sewall, S. Sewall Papers, Vol. 1: 164, 344, 411, 416-18, 436; Vol. 3: 293.
Sewall, S. E. Hist., Woburn, Mass., pp. 209-211.
Seybolt, R. F. Private Schools, pp. 4-5, 7-9.
Small, W. H. Early Schools, pp. 162-186.
Updegraff, H. Origin, Moving School, Mass., pp. 136-149.
Waters, T. F. Ipswich, Mass. Vol. 2: 274-5.
Willison, G. F. Saints & Strangers, p. 384.
Woody, T. Hist., Educ., Women. Vol. 1: 137-142, 164.

b. Town and Public Schools in New England

At first girls were allowed to attend the publicly supported schools generally when the schools were not used for the boys, such as before and after the boys attended or in the summer. Later, they attended with the boys or at coordinate sessions. The majority of the teachers were men, although in some instances women taught the girls or the whole school.

Allen, M. C. Hist., Wenham, Mass., p. 113.
Bentley, W. Diary. Vol. 1, see index (1) Susannah Babbidge, (2) Hannah Mascoll (3) Mary Bowditch, (4) Priscilla Gill and Sarah Knight. Vol. 2, see index (1), (2), (5), also pp. 32 & 437.
Blake, F. E. Hist., Dorchester Neck, Mass., p. 45.
Blake, J. W. Hist., Warwick, Mass., pp. 37-38.
Brooks, C. Hist., Medford, Mass., pp. 278, 281-283.
Butler, C. Hist., Groton, Mass., pp. 217-222, 354-355.
Dexter, E. G. Hist., Educ., pp. 427-428.
Dexter, E. A. Colonial Women, pp. 79-87.
Earle, A. M. Child Life, pp. 95-96.
Felt, J. B. Annals, Salem, pp. 164, 177, 354, 389.
Green, S. A. Journ., Sargent Holden, Mass. H.S. Proc. Ser. 2, Vol. 4: 386.
Hurd, I. H. Hist., Essex Co., Mass. Vol. 1: 131-132.
Johnson, C. Schools & Books, pp. 29-44, 135-145.
Lamson, D. F. Hist., Manchester, pp. 60, 206-209.
Meyer, A. N. Women's Work, p. 260.
Nelson, C. A. Waltham, Mass., pp. 71, 80.
Paige, L. R. Hist., Cambridge, Mass., pp. 365-373.
Sewall, S. E. Hist., Woburn, Mass., pp. 221-232.
Seybolt, R. F. Public Schools, pp. 1-11.
Seybolt, R. F. Apprenticeship & Apprenticeship Educ., pp. 36-51.
Small, W. H. Early Schools, pp. 164, 275, 286.
Smith, E. V. Hist., Newburyport, pp. 101-102.
Starbuck, A. Hist., Nantucket, p. 100.
Trumbull, J. R. Hist., Northampton. Vol. 1: 222, 439, 571-573.
Tucker, J. Old Schools & Teachers, Essex Inst. H. Colls. Vol. 7: 241-243.
Updegraff, H. Origin, Moving School, pp. 11-83, 150-170.
Waters, T. F. Ipswich, Mass. Vol. 2: 276-292.
Weeden, W. B. Hist., New Engl. Vol. 1: 221.
Willison, G. F. Saints & Strangers, p. 478.
Winsor, J. Mem. Hist., Boston. Vol. 2: 503; Vol. 4: 237.
Winthrop, J. Hist., New Engl. Vol. 2: 264.
Woody, T. Hist. Educ. Women. Vol. 1: 142-148, 155, 164.

c.   Early Private and Boarding Schools in New England

Private schools (some were partially supported by towns), some of which were boarding schools, sprang up in all the larger communities. Women were often the teachers and taught not only reading and writing but also music and the arts and crafts of the home. There were several notable teachers such as Sarah Knight who made significant contributions.

Bentley, W. Diary. See references under previous section.
Brooks, G. Dames and Daughters, pp. 75-102.
Dexter, E. G. Hist., Educ., pp. 428-430.
Dexter, E. A. Colonial Women, pp. 82-94.
Green, H. C. & M. W. Pioneer Mothers. Vol. 1: 442-455.
Hopkins, S. Life of Sarah Osborn.
Seybolt, R. F. Private Schools, pp. 11-83.
Small, W. H. Early Schools, pp. 170-178.
Wharton, A. H. Colonial Days, p. 41.
Woody, T. Hist. Educ. Women. Vol. 1: 149-160.

d. Tutorial Education of Women in New England

A few young women were allowed to study privately with the
school master, the minister, or a relative, in which case their education went well beyond the work done in the private schools and, in a
very few cases, paralleled that of the colleges.

Brown, A. Mercy Warren, pp. 23-26.
Holliday, C. Women's Life, pp. 92-93.
Woody, T. Hist. Educ. Women. Vol. 1: 133-136.

e. Later Female Academies, Seminaries and Charity Schools in
New England

The earliest academy for girls in New England was started in
1763 and was followed, after the Revolutionary War, by a number of
others. New subjects were added to the curriculum, and more emphasis was placed on the academic subjects. The charity school
movement was started in 1789 to give elementary education to the
girls from poor or indigent families.

Adams, S. W., & Stiles, H. R. Hist., Wethersfield, Mass.
    Vol. 1: 382.
Bentley, W. Diary. Vol. 2: 31, 155, 173-4, 215, 291, 315, 358-
    64, 405, 441.
Dexter, E. A. Career Women, pp. 1-20.
Dexter, E. A. Colonial Women, p. 87.
Hodgman, E. P. Hist., Westford, Mass., pp. 312-314.
Meyer, A. N. Woman's Work, p. 18.
Sewall Diary. Mass. H.S. Colls. Ser. 5, Vol. 7 (Diary Vol. 3):
    293.
Shipton, C. K. Secondary Educ., Puritan Colonies New Engl.
    Quart. Vol. 7: 646-661.
Small, W. H. Early Schools, p. 173.
Vanderpoel, E. N. Litchfield School, pp. 1-9.
Washburn, E. Hist., Leicester Academy, pp. 27-29.
White, A. C. Hist., Litchfield, Conn., pp. 110-120.
Woody, T. Hist. Educ. Women. Vol. 1: 339-342.

C. Schools of the Middle Atlantic Colonies

While provision was made for the education of the girls as well as the boys in the charters of each of the four colonies, two factors differentiated their development. The English took over New Netherlands and did not make education compulsory except for apprentices. In the other three colonies, Lutherans, Quakers, Moravians and other religious groups established schools almost at once in connection with their churches, where equal education was given to boys and girls.

a. Early Schools and Their Teachers

The early schools of the Middle Atlantic Colonies, like those of New England, were crude and limited to elementary subjects; however, they generally included both boys and girls, largely due to the religious beliefs of the settlers.

> Acrelius, I. Hist., New Sweden, pp. 351-352.
> Calhoun, A. Soc. Hist., Amer. Family. Vol. 1: p. 174.
> Clay, J. C. Annals, Swedes, pp. 43, 49.
> Earle, A. M. Child Life, p. 94.
> Earle, A. M. Colonial Days, N.Y., pp. 37-39.
> Halsey, A. F. Old Southampton, pp. 66-67.
> Pennypacker, S. Settlement, Germantown, pp. 109, 140, 189, 203.
> Powell, L. P. Hist. Educ. Del., pp. 12-26.
> Randall, S. S. Hist., Common School, N.Y., p. 3.
> Ridgely, M. L. What Them Befell, pp. 49-65.
> Rush, B. Account, German Inhabitants of Pa., p. 105.
> Van Rensselaer, J. K. Mana-ha-ta, pp. 10-11.
> Woody, T. Hist. Educ. Women. Vol. 1: 192, 195-207.

b. Private and Adventure Schools in the Middle Colonies

In the absence of laws governing the schools as in New England, many private schools sprang up, particularly in the cities. Most of them had religious foundations and were good elementary schools, but some of them were little more than financial ventures. Almost every newspaper carried advertisements of these schools. Each offered special inducement for students.

> Clement, J. Noble Deeds, pp. 213-217.
> Dexter, E. A. Colonial Women, pp. 88-93.
> Gottesman, R. T. Arts and Crafts, N.Y., 1726-1777, pp. 279, 311.
> Lee, F. B. Arch, N.J. Ser. 2, Vol. 2: 294.
> Nelson, W. Arch, N.J. Ser. 2, Vol. 4: 332.
> Powell, L. P. Hist. Educ., Del., p. 49.
> Scharf, J. T., & Wescott, T. Hist., Phila. Vol. 2: 962-963.
> Wharton, A. H. Colonial Days, p. 47.
> Woody, T. Hist. Educ. Women. Vol. 1: 217-230, 234-237, 333-339.

c. Town Schools in the Middle Colonies

It is impossible to differentiate sharply between church schools and town or public schools since, in many cases, the town and church were identical. The education of all the children was strongly emphasized so that even the children of poor parents attended the schools whether they paid tuition or not. The Penn Charter Public School was started by joint religious effort in 1697.

Earle, A. M. Colonial Days, N.Y., pp. 35-40.
Kilpatrick, W. H. Dutch Schools, pp. 30, 217-219.
Meyer, A. N. Woman's Work, p. 17.
New Jersey Hist. Soc. Morris Academy, N.J.H.S. Proc. Ser.
    1, Vol. 8: 18-31.
Woody, T. Hist. Educ. Women. Vol. 1: 198-201.

d. Tutorial Education of Girls in the Middle Colonies

Tutorial education was not uncommon in the Middle Colonies. Some of the wealthy settlers had indentured servants as tutors for their children. Most of the ministers took pupils to increase their incomes. Women tutors frequently advertised in the newspapers.

Dexter, E. A. Colonial Women, pp. 95-96.
Earle, A. M. Colonial Days, N.Y., p. 35.
Gottesman, R. S. Arts and Crafts, N.Y., 1777-1799, pp. 285-310.
Woody, T. Hist. Educ. Women. Vol. 1: 194.

e. The Charity School Movement in the Middle Colonies

As early as 1739 there was a charity school started by Trinity Church in New York City. A benefit concert was performed for its support in 1755. In 1796, Anne Parrish opened a charity school for girls in Philadelphia and later formed a society to insure the continuance of the school. The New York Association for the Education of Poor Female Children began its work in 1789. These and other efforts indicate the profound belief that the colonists had in the right of every girl to have an education.

Calhoun, A. W. Soc. Hist., Amer. Family. Vol. 1: 174.
Dexter, E. A. Career Women, p. 17.
Scharf, J. T., & Westcott, T. Hist., Phila. Vol. 2: 1475.
Sonneck, O. G. Early Concert Life, pp. 67-68, 161-163.
Weber, S. Charity School Movement, pp. 23-64.
Woody, T. Hist. Educ. Women. Vol. 1: 202-207.

D. The Education of Women in the Southern Colonies

It has been conservatively estimated that, before 1700, seventy-five per cent of the women in the Southern Colonies were illiterate and few ever attended school. The large estates tended to emphasize family education, which was largely tutorial. Old field schools were established at a central point between the estates and were public in that they served the several families of the neighborhood. The daughters of the indigent were trained by law in the weaving mills and given some elementary education.

a. Tutorial Education of Women in the South

Most of the education of the women in the Southern Colonies was tutorial. Some of the tutors were indentured servants who had been educated in England or Europe and had bound themselves to serve a master for their passage money. Others were adventurous scholars traveling through the colonies. A few were women. The tutorial plan of education, while leaving much to be desired, gave a few brilliant women an unusually fine training; and some of these went to England for further education.

Bruce, P. A. Inst. Hist., Va. Vol. 1: 299,301, 311, 323-329.
Bruce, P. A. Social Life, Va., pp. 231, 323-328.
Davis, J. Personal Adventures, pp. 15, 22-24, 78, 85-86.
Early, R. H. Byways, Va. Hist., pp. 155-157.
Fisher, S. G. Men, Women and Manners. Vol. 2: 321-323.
Richardson, H. D. Sidelights, Md. Hist. Vol. 1: Chap. 33.
Spruill, J. C. Women's Life, pp. 55, 185-187, 193-194.
Stanard, M. M. Colonial, Va., pp. 278-282, 287-294, 351-2.
Woody, T. Hist. Educ. Women. Vol. 1: 249, 261, 271-281.

b. Private Schools in the Southern Colonies

Private schools for girls began to appear after the middle of the eighteenth century, chiefly in the centers of population. These were day or boarding schools and ranged from the counterpart of the dame schools of New England to fashionable boarding schools where the girls were taught the elegant graces of society. The academic subjects were elementary and frequently taught by women.

Armstrong, Z. Notable Southern Families. Vol. 1: 39.
Bartlett, H. R. 18th Cent. Ga. Women, pp. 106-115.
Blandin, I. M. Hist. Higher Educ. Women, pp. 36-40, 43, 57,
    129-131, 153, 217-222, 273-274, 310-312.
Dexter, E. A. Colonial Women, pp. 82-83.
Dexter, E. A. Career Women, pp. 14-17.
Earle, A. M. Child Life, p. 94.
Hamilton, P. J. Hist., No. Amer. Vol. 5: 368-369.
Hirsch, A. H. Huguenots in So. Car., pp. 157-159.
Jones, H. Present State, Va., pp. 70, 83-94.

Prime, A. C.   Arts and Crafts, 1786-1800, p. 52
Spruill, J. C.   Women's Life, pp. 185, 197-200, 256-259.
Stanard, M. M.   Colonial Va., pp. 271-277.
Stith, E.   Will, W. M. Quart. Ser. 1, Vol. 5:   115.
Trumbull, J. R.   Hist., Northampton. Vol. 1:   222, 439, 571-573.
Tyler, L. G.   Model School, W. M. Quart. Ser. 1, Vol. 4:   1-14.
Tyler, L. G.   Educ. Colonial Va., W. M. Quart. Ser. 1, Vol. 6:
    1-6.
Waring, M. G.   Savannah's Private Schools, Ga. H. Quart. Vol.
    14:   324-334.
Woody, T.   Hist. Educ. Women. Vol. 1:   281-2, 292-295.
    (See also religious schools)

c.   Old Field and Other Free Schools in the South

Old Field schools helped to meet the educational needs of the children on the estates.   The school was often held in the schoolmaster's home, and generally all the white children of the neighborhood were eligible to attend.   Free schools were started in most of the cities by special endowments.   The first such school was opened in Virginia in 1642.   A few plantation owners held classes in elementary subjects for their negro slaves.

Blandin, I. M.   Hist. Higher Educ. Women, pp. 16-19.
Bruce, P. A.   Inst. Hist., Va. Vol. 1:   329-361.
Dalcho, F.   Acct. Church, So. Car., pp. 93-95.
Green, H. C. & M. W.   Pioneer Mothers. Vol. 1:   47.
Holliday, C.   Woman's Life, pp. 77-78.
James, E. W.   Norfolk Academy, W. M. Quart. Ser. 1, Vol.
    3:   3-8.
Knight, E. W.   Doc. Hist., Educ. Vol. 1:   178-219, 571-664.
Knight, L. L.   Ga.'s Landmarks. Vol. 2:   252-263.
McCrady, E.   So. Car. Royal Govt., pp. 46, 49-50, 449, 482-
    483.
McCrady, E.   So. Car. Proprietary Govt., pp. 339-340, 354,
    487-488, 494, 511-512, 700-701.
Maddox, W. A.   The Free School Idea, Va., pp. 1-62.
Richardson, H. D.   Sidelights, Md. Hist. Vol. 1:   169-170.
Spruill, J. C.   Women's Life, pp. 190, 255.
Stanard, M. M.   Colonial Va., pp. 262-270.
Tyler, L. G.   Educ., Colonial Va., W. M. Quart. Ser. 1, Vol. 6:
    71-85.
Tyler, L. G.   School Teachers, Va., W. M. Quart. Ser. 1, Vol.
    7:   178.
White, G.   Hist. Colls., Ga., pp. 21-31.
Woody, T.   Hist. Educ. Women. Vol. 1:   269-270.
    (See also religious schools)

3. The Education of Women by Religious Groups

Many of the religious groups in the colonies fostered the education of women. In each case, schools were started primarily to teach the specific religious principles held by the group. Knowledge of these principles was held necessary to the salvation of their souls. Hence, most of the curriculum in the early years was concerned with reading and understanding the tenets of the churches.

A. Catholic Schools for Women

The first school exclusively for girls in the United States was started in New Orleans in 1727 by a small group of Ursuline nuns. However, coeducational schools had been started in Florida and New Mexico as early as 1598 by Franciscan Friars. In Texas, the earliest schools were started about 1689 and, in California, by 1769. Georgetown Visitation School was started in Washington, District of Columbia, in 1798.

> Baudier, R. Catholic Church, La., pp. 103-107, 122, 123, 124, 136-138, 142.
> Blandin, I. M. Hist. Higher Educ. Women, pp. 20-30.
> Burns, J. A. Catholic School System, pp. 39-49, 55-62, 68-79, 113-114, 123-124, 141-143, 202-204.
> Burns, J. A., & Kohlbrenner, B. J. Hist., Catholic Educ., pp. 29-33, 55.
> Dexter, E. A. Career Women, p. 18.
> Fay, E. W. Hist. Educ., La., pp. 9, 17.
> Fortier, A. La. Studies, pp. 242-252.
> Goebel, E. J. Catholic Secondary Educ., pp. 26-32, 80-82, 94.
> Hodge, et al. Revised Memorial Benavides.
> James, G. W. In and Out, Old Missions, pp. 53-84.
> Jones, W. H. Hist., Catholic Educ., Colo., pp. 1-35.
> Knight, E. W. Doc. Hist., Educ. Vol. 1: 686-696.
> Lathrop, G. P. & R. H. Story of Courage, pp. 146-177.
> Woody, T. Hist. Educ. Women. Vol. 1: 329-330.

B. Puritan (Congregational) Education of Women

The Puritans were vitally concerned with the education necessary to understand the principles of their religion; and since women's souls also had to be saved, laws were passed requiring all children to learn to read and write. The Overseers visited the homes and catechised the girls as well as the boys. Beyond this meager learning, the Puritans tended to discourage any efforts to educate the girls in their communities.

> Bentley, W. Diary, pp. 29-32.
> Mason, M. P. Church-State Relationships, Conn., pp. 8-16, 36-41.
> Mather, C. Diary, Mass. Hist. Soc. Colls. Ser. 7, Vol. 7: 457-458, 477.
> Morgan, E. S. Puritan Family, pp. 45-61.
> Sewall, S. Hist., Woburn, Mass., pp. 66-68.

Stewart, G. Hist., Religious Educ., Conn., pp. 3-93, 155-193.
(See also education in New England)

C. Education of Women by the Church of England (Episcopalian)

The Episcopalian Church as the official Church of England "strictly required and admonished parents" to educate their children in Christian principles. Through their Society for the Propagation of the Gospel in Foreign Parts, they started coeducational schools in most of the southern colonies and in New York. However, they did not encourage advanced education for women.

Calhoun, A. Soc. Hist., Amer. Family. Vol. 1: 193.
Clement, J. Noble Deeds, pp. 213-217.
Holtz, A. A. Moral, Religious, Educ., pp. 21-22, 25-27.
Kemp, W. W. Support, Schools, N.Y.
McCrady, E. So. Car. Royal Govt., pp. 482-487.
McCrady, E. So. Car. Proprietary Govt., p. 449.
Pratt, D. J. Annals, Public Educ., N.Y., pp. 109-110.
Raper, C. L. Church & Private Schools, pp. 21-24.

D. Education of Women by the Lutheran and Other Reform Church Groups

The Lutherans, Pietists and Mennonites started church schools to educate both the boys and girls. The curriculum was elementary, and generally taught by the pastor. The church school was frequently the only school in the community.

Holtz, A. A. Moral, Religious, Educ., pp. 21-25.
Weber, S. Charity School Movement, pp. 19-20.
Wickersham, J. P. Hist., Educ., Pa., pp. 140-141.
Woody, T. Hist. Educ. Women. Vol. 1: 209-216.

E. Education of Women by the Moravians

The Moravians were the first group of colonists to show an interest in the advanced education of women. They opened a female academy at Bethlehem, Pennsylvania. They also started schools in New York, Delaware, New Jersey and North Carolina.

Biddle, G. B., & Lowrie, S. D. Notable Women, Pa., pp. 34-35.
Blandin, I. M. Hist. Higher Educ. Women, pp. 31-35.
Dexter, E. A. Career Women, p. 18.
Fries, A. L. Road to Salem.
Haller, M. Moravian Educ. in Pa., Moravian Hist. Soc. Trans.
    Vol. 15: 1-397.
Meyer, A. N. Woman's Work, p. 17.
Myers, E. L. Moravian Sisters, pp. 141-160.
Raper, C. L. Church & Private Schools, No. Car., pp. 86-91.
Reichel, L. T. Hist., Church, United Brethren, pp. 199-201.

Reichel, W. C. Hist., Bethlehem Female Seminary, pp. 29-187.
Roof, K. M. Colonel William Smith and Lady, p. 19.
Rush, B. Account, German Inhabitants, Pa., pp. 49-50.
Wickersham, J. P. Hist., Educ., Pa., pp. 151-279.
Woody, T. Hist. Educ. Women. Vol. 1: 179, 216-217, 330-333, 339-341.

F.   Education of Women by the Quakers

Quaker women were not only educated with the men of the church, but they took an active part in the educational programs as members of promotional committees as teachers and as active workers on the supervisory boards. Wherever a settlement of Quakers was made, the women assisted in the establishment of a church school. When poverty became an educational problem, they started a charity school.

Calhoun, A. Soc. Hist., Amer. Family. Vol. 1: p. 201.
Comfort, W. W. Quakers, p. 26.
Dexter, E. A. Colonial Women, pp. 96-97.
Evans, W. & T. Friends Library, Vol. 1: 461.
Holtz, A. A. Moral & Religious, Educ., p. 35.
Klain, Z. Educ. Activities, Quakers, New Engl.
Klain, Z. Quaker Contributions, Educ., pp. 284-296.
Scharf, J. T., & Westcott, T. Hist., Phila. Vol. 2: 1475.
Woody, T. Quaker Educ., N.J.
Woody, T. Quaker Educ., Pa.
Woody, T. Hist. Educ. Women. Vol. 1: see index under Quaker Educ.

4.   Apprenticeship Education of Women

Apprenticeship education was made compulsory in most of the colonies due to the great need for trained workers. In New England, the law was stretched to cover all youths. In the southern colonies, it was applied only to the poor. Girls were taught household duties and elementary reading and writing. Later, they were put in the nascent cloth factories.

A.   In the New England Colonies

In New England all girls, apprenticed or "bound out," were required by law to be given an elementary education. If a parent (or master or mistress) did not educate a girl, the civil authority removed her from the home and placed her with a master (or mistress) who would guarantee to give the girl the required education.

Atwater, E. E. Hist., New Haven, pp. 261-292.
Jernegan, M. W. Laboring and Dependent Classes, pp. 59-128.
Leonard, E. A. Origins, Personnel Services, pp. 10-11, 13-14.
Morgan, E. S. The Puritan Family, pp. 37-38.
Seybolt, R. Apprenticeship and Apprenticeship Educ., pp. 25-34, 36-65.

B. In the Middle Atlantic Colonies

Apprenticeship education laws existed in the Middle Atlantic colonies but were not applied as rigorously as in New England. Masters were urged to teach their apprentices the three R's; and where it was obviously an advantage, they did so.

Calhoun, A. Soc. Hist., Amer. Family. Vol. l: 193.
Earle, A. M. Colonial Days, N.Y., p. 86.
Seybolt, R. Apprenticeship and Apprenticeship Educ., pp. 66-103.
Wickersham, J. P. Hist., Educ., Pa., pp. 28-29.
Woody, T. Quaker Educ., N.J.
Woody, T. Hist. Educ., Women. Vol. l: 256-265.

C. In the Southern Colonies

The apprenticeship education laws in the southern colonies were strong on manual training and weak or vague on academic training. Also, the laws applied exclusively to the children who were from indigent homes, illegitimate, or poor orphans. Many of the children were forced to come to the city factories and work as they trained.

Bruce, P. A. Econ. Hist., Va. Vol. 2: 455.
Bruce, P. A. Inst. Hist., Va. Vol. l: 310-315.
Hening, W. W. Statutes at Large, Va. Vol. 3: 375-376; Vol. 8: 134-135, 376-377; Vol. 12: 197.
Jernegan, M. W. Laboring and Dependent Classes, pp. 131-171.
Klain, Z. Quaker Contributions, Educ., N. C., pp. 297-299.
Knight, E. W. Doc. Hist., Educ. Vol. l: 32-61.
Spruill, J. C. Women's Life, p. 189.
Tyler, L. G. Educ., Va., W. & M. Quart. Ser. l, Vol. 5: 219-223; Vol. 6: 1-6, 71-89.
Woody, T. Hist., Educ., Women. Vol. l: 268-269.

5. The Subjects Taught the Girls in the Colonial Schools

A. Listing of Subjects Taught

The subjects taught in the colonial schools concerned domestic duties, social graces and academic subjects. The emphasis varied from domestic duties for apprentices to social graces for the southern girl and the academic subjects for the few brilliant students.

Bagnall, W. R. Textile Industry, pp. 18-31.
Bolton, C. K. Scotch-Irish Pioneers, p. 305.
Bolton, E. S., & Coe, E. J. Amer. Samplers, pp. 355-387.
Bowne, E. S. Girl's Life, pp. 8, 11, 15.
Burns, J. A. Catholic Schools System, pp. 42, 47-48, 55-60, 73-78.

Dexter, E. A. Colonial Women, pp. 88-94.
Dexter, E. A. Career Women, pp. 9, 12, 14-15.
Dow, G. F. Arts and Crafts, New Engl., pp. 267, 273-276, 281-282, 288-289.
Goebel, E. J. Catholic Secondary Educ., pp. 35-37, 43-45.
Gottesman, R. S. Arts and Crafts, N.Y., 1726-1776, pp. 275-278, 298-9.
Gottesman, R. S. Arts and Crafts, N.Y., 1777-1799, pp. 5, 370.
Lamson, D. F. Hist., Manchester, p. 285.
McCrady, E. So. Car. Royal Govt., pp. 490-491.
Meriwether, C. Colonial Curriculum, pp. 23-40.
Myers, A. C. Journ., Sally Wister, pp. 13-16.
Pennypacker, S. W. Settlement, Germantown, pp. 189-202.
Seybolt, R. F. The Private Schools, pp. 88-89.
Weeden, W. B. Hist., New Engl. Vol. 1: 282-283.
Woody, T. Hist., Educ., Women. Vol. 1: see index, curriculum.

B.   Textbooks Used in the Colonial Schools

The Hornbook and primer were replaced in time by more advanced textbooks. After the Revolutionary War, the textbooks of the academies for girls included books on grammar, philosophy, and some mathematics. However, most of the textbooks remained collections of superficial moralizing bits of information.

Bennett, J. Letters, Young Lady. Vols. 1 & 2.
Bingham, C. Amer. Preceptor.
Bingham, C. Young Lady's Accidence.
Burton, J. Lectures, Female Educ., Manners.
Darwin, E. Plan, Female Educ.
Dilworth, T. Schoolmaster's Assistant.
Earle, A. M. Child Life, pp. 117-190.
Fordyce, J. Sermons, Young Women.
Foster, H. W. Boarding School.
Halsey, R. V. Forgotten Books.
Johnson, C. Schools and Books, pp. 45-99.
Kilpatrick, W. F. Dutch Schools, pp. 149, 223-225, 227, 229.
Schlesinger, A. M. Learning How to Behave, pp. 1-15.
Spruill, J. C. Women's Life and Work, p. 202.
Stewart, G. Hist., Religious Educ., Conn., pp. 94-122, 194-217.

C.   Books and Libraries in Colonial Days

Since much of the education of girls during the colonial period was carried on in the home, it is of interest to note the extent of the libraries and kinds of books available to the girls. In general, the libraries were very limited and devoted largely to religious subjects.

Acrelius, I. A Hist., New Sweden, pp. 366-368.
Bayer, H. C. The Belgians, p. 346.
Bruce, P. A. Inst. Hist., Va. Vol. 1: 405-439.

Dalcho, F. Acct. Church, S. C., pp. 37-39.
Earle, A. M. Customs and Fashions, pp. 257-288.
Edmunds, A. J. First Books Imported, Phila., P.M.H.B. Vol.
　　30: 300-308.
Ford, W. C. Boston Book Market.
Hirsch, A. H. Huguenots, So. Car., pp. 161, 250-251.
McCrady, E. So. Car. Royal Govt., pp. 509-510.
Powell, L. P. Hist., Educ., Del., pp. 14-15.
Richardson, H. D. Sidelights, Md. Hist. Vol. 1: 119-122.
Stanard, M. M. Colonial Va., pp. 295-307.
Stearns, B. M. Early Phila. Mag. for Ladies, P.M.H.B. Vol.
　　64: 479-482.
Van Rennselaer (Mrs.) J. K. Mana-ha-ta, pp. 271, 383.
Wertenbaker, T. J. First Americans, pp. 237-282.
Wickersham, J. P. Hist., Educ., Pa., p. 17.
Wm. & M. Quart. Libraries, Colonial Va. Ser. 1, Vol. 3:
　　246-248.
Woody, T. Hist., Educ., Women. Vol. 1: 230-234, 252.

6. Glimpses of the School Life of the Girls

Diaries and chronicles of the school girls give us glimpses into their problems and delights.

Bowne, E. S. Girl's Life.
Foster, H. W. The Boarding School, pp. 8-10.
Earle, A. M., & Winston, A. G. Diary, Anna Winslow.
Myers, A. C. Journ. Sally Wister.
Vanderpoel, E. N. Litchfield School.

VIII

WOMAN'S DOMAIN -- THE HOME

As soon as possible after the establishment of each of the settlements, the colonists moved out of their first crude shelters and built houses to accomodate not only the family itself but also the wide range of home industries that were necessary to the maintenance and growth of the colony. The homes were literally the centers of industry; and it was as managers, or proprietors, of the homes that the colonial women made their major contributions. Some managed estates and experimented in agriculture; others produced saleable goods of many kinds; still others taught school, or transacted their shipping, sales and other businesses in their homes.

1. General Statements

Calhoun, A. Soc. Hist. Amer. Family. Vol. 1: 51-66, 67-82, 128-151,
　　153-272, 299-312.

Chastellux, Marquis de. Travels, pp. 251-256.
Crawford, M. C. Famous Families of Mass. Vols. 1 & 2, see index.
Earle, A. M. Margaret Winthrop.
Grant, A. Memoirs. Vols. 1 & 2.
Holliday, C. Women's Life, pp. 136-142.
Mason, E. V. Journal, Young Lady of Va.
Morison, S. E. Story of the "Old Colony."
Randolph, S. N. Domestic Life, Thomas Jefferson.
Rogers, A. A. Family Life in 18th Cent. Va.
Smith, H. Colonial Days, pp. 61-88.
Stanard, M. M. Colonial Va., pp. 102-135.
Torbert, A. C. Eleanor Calvert.
Van Doren, C. Jane Mecom.
Winsor, J. Mem. Hist., Boston. Vol. 1: 518-519.

2.   Women as Wives in the Colonial Home

Pioneer conditions made independent life almost impossible, both for men and women, even when they possessed considerable property and servants. Women married early and remarried as circumstances required, often three or four times.

A.   Marriages

a.   Courtship and Early Marriage

In all of the colonies the girls married while they were very young. Twelve, thirteen, and fourteen year-old-brides often assumed the responsibility for maintaining a home.

Adams, C. F. Church Discipline, New Engl., Mass. H. S. Proc.
    Ser. 2, Vol. 6: 503-510.
Andrews, C. M. Colonial Folkways, pp. 86-90.
Baber, R. E. Marriage & Family, pp. 28-39.
Bancroft, H. H. Works. Vol. 34: 307-310.
Bradford, W. Hist., Plymouth, p. 116.
Brickell, J. Natural Hist., No. Car., p. 31.
Calhoun, A. Soc. Hist. Amer. Family. Vol. 1: 54-57, 61-63,
    129-130, 202.
Comfort, W. W. Quakers, p. 24.
Dexter, E. A. Colonial Women, pp. 138-139.
Dunton, J. Life & Errors, p. 137.
Hall, C. C. Early Md., pp. 352-353.
Hart, A. B. Commonwealth Hist., Mass. Vol. 2: 361-364.
Holiday, C. Women's Life, p. 258.
Jones, R. M. Quakers, Amer., pp. 147, 547.
Morgan, E. S. The Puritan Family, pp. 39-44.
Morgan, E. S. Puritans and Sex, New Engl. Quart. Vol. 15:
    591-607.
Myers, A. C. Hannah Logan's Courtship.

Oberholtzer, E. P. Hist., Phila. Vol. 1: 64-65.
Powell, C. L. Marriage, New Engl., New Engl. Quart. Vol. 1:
    323-334.
Raper, C. L. Church & Private Schools, p. 12.
Sachse, J. R. German Pietists, p. 383.
Spruill, J. C. Women's Life, pp. 48, 140.
Stanard, M. M. Colonial Va., pp. 166-185.
Stiles, H. R. Bundling, pp. 14-16, 76-80, 107.
Streeter, S. F. Early Hist., Md., pp. 278-279.
Weeden, W. B. Hist., New Engl. Vol. 1: 217-220, 284, 293-295,
    412.
Winsor, J. Mem. Hist., Boston. Vol. 1: 518-519.
Woody, T. Hist. Educ. Women. Vol. 1: 241.

b. Later Marriages

Women who survived their husbands generally remarried in a
few weeks or months. Widows were considered better prospective
wives because they had already had experience in running a household.

Bruce, P. ι. Social Life, Va., pp. 223-238.
Calhoun, A. Soc. Hist. Amer. Family. Vol. 1: 70-71.
Earle, A. M. Child Life, p. 12.
Downey, F. A Governor Goes A-Wooing, V.M.H.B. Vol. 55:
    6-19.
Hiden, Mrs. P. W. Three Rectors & Their Wife, W. M. Quart.
    Ser. 2, Vol. 19: 34-41, 299-301.
Lee, F. B. Arch. N. J. Ser. 2, Vol. 2: 137.
Mather, C. Diary, Mass. H. S. Colls. Ser. 7, Vol. 7: 457, 477.
Woody, T. Hist. Educ., Women. Vol. 1: 248.

c. Fecundity

The early marriages and repeated remarriages of the colonial
women tended to increase their childbearing. In 1675 the average New
England family consisted of 9.02 persons. Many instances are recorded of women bearing seventeen to twenty children.

Calhoun, A. Soc. Hist. Amer. Family. Vol. 1: 87-89, 192.
Earle, A. M. Child Life, p. 12.
Holliday, C. Women's Life, pp. 114-116.
Nelson, W. Arch. N. J. Ser. 1, Vol. 27: 541-542.
Spruill, J. C. Women's Life, p. 48, 140.
Weeden, W. B. Hist. New Engl. Vol. 1: 284.

B. The Position of the Wife in the Colonial Home

Wives were generally second in command in the home and took over
the responsibilities of absent husbands on occasion. They supervised most
of the productive work of the household and, in some cases, that of the land

as well. They were responsible for the training of their daughters and servants in the work of the home.

Brown, A. Mercy Warren, pp. 78-9.
Calhoun, A. Soc. Hist. Amer. Family. Vol. 1: 83-103, 273-283.
Early, R. H. Byways, Va., pp. 152-159.
Griffin. Journal, pp. 161-162
Hanscom, E. D. Heart of Puritan, pp. 32-33, 35-36, 59-82.
Holliday, C. Women's Life, pp. 97-102, 142-147, 246-290.
Moller, Herbert. Sex Composition of Colonial Amer., W. M. Quart.
    Ser. 3, Vol. 2: 145-153.
Reynard, E. The Narrow Land, pp. 178-204.
Simonhoff, H. Jewish Notables, pp. 17-20, 25-28.
Spruill, J. C. Women's Life, pp. 43-44, 64-65, 77-78.
Spruill, J. C. Southern Housewives, N.C.H.R. Vol. 13: 25-46.
Stanard, M. M. Colonial Va., pp. 348-352.
Twichell, J. H. Old Puritan Love Letters.
Wharton, A. H. Colonial Doorways, pp. 177-196.
Woody, T. Hist. Educ. Women. Vol. 1: 257.

C.   Colonial Wives as Helpmates

Colonial wives helped their husbands in their joint productive endeavors and in the fostering of the personal careers of their husbands.

Adams, C. F. Familiar Letters.
Anderson, J. Memorable Women. Vol. 1: 120-155.
Andrews, C. M. Colonial Folkways, pp. 85-86.
Andrews, M. P. Hist. Md. Vol. 1: 267-268.
Andrews, M. P. Va., pp. 111-112.
Andrews, M. P. Soul of a Nation, pp. 148, 169, 247, 299.
Bacon, Elizabeth. Letter, W. M. Quart. Ser. 1, Vol. 9: 4-6.
Baird, C. W. Hist. Huguenot Emigration. Vol. 2: 112-114, 182-183,
    396-397.
Barnard, E. K. Dorothy Payne.
Biddle, G. B., and Lowrie, S. D. Notable Women, Pa., pp. 7-10,
    40-42.
Bradford, G. Wives, pp. 55-88.
Bradford, W. Hist. Plymouth, p. 146.
Brooks, G. Dames and Daughters, pp. 113-168, 215-244.
Brown, A. Mercy Warren.
Brown, M. L. Mr. & Mrs. Wm. Bingham, P.M.H.B. Vol. 61: 286-324.
Browning, C. H. Mother of Mary, the Mother of Wash., P.M.H.B.
    Vol. 36: 217-221.
Calder, I. M. New Haven Colony, p. 158.
Calhoun, A. Soc. Hist. Amer. Family. Vol. 1: 92, 278-279, 281-283.
Conkling, M. C. Memoirs, pp. 1-59, 69-167.
Crawford, M. A. Romance New Engl. Rooftrees, pp. 117-129.
Davenport, J. Letters, Mass. H. S. Colls. Ser. 4, Vol. 7: 487-532.
Davis, C. F. Cicely Farrar & Temperance Baley, W.M. Quart.
    Ser. 2, Vol. 21: 180-183.

Desmond, A. C. Martha Washington.
Desmond, A. C. Alexander Hamilton's Wife.
De Windt, I. P. Correspondence.
Doggett, C. Smyrna Colony, pp. 17-18.
Drinker, S. Hannah Penn.
Duane, W. Diary, Christopher Marshall, pp. 176-177.
Earle, A. M. Colonial Days, N. Y., p. 160.
Eckman, Jeanette. Dutch in New Castle, Del. Hist. Mag. Vol. 4:
246-301.

Ellet, E. F. Women Amer. Revolution. Vol. 1: 24-73, 119-142.
Fisher, S. G. Men Women Manners. Vol. 1: 195-204.
Green, H. C., & M. W. Pioneer Mothers. Vol. 1: 283-299.
Hanscom, E. D. Heart of a Puritan, pp. 59-82.
Hill, F. A. The Mystery Solved.
Hirsch, A. H. Huguenots So. Car., pp. 174-229.
Holliday, C. Women's Life, pp. 86-226.
Holloway, L. C. Ladies, White House, pp. 1-39, 40-87, 88-126.
Hoppin, C. A. Bride of Wakefield, Tyler's Quart. Vol. 9: 224-230.
Huguenot, So. Car. Transc. Vol. 4: 48-56, 1897 re Judith Manigault.
Hull, W. I. William Penn, pp. 57-61.
Humphrey, G. Women, Amer. Hist., pp. 55-71.
Humphreys, M. G. Catherine Schuyler.
James, B., & Jameson, J. Journ. Jaspar Dankaert. See index M.
Phillipse.

Jervey, Th. T. The Harlestons, S.C.H.G. Mag. Vol. 3: 154.
Keith, C. P. Wife & Children, Sir Wm. Keith, P.M.H.B. Vol. 56: 1-8.
Lamb, M. Hist. N. Y. Vol. 1: 128-129.
Lebeson, A. B. Jewish Pioneers, pp. 178-182.
Logan. Part Taken by Women, pp. 112-217. See index Women's names.
Ludwell, P. Boundary Line Proceedings, V.M.H.B. Vol. 5: 9-10.
McLean (Mrs.), D. Baroness de Riedesel, N.Y. State H.A. Proc. Vol:
3: 39-44.

Mellick, A. D. Story, Old Farm, p. 153.
Mitchell, E. V. American Village, p. 226.
Moore, C. Family Life, George Washington, see index.
Morgan, E. S. Puritan Dilemma, pp. 6-68, 204.
Mowatt, C. S. St. Augustine under British Flag, Fla. H.Q.R. Vol. 20:
131-150.

Myers, A. C. Narratives, Penna., pp. 80-81.
Neill, E. D. Va. Carolorum, pp. 346, 379, 391-392, 400.
Peare, C. O. William Penn. See index Hannah Penn.
Pound, A. The Penns. See index Hannah Penn.
Ramsay, D. Hist. So. Car. Vol. 1: 5-8.
Reed, W. B. Life, Esther Reed.
Reed, W. B. Life, Joseph Reed. Vol. 2: 253-279.
Richards, L. E. Abigail Adams.
Richardson, H. D. Sidelights Md. Hist. Vol. 2: 174-176.
Roof, K. M. Colonel Smith and Lady.
Sale, E. T. Belles & Cavaliers, pp. 41-55, 64-74, 145-151.
Sawyer, Wm. Gov. Printz' Daughter, Pa. H. Mag. Vol. 25: 109-114.

Schlesinger, E. B. Cotton Mather, W. M. Quart. Ser. 3, Vol. 10: 181-189.
Scudder, H. E. Men and Manners, pp. 100-103, 138-160, 167-176.
Sewall, S. Diary, Mass. H.S. Colls. Ser. 5, Vols. 5, 6, 7 (Diary Vol. 2), p. 93.
Southall, J. P. Lady Yardley & Cicely Farrar, V.M.H.B. Vol. 50: 74-88, Vol. 51: 83, 381-382, Vol. 55: 259-266.
Springer, M. E. Elizabeth Schuyler.
Spruill, J. L. Women's Life, pp. 13-14, 44, 78, 80.
Terhune, M. V. Mary Washington.
Twichell, J. H. Old Puritan Love Letters.
Tyler's Quart. Lady Yardley, Vol. 2: 115-129.
Van Rensselaer, J. H. Mana-ha-ta, pp. 129-130, 300-306.
Vawter, M. H. Va. Ancestors, Tyler's Quart. Vol. 31: 82-99, 187-200.
Walker, Lewis B. Life Margaret Shippen, P.M.H.B. Vols. 24, 25, & 26, see index.
Washington, G. Account Book, P.M.H.B. Vols. 29, 30 & 31, see index.
Waters, T. F. John Winthrop, Mass. H.S. Colls. Ser. 4, Vol. 7, see index Mrs. John Davenport.
Watson, J. F. Annals, Phila. Vol. 1: 573-574.
Wertenbaker, T. J. Va. Under Stuarts, pp. 64-67.
Wharton, A. H. Salons.
Wharton, A. H. Colonial Days, pp. 67-68.
Wharton, A. H. Martha Washington.
Wharton, A. H. Through Colonial Doorways, pp. 177-196.
White, E. N. Mary Browne.
Whitton, M. O. First, First Ladies, pp. 3-19, 30-38, 39-53.
Wm. & M. Quart. Early Physicians, W. & M. Quart. Ser. 1, Vol. 14: 96-100.
Williams, J. R. Fithian's Journ., See index., Frances Ann Carter.
Wister (Mrs.) O. J., & Irwin, A. Worthy Women, pp. 279-328.
Woody, T. Hist. Educ. Women. Vol. 1: 165, 257.
Yardley, J. H. Before Mayflower, pp. 62, 87-89, 106, 112.

D.   Errant Colonial Wives

Most of the colonial wives accepted the restraints of their position, but a few, from good or evil intent, broke away from conventions and caused scandal in the towns.

Allen, M. C. Hist. Wenham, Mass., p. 61.
Bancroft, H. H. Works. Vol. 34: 306-307.
Calhoun, A. Hist. Amer. Family. Vol. 1: 313.
Dexter, E. A. Colonial Women, p. 186.
Earle, A. M. Colonial Dames, pp. 96-98.
Nelson, W. Arch. N.J. Ser. 1, Vol. 11: 239, Vol. 19: 401, Vol. 24: see index wives eloped, Vol. 25: 133, 149, 312, Vol. 26: see index wives eloped, Vol. 27: see index wives eloped, Vol. 28: see index wives eloped, Vol. 29: 77, 96, 101, 129, 297, 435, 504. Ser. 2, Vol. 3: see index wives eloped, Vol. 4: 222, 368, 499.

Singleton, E. Social Life, N.Y., pp. 373-396.
Stryker, W. Archives, N.J. Ser. 2, Vol. 1, see index "rights of wives"
    & names of women.
Winslow, O. E. Meetinghouse Hill, pp. 182-184, 186.
Woody, T. Hist. Educ. Women. Vol. 1: 187-190, 254-255.

Women Homemakers in Colonial Times

A.   Women as Proprietors and Managers of the Homestead

    In all of the colonies women were given grants of land, either as
"feme sole" or in conjunction with a grant to their husbands. By purchase
and inheritance the tracts of land owned by the women were often greatly increased, in some cases to include several thousands of acres. In many instances, the management of the land was in the hands of women.

    a.   In the New England Colonies

    Women and children worked in the first fields that were cleared
for planting. The individual plots were not large; but the crops included, mainly, vegetables and fruits for the families, grasses and
grains for the animals, and flax for linen cloth.

    Adams, J. T. Provincial Society, pp. 11, 88.
    Andrews, Charles M. Rivertowns, pp. 47, 56-7.
    Atwater, E. E. Hist., New Haven, Conn., pp. 109-111.
    Beedy, H. C. Mothers, Maine, pp. 139-147.
    Blake, F. E. Princeton, Mass. Vol. 1: 85-87.
    Bradford, W. Hist., Plymouth, p. 146.
    Bradstreet, Ann. Will, Essex Inst. H. Colls. Vol. 4: 185-190.
    Brandon, E. T. Records, Cambridge, pp. 5, 10, 19.
    Briggs, L. V. Hist., Cabot Family. Vol. 1: 52-54.
    Cartwright, E. E. Will, 1640, Essex Antiq. Vol. 1: 30-31.
    Chastellux, Marquis de. Travels, pp. 266-267, 279-282.
    Cummings, J. Will, Essex Antiq. Vol. 1: 187-188.
    Dexter, E. A. Colonial Women, pp. 98-125.
    Dillingham, S. Will, 1636, Essex Antiq. Vol. 1: 13-14.
    Earle, A. M. Colonial Dames, pp. 45-50.
    East, R. A. Business Enterprise, p. 21.
    Grant, A. M. Memoirs, p. 46.
    Lowle, Elizabeth. Will, Essex Antiq. Vol. 4: 154.
    Porter, Helen C. (ed.). Will of Mary Washington, Conn. Mag.
        Vol. 11: 216.
    Scarlet, A. Will, 1643, Essex Antiq. Vol. 1: 100-101.
    Waters, T. F. Ipswich, Mass. Vol. 2: 258.
    Weeden, W. B. Hist., New Engl. Vol. 1: 56, 90.
    Winsley, Ann. Estate, Essex Inst. H. Coll. Vol. 7: 71-72.
    Worcester, S. A. Colls., Bridget Usher. Vol. 3: see index
        under her name & other women. Vol. 4: see index wo-
        men's names.

Worth, H. B. Nantucket Lands & Landowners, Nantucket H. A.
Proc. Vol. 2: 75-76, 300-335.

b.   Women Proprietors in the Middle Atlantic Colonies

The land owned by women in the Middle Atlantic colonies tended
to be more extensive than in New England. Women proprietors of
estates or truck gardens advertised their produce for sale frequently
in the newspapers.

Biddle, G. B., and Lowrie, S. D. Notable Women, Pa., pp. 2-4,
     7-10, 17-19.
Desmond, A. C. Mary Philipse: Heiress. N.Y. State H. A.
     Proc. Vol. 45: 22-30.
Dexter, E. A. Colonial Women, pp. 100-109, 114-116.
Earle, A. M. Colonial Dames, pp. 49-52.
Ellis, F. Hist., Lancaster Co., Pa., pp. 201, 244, 748, 926.
Fosdick, L. J. French Blood, Amer., p. 393 ff.
Gerard, G. W. Lady Deborah Moody.
Green, H. C. and M. W. Pioneer Mothers. Vol. 1: 221-223.
Hazard, S. Annals, Pa., pp. 219-220, 399-401, 403.
Humphreys, M. G. Catherine Schuyler, pp. 29-78.
Marcus, J. R. Early Amer. Jewry. Vol. 2: 358.
Melish, J. Travels. Vol. 1: 121 ff.
Nelson, W. Archives, N.J. Ser. 1, Vol. 27: 437-438.
     Ser. 2, Vol. 3: 228-271.
Parsons, J. C. Diary J. Hiltzheimer, p. 57 ff.
Putnam, Ruth. Annetje Jans' Farm, Half Moon Series. Vol. 1:
     61-97.
Prowell, G. R. Hist., Camden Co., Pa., p. 646.
Ross, P. Hist., Long Is. Vol. 1: 568.
Rupp, I. S. Hist., Lancaster Co., Pa., pp. 90-108.
Rush, B. Account, German Inhabitants, p. 25.
Thompson, B. F. Hist., Long Island, pp. 83-84.
Van Laer, A. J. Correspondence, Maria Rensselaer.
Van Rensselaer, (Mrs.) J. K. Mana-ha-ta, pp. 18-38, 109-111.
Winthrop, J. Hist., Plymouth. Vol. 2: 126.

c.   Women Proprietors in the Southern and South Western Settlements

Women proprietors in the Southern colonies were outstanding for
their agricultural experimentation. They had swamps drained and
highlands cleared for production. They became experts in the raising
of indigo, cotton, tobacco, figs and other tropical fruits, olive and mul-
berry trees, medicinal herbs, and flowers as well as vegetables, fruits,
and grains. Several women also became experts in animal husbandry.
In the southwestern settlements they owned and operated large ranches.

Ames, S. M. Studies, Va., pp. 18-35, 56, 73, 134.
Andrews, C. M. Colonial Folkways, pp. 86-139.
Andrews, M. P. Hist., Md. Vol. 1: 267.
Amory, M. Will, S.C.H.G. Mag. Vol. 12: 73-74.
Bancroft, H. H. Works. Vol. 34: 306-307.
Bartlett, H. R. 18th Cent. Ga. Women, pp. 63-65.
Beale, G. W. Mary Washington, V.M.H.B. Vol. 8: 283-287.
Beverly, R. Hist., Va., pp. 54-60.
Bibbens, R. M. Beginnings, Md., pp. 69-70.
Booker, M. Will, Tyler's Quart. Vol. 18: 171-172.
Brooks, G. Dames and Daughters, pp. 59-75, 103-132.
Browne, W. H. Md., Hist. Palatinate, pp. 64, 148.
Bruce, P. A. Econ. Hist., Va. Vol. 1: 100, 328, 469, Vol. 2: 88, 174, 182-184, 249.

Calhoun, A. Soc. Hist. Amer. Family. Vol. 1: 278, 283.
Calvert, M. Will, Lower Norfolk Co. (Va.) Antiq. Vol. 1: 115-116, 119-120.
Calvert Papers. First Selection, p. 165.
Carey, M. Will, W. M. Quart. Ser. 1, Vol. 20: 289-292.
Carter, R. Letter, V.M.H.B. Vol. 6: 88-90.
Chavez, Fray A. Origins, N.M. Families, See index.
Commons. Doc. Hist. Amer. Indust. Soc. Vol. 1: 265-266, 309.

Dexter, E. A. Colonial Women of Affairs, pp. 98-125.
Dexter, E. A. Career Women, pp. 188-190.

Earle, A. M. Colonial Dames, pp. 45-50, 78-83, 85-86.
Fisher, S. G. Men, Women and Manners. Vol. 2: 321.
Fleet, B. Va. Colonial Abstracts. Vol. 10: 13, 35, 36, 59.

Gordon, A. I. Will, W. M. Quart. Ser. 1, Vol. 14: 211-213.
Green, H. C. and M. W. Pioneer Mothers. Vol. 1: 455-485.
Grimes, J. Bryan. Abstracts of No. Car. Wills. See index.

Harrison, S. Will, Tyler's Quart. Vol. 9: 132.
Hayward, M. Wash. Will, Tyler's Quart. Vol. 28: 165-166.
Henry (Mother of Patrick). Will, W. M. Quart. Ser. 2, Vol. 8: 117-119.
Hillhouse, M. P. Hist. Colls., pp. 144-146.
Jervey, T. T. Will, Affra Coming, S.C.H.G. Mag. Vol. 12: 75.
Knight, L. L. Georgia's Landmarks. Vol. 1: 379.
LeNoble, C. Will, Huguenot S. S. C. Trans. No. 13: 25-29.
Logan. Part taken by women, pp. 106-112, see index.
Lossing, B. J. Mary and Martha Washington.
McCrady, E. So. Car., Proprietory Govt., see index.
McCrady, E. So. Car., Royal Govt., pp. 267-270, 536.
Macon, E. Will, W. M. Quart. Ser. 1, Vol. 14: 265-267.
Marcus, J. R. Early Amer. Jewry. Vol. 2: 356-360.
Parran, A. Register Md. Heraldic Families. Vol. 1: 19, 21, 29.
Peniston, E. Will, V.M.H.B. Vol. 48: 104-105.
Phillips, U. B. Life and Labor, Old South, pp. 95-96.
Phillips, U. B. Plantation and Frontier. Vol. 1: 265-266.
Pryor, S. A. Mother of Washington.
Putnam, E. The Lady, pp. 302-304, 311.

Ramey, M. E. Margaret Brent.
Ramsay, D. Hist. S. C. Vol. 2: 209-212, 220.
Ravenel, H. H. Eliza Pinckney.
Ravenel, H. H. Charleston, pp. 10-11, 19, 20, 35, 158, 345.
Sass, Herbert R. Love & Miss Lucas, Ga. H. Rev. Vol. 10: 312-320.
Smith, G. G. Story Ga., pp. 31-32.
Spruill, J. C. Women's Life, pp. 65, 68, 78, 278, 305-312.
Temple, A. Will, 1781, W. M. Quart. Ser. 1, Vol. 13: 140.
Turner, N. B. Mother, Washington.
Twitchell, R. E. Spanish Arch., N. M. Vol. 1, see index.
Tyler, L. G. Narratives, Va., p. 267, see index.
Whaley, Mary. Will, W. M. Quart. Ser. 1, Vol. 4: 13-14.
Wharton, A. H. Colonial Days, pp. 75-76.
White, G. Hist. Colls. Ga., pp. 21-31.
Woody, T. Hist. Educ. Women. Vol. 1: 257-258.

B.   Colonial Houses

The first dwellings in the northern and middle colonies were little more than caves dug in the hillsides. Later, log cabins and more elaborate and comfortable houses were built.

a.   Earliest Dwellings

When the pilgrims landed at Plymouth they "burrow(ed) themselves in the earth . . . under some hillside, casting the earth aloft upon timber." In New Netherlands the first colonists dug a square pit and lined it with wood and bark. In Virginia the colonists used split, green wood for walls and roof and chinked the holes with clay and mud.

Bemis, A. F., and Burchard, J. Evolving House. Vol. 1: 260-291.
Briggs, M. S. Homes, Pilgrim Fathers.
Dow, G. F. Everyday Life, pp. 13-27.
Earle, A. M. Home Life, pp. 1-2, 53.
Earle, A. M. Colonial Days, N. Y., pp. 74, 98.
Holliday, C. Women's Life, pp. 8-9.
Langdon, W. C. Everyday Things, 1607-1706, pp. 1-37.
Price, J. H. Va., p. 34 ff.
Shurtleff, H. R. Log Cabin Myth, pp. 49, 51, 79, 87-88, 90, 146.
Stanard, M. M. Colonial Virginia, pp. 55-101.
Van Rennselaer, (Mrs.) J. K. Mana-ha-ta, pp. 14-15, 31-33, 36-37, 75-76.
Wharton, A. H. Colonial Days, pp. 15-16, 66-88.

b.   Later Houses

The first houses, built from logs and rough-hewn wood, were cold and drafty. In the course of fifty years a new style of house was developed around a central fireplace. Bricks were made in Virginia by 1611 and in New Plymouth by 1627. They replaced the wood and clay that had been used in the chimneys. Thatched roofs disappeared, and soon two-storied homes appeared with many rooms. Outhouses for the spinning, weaving, food processing, and other household tasks were built near the main house.

Bemis, A. F., Burchard J. Evolving House. Vol. 1: 260-291.
Briggs, M. Homes of the Pilgrim Fathers, pp. 136-175.
Bruce, P. A. Econ. Hist. Va. Vol. 2: 155.
Corry, J. P. Houses, Colonial Ga., Ga. Hist. Quart. Vol. 14: 181-201.
Earle, A. M. Colonial Days, N. Y., p. 98.
Eberlein, H. D. Architecture, Colonial Amer.
Fithian, P. V. Journal & Letters, pp. 107-108.
Morison, S. E. The Story of "Old Colony," pp. 174-178.
Ravenel, B. S. Architects, Charleston, So. Car., pp. 1-91.
Shurtleff, H. R. Log Cabin Myth, pp. 49-51, 79, 87-90, 146.
Spruill, J. C. Women's Life, pp. 22-24, 64-67.
Spruill, J. C. Va. & Car. Homes, N.C.H. Rev. Vol. 12: 320-340.
Stanard, M. M. Colonial Va., pp. 55-101.
Terhune, M. V. Some Colonial Homesteads.
Terhune, M. V. More Colonial Homesteads.
Van Rensselaer, J. K. Mana-ha-ta, pp. 31-33, 36-37, 75-76, 325.
Weeden, W. B. Econ. Hist. New Engl. Vol. 1: 218.
Wertenbaker, T. J. First Americans, pp. 283-297.
Whipple, S. L., and Waters, T. F. Puritan Homes, Ipswich H. Publ. No. 27: 1-86.

C.   The Furnishings of the Colonial Homes

Inventories and other colonial documents show the meager furnishing of the early homes. Only equipment necessary to maintain the home and produce material was available during the first one hundred years. Later, the homes became more comfortable and ornate.

Acrelius, I. Hist. New Sweden, pp. 156-159.
Bayer, H. G. The Belgians, p. 330.
Bemis, A. F., & Burchard, J. The Evolving House. Vol. 1: 263, 270, 283, 290.
Bruce, P. A. Econ. Hist. Va. Vol. 1: 339-340. Vol. 2: 167, 172-173, 176-177, 183-184.
Dexter, E. A. Colonial Women, p. 109.
Dow, G. F. Everyday Life, pp. 28-90.
Drinker, C. K. Not So Long Ago, pp. 3-47.
Earle, A. M. China Collecting.
Earle, A. M. Home Life, pp. 76-77, 80, 100, 133,
Eberlein, H. D. Colonial Interiors.
Hanscom, E. D. Heart of a Puritan, p. 32.
Hirsch, A. H. Huguenots, So. Car., pp. 247-250.
Little, F. Early American Textiles, pp. 206-247.

Morison, S. E. Story of "Old Colony," pp. 176-177.
Perley, Sidney. Heating Olden Times, Essex Antiq. Vol. 1: 183-186.
Phillips, U. B. Plantation and Frontier. Vol. 1: 296-298.
Richardson, H. D. Sidelights, Md. Hist. Vol. 1: 25-56. Vol. 2: 101.
Spruill, J. C. Women's Life, pp. 23-24, 37.
Stanard, M. M. Colonial Va., pp. 56, 94.
Tryon, R. M. Household Manuf., pp. 221-225.
Van Rensselaer, (Mrs.) J. K. Mana-ha-ta, p. 147.
Watson, J. F. Annals Phila., pp. 175-182.
Weeden, W. B. Econ. Soc. Hist. New Engl. Vol. 1: 106-107, 212-217,
229, 283-285, 414-417. Vol. 2: 804-806.
Williams, J. R. Fithian's Journ. pp. 251-268.
Willison, G. F. Saints and Strangers, pp. 386-387.

D.   The Duties and Responsibilities of the Colonial Homemaker

The duties and responsibilities of colonial homemakers included
every aspect of the life of the household, from defensive warfare with the
Indians to the production of necessary items for sale in the marketplace.

a.   Supervision and Care of the Household

The supervision and care of the household included multitudinous
tasks, many of which were actually done by the apprentices, bound-out
children and slaves. The homemaker was responsible for seeing that
each task was completed correctly and in time to meet the needs of
the family.

Arthur, J. P. Western No. Car., pp. 256-258.
Bartlett, H. R. 18th Cent. Ga. Women, pp. 116-122.
Beedy, H. C. Mothers, Maine, pp. 139-147.
Bemis, A. F. & Burchard, J. Evolving House. Vol. 1: 275.
Brickell, J. Natural Hist., No. Car., p. 32.
Bruce, P. Econ. Hist. Va. Vol. 2: 15.
Calhoun, A. Soc. Hist. Amer. Family. Vol. 1: 168-169, 200-203,
281, 283.
Commons, J. R. et al. Doc. Hist. Amer., Indust. Soc. Vol. 2:
271-272, 334.
Duane, W. Diary Christopher Marshall, pp. 157-158, 167, 171.
Earle, A. M. Home Life, pp. 1-51, 150.
Earle, A. M. Colonial Dames, pp. 276-315.
Earle, A. M. Margaret Winthrop, pp. 55-56.
Felt, J. Annals Salem, pp. 1-102.
Green, H. C. and M. W. Pioneer Mothers. Vol. 1: 36-, 397-
485.
Hart, A. B. Com. Hist. Mass. Vol. 2: 366-371.
Holliday, C. Women's Life, pp. 105-114, 147-151.
Humphreys, M. G. Catherine Schuyler, pp. 8-11, 22.
Huntington, A. S. Under Colonial Roof-Tree, pp. 26-104.
Josselyn, J. New Engl. Rarities, pp. 1-114.

Macy, O. Hist., Nantucket, pp. 40-41.
Morgan, E. S. The Puritan Family, pp. 9-27.
Myers, A. C. Journal, Sally Wister, pp. 13-17.
Rush, B. Account, German Inhabitants, Pa., pp. 66-67.
Smith, H. Colonial Days, pp. 109-122.
Spruill, J. C. Women's Life, pp. 44-45, 76, 80-82, 110.
Spruill, J. C. Southern Housewives, N.C.H. Rev. Vol. 13: 25-
46.
Talbot, M. Educ. Women, pp. 7-8.
Tryon, R. M. Household Manuf., pp. 61-62, 227-236.
Weeden, W. B. Hist., New Engl. Vol. 2: 861-862.

b.   Production and Care of Food

The production, processing, preserving , and preparing of food
for the family was one of the major responsibilities of the colonial
homemaker.

Abbott, E. Women, Industry, p. 15.
Andrews, C. M. Colonial Folkways, pp. 98-109.
Bemis, A. F., and Burchard, J. Evolving House. Vol. 1: 275-
277.
Beverly, R. Hist., Va., pp. 138-141.
Bradford, W. Hist., Plymouth, pp. 99-100, 115-116, 121, 166, 175.
Bricknell, J. Natural Hist., No. Car., p. 32.
Bruce, P. A. Econ. Hist., Va. Vol. 1: 328, 469, Vol. 2: 15,198.
Calhoun, A. W. Soc. Hist. Amer. Family. Vol. 1: 168-169, 278-
281.
Dexter, E. A. Colonial Women, pp. 111-125.
Earle, A. M. Child Life, pp. 29-31.
Earle, A. M. Colonial Dames, pp. 85-86, 281.
Earle, A. M. Colonial Days, N.Y., p. 134.
Earle, A. M. Home Life, pp. 145-147, 150-155, 158-159, 168-169,
172.
Earle, A. M. Old Time Gardens.
Fithian, P. V. Journal & Letters, p. 105.
Holliday, C. Women's Life, pp. 7-8, 113.
Rush, B. Account, German Inhabitants, Penna., p. 25.
Singleton, E. Social, N.Y., pp. 342-364.
Spruill, J. C. Women's Life, pp. 22, 64-68, 81-82, 278, 305,
308-312.
Tryon, R. M. Household Manuf., pp. 219-225.
Van Rensselaer, (Mrs.) J. K. Mana-ha-ta, pp. 157-162, 266.
Waters, T. F. Ipswich. Vol. 2: 48, 258.
Weeden, W. B. Hist., New Engl. Vol. 1: 90, 416, Vol. 2: 540-
541.
Woody, T. Hist. Educ., Women. Vol. 1: 265-268.
Wylie, J. C. Mrs. Washington's Book of Cookery, P.M.H.B.
Vol. 27: 436-440.

c. Clothing the Family

For the colonial women, the production of cloth went far beyond the needs of her family. It was one of the first of the household industries to leave the home. It has therefore been given a classification under the Occupations of Women. See Chapter IX.

d. Colonial Mothers and the Training of the Children in the Home

Colonial mothers trained their daughters, women servants, and slaves in the household tasks. In some cases, they also gave their children and the servants who were bound-out to them an elementary education in academic subjects. In a few instances, the mothers extended this education to their slaves.

Unencumbered child life was short and grim. So great was the need, particularly in the northern colonies, that children were set to tasks as soon as they could walk; and the work-load increased as rapidly as possible. Child labor was common in all the colonies.

Butts, S. H. Mothers, Ga., pp. 17-18, 74-75, 92, 96-97, 99-100, 139-140.

Calhoun, A. Soc. Hist., Amer. Family. Vol. 1: 105-127, 285-298.

Conkling, M. C. Memoirs, pp. 1-59.

Earle, A. M. Child Life, pp. 191-304.

Earle, A. M. Home Life, pp. 252-280.

Green, H. C. and M. W. Pioneer Mothers, Vol. 1: 155-198.

Hanscom, E. D. Heart of Puritan, pp. 85-118.

Hart, A. B. Colonial Children, pp. 165-200.

Holliday, C. Women's Life, pp. 74-75, 84, 124-136.

Kiefer, Sr. Monica. Early Amer. Childhood, P.M.H.B. Vol. 68: 3-37.

Moore, C. Family Life, George Washington, pp. 13, 22, 28, 43, 80, 134-139.

Morgan, E. S. Puritan Family, pp. 78-89.

Simonhoff, H. Jewish Notables, pp. 17-20, 25-28.

Spruill, J. C. Women's Life, pp. 55, 64.

Willison, G. F. Saints and Strangers, p. 469.

e. Care of the Sick and Elderly in the Home

Homemakers were often the only available persons to care for the sick. They learned to give first aid and elementary nursing care. They raised herbs and made tonics, medicines, salves, and ointments for treatment of the ailing.

Briggs, L. W. Charleston Gardens.

Dexter, E. A. Colonial Women, pp. 69-71.

Earle, A. M. Customs & Fashions, pp. 331-387.

Earle, A. M. Old Time Gardens, pp. 107-131.

Earle, A. M. Sun Dials and Roses.
Holliday, C. Woman's Life, pp. 6, 113.
Spruill, J. Women's Life, p. 81.

f. Supervision of the Social Life of the Home and Community

At first the social life of colonial women consisted mainly in sharing some task with her neighbors, such as spinning or quilting bees and corn huskings. Later, particularly in the cities, social life lost its utilitarian aspects and became an elaborate program of pleasure and relaxation.

Bliss, W. R. Old Colony Town.
Bridenbaugh, C. Cities, Wilderness, pp. 386-459.
Bruce, P. A. Social Life, Va., pp. 157-169.
Crawford, M. C. Romantic Days.
Crawford, M. C. Social Life, New Engl.
Earle, A. M. Colonial Days, N.Y.
Earle, A. M. Customs and Fashions, N. E.
Earle, A. M. In Old Narragansett.
Ellet, E. F. Court Circles, pp. 15-41.
Fisher, S. G. Men, Women, Manners.
Goodwin, M. W. Colonial Cavalier.
Griswold, R. W. Republican Court.
Mason, E. Journ., Young Lady, Va.
Scudder, H. E. Men & Manners, pp. 36-40.
Singleton, E. Social Life, N.Y., pp. 3-168.
Smith, H. Colonial Days, pp. 167-328.
Stanard, M. M. Colonial Va., pp. 136-167.
Tittle, W. Colonial Holidays.
Van Rensselaer (Mrs.) J. K. Mana-ha-ta, pp. 72-84, 213-245, 260-275.
Weeden, W. B. Hist., New Engl. Vol. 1: 223-225, 295-302.
Wharton, A. H. Colonial Days, pp. 195-237.

4. Women as Servants in the Home

The work of women servants in the home ranged from rough, heavy field work on the farms through all kinds of household chores, to respected tasks such as teaching, nursing, and supervisory work. The women servants who were slaves or bound-out servants were not paid for their services directly but given food, clothing, and shelter. Other women servants were given very meager wages, whether they were white, Indian or Negro.

Andrews, C. M. Colonial Folkways, pp. 186-189.
Bruce, P. A. Econ. Hist., Va. Vol. 2: 15, 33-37, 49-52
Calhoun, A. W. Soc. Hist., Amer. Family. Vol. 1: 313.
Dexter, E. A. Colonial Women, p. 113.
Dow, G. F. Arts and Crafts, pp. 185, 187, 188, 193, 194, 196, 199.
Earle, A. M. Home Life, pp. 150, 252-253.

Earle, A. M. Colonial Days, N.Y., p. 86.
Gottesman, R. S. Arts and Crafts, 1726-1776, pp. 335, 337, 339, 341-343.
Greene, L. J. Negro in Colonial New Engl., pp. 110, 119-120.
Hall, C. C. Early Md., pp. 290-291.
Hanscom, E. D. Heart of Puritan, pp. 40-41.
Holliday, C. Women's Life, p. 109.
Morgan, E. S. Puritan Family, pp. 62-77.
Phillips, U. P. Plantation and Frontier. Vol. 1: 340-343, Vol. 2: 93.
Spruill, J. C. Women's Life, p. 77.
Waters, T. F. Ipswich, Mass. Vol. 2: 255.
Woody, T. Hist. Educ. Women. Vol. 1: pp. 190-192, 258-261, 265-268.

IX

COLONIAL WOMEN IN THE PRODUCTIVE LIFE OF THE

COMMUNITIES

1. Women in Occupational Life

Colonial women entered into every aspect of the productive life of the colonies. It is hard to find a productive endeavor of any kind carried on by the men
that was not entered also by a woman, at one time or another, as worker, super-
visor or owner.

Ames, S. M. Studies, Va., pp. 111-146.
Hart, A. B. Com. Hist., Mass. Vol. 2: 371-373.
Tryon, R. M. Household Manuf., pp. 53-60.

A. Colonial Women in the Field of Medicine

a. General statements

Women acted as physicians, midwives, and nurses in all of the
early settlements. They also produced medicines, salves, and ointments.

Browne, C. Diary, V.M.H.B. Vol. 32: 305-320.
Calder, I. M. Colonial Captivities, pp. 169-200.
Cobbledick, M. R. Status of Women, p. 81.
Cutbush, E. Observations, Army Matron, pp. 205-206.
Dexter, E. A. Career Women, pp. 29-49.
Green, S. A. Journ. Sergeant Holden, p. 29.
Gregory, S. Letter, Ladies.
Hunt, G. Journ. Continental Congress. Vol. 2: 294, 297, Vol.
    4: 858, Vol. 18: 878.
Hurd-Meade, K. C. Hist. Women Medicine, pp. 409-417.
Hurd-Meade, K. C. Medical Women, Amer. Med. Rev., Rev. Vol.

39: 101-105.
Meyer, A. N. Woman's Work, pp. 139-142.
Nutting, M., Dock, L. Hist. Nursing. Vol. 2: 342 ff.
Packard, F. R. Hist., Medicine in U.S. Vol. 1: 49-50.
Tandy, Elizabeth. Community Medicine, N.Y. State H.A.
Quart. Vol. 4: 49-54.

b.   New England Women in Medicine

The New England midwives were trained by experience, and some attended over a thousand births. They had a considerable knowledge of herbs, ointments, and simple nursing care. A few received some training in general medicine.

Anderson, J. Memorable Women. Vol. 1: 189-190.
Bentley, W. Diary. Vol. 2: 308, Vol. 3: 71-73.
Bliss, W. R. Old Colony Town, p. 53.
Bridenbaugh, C. Cities Wilderness, pp. 90, 243.
Dall, C. H. College, Market and Court, p. 226 footnote.
Dexter, E. A. Colonial Women, pp. 58-66, 67-68, 72.
Dow, G. F. Holyoke Diaries, pp. 141-152.
Hanson, J. W. Hist. Gardiner, Me., p. 65.
Holman, M. C. Amer. Womanhood, Conn. Mag. Vol. 11: 251-254.
Macy, W. F. Nantucket Scrapbasket, pp. 69-70, 93-94.
Osterweis, R. G. Three Cent. New Haven, pp. 36-37.
Pringle, J. R. Hist. Gloucester, Mass., pp. 39-40.
Roof, K. M. Colonel Smith and Lady, p. 226.
Sewall, S. Sewall Papers. Vol. 1: 40, Vol. 2: 51, 410, Vol. 3: 11, 14.
Temple, J., Sheldon, G. Hist. Northfield, Mass., pp. 68, 164, 363.
Thompson, Z. Hist. Vermont. Part 3: 110.
Watertown. Records. Vol. 2: 115, 120 see index women's names, nursing indigent.
Weeden, W. B. Hist., New Engl. Vol. 1: 81.
Winthrop, J. Hist., New Engl. Vol. 1: 313-316.
Woody, T. Hist. Educ., Women. Vol. 1: 163-164.
Worcester Soc. Antiq. Colls. Vol. 4: 29, 31, 40, 47, see index women's names.

c.   Women in Medicine in the Middle Atlantic Colonies

The midwives were regularly licensed by the Dutch settlers in New Amsterdam, and a house was provided for them by the government. Many of the women, as midwives or nurses, gave free service to the poor and to the Indians. In 1658, a hospital was started in New York City with a matron in charge. In 1765, Dr. Shippen opened training classes for midwives in Philadelphia.

Bridenbaugh, C. Cities Wilderness, pp. 245, 405.
Calhoun, A. Soc. Hist., Amer. Family. Vol. 1: 171.
Carlisle, R. Account Bellevue Hospital, p. 4 ff.
Dexter, E. A. Colonial Women, pp. 59, 66-71, 73-77.
Drinker, C. K. Not So Long Ago, pp. 48-142.
Earle, A. M. Colonial Days, N.Y., pp. 90-91.
Ellet, E. F. Domestic Hist. Amer. Rev., p. 43.
Gottesman, R. S. Arts and Crafts, 1726-1776, p. 308.
Green, H. C., and M. W. Pioneer Mothers. Vol. 1: 155-158.
Johnston, F. C. Pioneer Physicians, Wyoming H.G. Mag,
    May 11, 1888, pp. 55-58.
Kelker, Luther R. (ed.) List of Patients, P.M.H.B. Vol. 26:
    92-100.
Nelson, W. Arch. N.J. Ser. 1, Vol. 19: 383; Vol. 27: 445;
    Ser. 2, Vol. 3: 52; Vol. 4: 398, 508.
Prowell, G. K. History, Camden Co., N.J., pp. 237-241.
Stryker, W. Arch. N.J. Ser. 2, Vol. 1: 530.
Van Rensselaer (Mrs.) J. K. Mana-ha-ta, pp. 8, 355.
Watson, J. F. Annals, Phila., p. 399.
Woody, T. Hist. Educ. Women. Vol. 1: 227-228.

d. Southern Colonial Women in Medicine

The women who were midwives or "doctoresses" were respected, and a few had received elementary medical training. The
nurses often acted as midwives, especially among the poor.

Baudier, R. Catholic Church, La., pp. 107, 138, 183.
Blanton. Medicine, Va., 17th Cent., pp. 159-174.
Browne, W. H., & Hall, C. C. Arch., Md. Vol. 4: 268-446, 483;
    Vol. 10: 122, 415; Vol. 12: 245, 257, 298; Vol. 41: 332.
Hening, W. W. Statutes at Large, Va., Vol. 1: 552; Vol. 8: 22,
    379; Vol. 11: 47, 161, 167, 384; Vol. 12: 199, 273, 378.
Palmer, W. P. Calendar Va. State Papers. Vol. 3: 36, 222;
    Vol. 8: 83, 161, 185, 195, 227.
Redman, A. Petition, Nurse Md. H. Mag. Vol. 17: 379.
Sisco, L. D. People Charles Co., Md. Md. H. Mag. Vol. 23:
    344-363.
Spruill, J. C. Women's Life, pp. 50, 267-275.
V.M.H.B. Nurses, Army. Vol. 14: 186-187.
Wallace, D. D. Hist. S.C. Vol. 1: 389.
W. M. Quart. Nurse at College & Midwifery. Ser. 1, Vol. 3:
    131; Ser. 2, Vol. 2: 204.
Woody, T. Hist. Educ. Women. Vol. 1: 263-264.

B. Colonial Women Owners of Taverns

Women, generally widows, were frequently licensed to keep taverns
in all the colonies. At first, the taverns were used chiefly to accommodate
travelers but later were expanded and used as centers of entertainment,

business transactions and political meetings.

a.   In New England

Some women tavern owners were restricted in their sale of
alcoholic beverages; others were licensed to sell beer or wine.
The inns varied from small home boarding houses to regular hostelries where people met to transact business, discuss politics, or be
entertained.

Abbott, E. Women, Industry, p. 13.
Ashbury, F. Journal. Vol. 2: 280, 318.
Bridenbaugh, C. Cities, Wilderness, pp. 108-109 ff.
Bridenbaugh, C. Gentleman's Progress, pp. 106-107, 155.
Cogswell, E. C. Hist. Nottingham, N.H., p. 86.
Crawford, M. C. New Engl. Inns, pp. 170, 182, 285-287.
Dexter, E. A. Colonial Women, pp. 1-8, 10, 12-17, 26, 49-51,
    205-206.
Dexter, E. A. Career Women, pp. 117-118, 120-121, 124.
Drake, S. A., & Watkins, K. W. Old Boston Taverns, see index.
Earle, A. M. Stage Coach and Tavern Days, pp. 17-18, 20, 40,
    69, 76-77, 94, 209.
Felt, J. B. Annals, Salem, p. 175.
Knight, S. Journal, pp. 16, 19, 38, 44-46, 62.
Lathrop, E. L. Early Amer. Inns, p. 102.
Morison, S. E. Builders, Bay Colony, pp. 203-204.
Nourse, H. S. Records, Lancaster, Mass., p. 329.
Rochefoucault-Liancourt, F. Travels. Vol. 2: 212.
Sayles, L. B. Brave Knight, 17th Cent., Conn. Mag. Vol. 7:
    334-338.
Starbuck, A. Hist. Nantucket, p. 655.
Weeden, W. B. Hist., New Engl. Vol. 1: 114, 195, 207.
Wenham Hist. Soc. Wenham Records, pp. 145-150.

b.   In the Middle Atlantic Colonies

Women tavern owners in the Middle Atlantic colonies soon developed specialties and succeeded in running suburban hostelries which
they advertised regularly in the newspapers.

Ashmead, H. G. Hist., Chester, Del., p. 86.
Davis, J. Personal Adventures, pp. 347-348, 371.
Dexter, E. A. Colonial Women, pp. 7-12.
Dexter, E. A. Career Women, pp. 116-117, 119-120, 127-129.
Earle, A. M. Colonial Days, N.Y., pp. 162, 207.
Earle, A. M. Stage Coach and Tavern Days, p. 85.
Griffin, A. Journ. pp. 135-137.
Lathrop, E. L. Early Amer. Inns. pp. 120, 127.
Lebeson, A. B. Pilgrim People, p. 68.
Lee, Francis. Arch., N.J. Ser. 2, Vol. 2: 252.

Manges, F. M. Women Shopkeepers, pp. 71-96, 115.
Nelson, W. Arch. N.J. Ser. 1, Vol. 24: 234, 365, 547; Vol. 25:
16, 29, 38, 338; Vol. 26: 334, 591; Vol. 27: 285, 461, 554,
614; Vol. 28: 343; Ser. 2, Vol. 3: 479-480.
Nevins, A. Amer. Soc. Hist., pp. 70-71, 73-74.
Scharf, J. T., Wescott, T. Hist. Phila. Vol. 2: 982-983, 1687.
Stryker, W. Arch., N.J. Ser. 2, Vol. 1: 251.
Whitehead, W. A. Arch., N.J. Ser. 1, Vol. 7: 181, 224, 449-450.

c. In the Southern Colonies

The taverns in the Southern colonies were needed not only to accommodate travelers but as meeting places for the owners of the large estates. The inns became centers of community entertainment, political debates, and business transactions. Many women were licensed to run the taverns, and a number became famous for their food and entertainment.

Andrews, G. Reminiscenses, Ga., pp. 36-38.
Bartlett, H. R. 18th Cent. Ga. Women, pp. 70-71.
Davis, J. Personal Adventures, pp. 17-19, 43, 45-46, 60-61,
79-80, 82-83, 85.
Dexter, E. A. Colonial Women of Affairs, p. 206.
Dexter, E. A. Career Women, pp. 118-119, 120-121, 123, 125, 128.
Lathrop, E. L. Early Amer. Inns, p. 204.
McCrady, E. So. Car. Royal Govt., p. 606.
Spruill, J. C. Women's Life, pp. 95, 294-302.
Washington, G. Diaries. Vol. 4: 21-22, 35, 48, 119.
Wm. & M. Quart. Mary Brough. Ser. 1, Vol. 12: 82.
Woody, T. Hist. Educ. Women. Vol. 1: 258-259.

C. Colonial Women in the Production of Clothing

a. General Statements

Next to supplying food, clothing was the most persistent problem that colonial women faced. They raised flax, herded sheep, spun thread, wove cloth, and made and repaired suits, dresses and coats for their families, servants, and sometimes for sale. They taught the arts of knitting and making cloth and clothing and were among the first workers in the new factories.

Coman, K. Indust. Hist. U.S. Vol. 1: 64-65, 114.
Earle, A. M. Home Life, pp. 166-251.
Eberlein and McClure. Amer. Antiq., pp. 272-285.
Tryon, R. M. Household Manuf., pp. 62-122, 192-196, 202-213.
Woody, T. Hist. Educ. Women. Vol. 1: 192.

b. Clothmaking in the Colonial Home

(1)   In New England

The need for cloth was so urgent in the New England colonies that in 1640 a Court order was passed to encourage the production of cotton, linen, and woolen cloth. Bounties and premiums were offered from time to time. In 1656, families were assessed a given quantity of yarn or cloth according to the number and ability of the members of the household. Women and children were expected to spend their free time at the wheel or loom. Schools were started to train young workers.

Bagnall, W. R. Textile Indust., U.S., pp. 5-10, 50-52, 58-59.
Beedy, H. C. Mothers Maine, pp. 149-150.
Bemis, A. F., & Burchard, J. Evolving House. Vol. 1: 275.
Bolton, C. K. Scotch-Irish Pioneers, pp. 49-55, 100.
Coman, K. Indust. Hist. U.S. Vol. 1: 117.
Dow, G. F. The Arts and Crafts, p. 281.
Earle, A. M. Home Life, pp. 180, 184, 188-189, 202, 239.
Fisher, S. G. Men, Women and Manners. Vol. 1: 273.
Gottesman, R. S. Arts and Crafts, 1726-1776, pp. 260, 263.
Little, F. Amer. Textiles, pp. 31, 36-37, 39, 64, 70.
Mason, G. C. Reminicences, Newport, p. 358.
Meyer, A. N. Woman's Work, p. 276.
Philbrick, E. Spinning, Essex Antiq. Vol. 1: 51, 87-92.
Weeden, W. B. Hist. New Engl. Vol. 1: 1, 170-171, 173, 176-177, 193-194, 197-198, 200, 305-307.
Wharton, A. H. Colonial Days, p. 93.

(2)   Clothmaking in the Homes of the Middle Atlantic Colonies

The German settlers in the Middle Atlantic colonies, both men and women, soon became famous for their linen cloth and knitted goods. Laws were passed offering premiums for finished cloth and schools were started to train the boys and girls in all the processes.

Bagnall, W. R. Textile Indust., U.S., pp. 5-10, 18, 23, 27, 52-54, 70-71.
Benson, A., & Hedin, N. Swedes, Amer., pp. 77-86.
Colton, J. M. Annals, Manhattan, p. 36.
Earle, A. M. Home Life, pp. 181, 190, 259.
Little, F. Amer. Textiles, p. 45.
Melish, J. Travels, Vol. 1: 394-395.
Nelson, W. Arch., N.J. Ser. 2, Vol. 3: 366.
Rutherford, J. Notes, N.J., N.J.H.S. Proc. Ser. 2, Vol. 1: 85-86.
Van Rensselaer, (Mrs.) J. K. Mana-ha-ta, pp. 46, 152, 185.

(3)   Clothmaking in the Southern Colonial Homes

In the southern colonies, cloth production was done by slaves, orphans, children of indigent and poor families, and women of poor families. Laws were passed offering bounties on production, and counties were ordered to send children to the towns to be trained as workers.

Ashe, S. A. Hist. No. Car. Vol. 2: 167-168.
Beverly, R. Hist. Va., p. 239.
Bricknell, J. Natural His., No. Car., p. 32.
Bruce, P. A. Econ. Hist. Va. Vol. 1: 100, 239, 246, 328, 469. Vol. 2: 259-260, 454-459, 460-471.
Earle, A. M. Home Life, pp. 182-183, 189-190.
Little, F. Amer. Textiles, pp. 14, 67.
Melish, J. Travels. Vol. 1: 32-33.
Phillips, U. P. Plantation and Frontier. Vol. 1: 186-189, Vol. 2: 314-317, 321-325.
Spruill, J. Women's Life, pp. 74-75, 80-82.
Woody, T. Hist. Educ. Women. Vol. 1: 243, 260-261.

(4)   Silk Culture in the Colonies

Silkworms were sent to Virginia in 1623, and repeated attempts were made to foster the production of silk cloth in most of the colonies. Three women are famous for their encouragement of the industry, e.g., Eliza Pinckney, Grace Fisher and Susanna Wright. In spite of the encouragement, the industry failed to develop.

Bagnall, W. R. Textile Indust., U.S., p. 23.
Biddle, G. B., & Lowrie, S. D. Notable Women, Pa., pp. 24-25.
Bruce, P. A. Econ. Hist. Va. Vol. 1: 240-242, 366-368.
DeBrahm, J. G. Hist. Three Provinces, pp. 21-22, 49-50, 53.
Fisher, S. G. Men, Women, Manners. Vol. 2: 321.
Hamer, M. B. Silk Indust., Ga., N.C.H. Rev. Vol. 12: 125-148.
Little, F. Amer. Textiles, pp. 20, 126-155.
McKinstry, M. T. Silk Culture, Ga. H. Quart. Vol. 14: 225-235.
Meyer, A. N. Woman's Work, p. 278.
Mitchell, E. V. Amer. Village, p. 245.
Neill, E. D. Va. Carolorum, pp. 240-241.
Nelson, W. Arch., N.J. Ser. 1, Vol. 27: 176-177, 353-354, 588-589, Vol. 29: 331.
Sale, E. T. Belles & Cavaliers, pp. 109-116.
Salley, A. S. Early Carolina, pp. 143, 175.
Spruill, J. C. Woman's Life, p. 16.

Stanard, M. M. Va.'s First Century, pp. 124, 190, 232-234, 242-244.

Tryon, R. M. Household Manuf., p. 214.

(5)   Weavers in the Communities

In 1719, a large group of Irish weavers emigrated with their families to New England. The weavers who emigrated later often became itinerant weavers and went from town to town and wove the yarn prepared by the women. A few of the itinerant weavers were women. They mark the transition from home to factory production.

Bolton, C. K. Scotch-Irish Pioneers, pp. 49-55, 100.
Earle, A. M. Narragansett, pp. 45-46.
Little, F. Amer. Textiles, pp. 34, 58.
Mitchell, E. V. Amer. Village, p. 238.
Sheldon, G. Hist. Deerfield, Mass. Vol. 1: 606.
Weeden, W. B. Hist. New Engl. Vol. 1: 305; Vol. 2: 494-495.

c.   The Beginnings of Cloth Manufacturing in the Colonies

As soon as the colonists had met their family needs, they produced cloth for sale. Small home factories were developed. Later, cooperative factory ventures were undertaken to supplement home production. Toward the close of the eighteenth century machinery improvements outdistanced the home methods.

(1)   Nascent Factories in the Colonial Homes

The home factories were small and almost completely self-contained. The members of the household produced the thread and spun and wove it into cloth. Most of the work was done by women and children, with the occasional help of an itinerant weaver for the heavier woolen cloths.

Bishop, J. L. Hist. Amer. Manuf. Vol. 1: 410-423.
Clark, V. S. Hist. Manuf., U.S. Vol. 1: 31, 157-164.
Dexter, E. A. Career Women, pp. 199-201.
Kohn, A. Cotton Mills, S. C., pp. 1-12.
Little, F. Amer. Textiles, pp. 73-74.
Montgomery, J. Cotton Manuf., U.S., p. 143.

(2)   School Clothing Factories

In 1730, a spinning school was started in Boston. Later, other schools utilized the services of children and apprentices to produce cloth. In some of the colonies, attendance at the spinning schools was mandatory for children from poor families.

Abbott, E. Women, Industry, p. 20.
Bagnall, W. R. Textile Indust., U.S., pp. 18-19, 29-31.
Bolton, C. K. Scotch-Irish Pioneers, p. 305.
Clark, V. S. Hist. Manuf., U.S. Vol. 1: 188-214.
Coman, K. Indust. Hist., U.S. Vol. 1: 117.
Gottesman, R. S. Arts and Crafts, 1777-1779, p. 288.
Leonàrd, E. A. Origins, Personnel Services, pp. 10-11,
    13-14.

(3) Attitudes Toward the New Factories

The early factories were considered a boon to civilization
because they increased the quantity of production, utilized the
energies of children and women not otherwisé employed, and
assisted in developing economic independence from England.

Calhoun, A. Soc. Hist., Amer. Family. Vol. 2: 172-174.
Coman, K. Indust. Hist., U.S., p. 147.
Weeden, W. B. Hist. New Engl. Vol. 1: 196.
Woody, T. Hist., Educ., Women. Vol. 2: 6-7.

(4) Factories Supported as Charity Ventures

Benevolent societies started factories for destitute women
in New York, Massachusetts, and Rhode Island. In 1791, New
Hampshire passed a law to facilitate the use of the poor and idle
in factories. Children were also put to work in these factories.

Calhoun, A. Soc. Hist., Amer. Family. Vol. 2: 173-174.
Gottesman, R. S. Arts and Crafts, 1726-1776, p. 258-259.
Little, F. Amer. Textiles, pp. 76-80.
Weeden, W. B. Hist. New Engl. Vol. 1: 196.

(5) Early Factories

Toward the end of the eighteenth century, sufficient cap-
ital and machinery had been developed to start commercial
ventures in the production of cotton, linen, and woolen cloth in
most of the colonies. Most of the workers were women and
children.

Bagnall, W. R. Textile Indust., U. S., pp. 92-95, 173-174.
Bishop, J. L. Hist., Amer. Manuf. Vol. 1: 296-347, 383-
    410.
Briggs, L. V. Hist., Cabot Family. Vol. 1: 157-161.
Clark, V. S. Hist., Manuf., U. S. Vol. 1: 156-158, 188-214.
Coman, K. Indust. Hist., U. S., pp. 114-115, 118.
Mitchell, B. William Gregg, pp. 60-63, 200-201.
Montgomery, J. Cotton Manuf., U. S., pp. 75-76, 82-84,
    85-90, 106-107, 141-155.

Tryon, R. M. Household Manuf., U.S., pp. 62-122, 192-196,
202, 213, 243-264.
Weeden, W. B. Hist. New Engl. Vol. 1: 387-394; Vol. 2:
679-681, 731-733, 788-791, 849-855.
White, G. S. Samuel Slater, pp. 47-99.
Woody, T. Hist., Educ. Women. Vol. 1: 260-261.

d.   Costumes and Fashions of Colonial Dames

Puritan costumes were plain and mostly of homespun materials.
In the Middle Atlantic colonies, the dress varied from the simple costumes of the Quakers to the more elaborate dress of many of the city
dwellers. In the southern colonies, the landed gentry dressed in the
fashions of England and the slaves in homespun cotton clothes.

(1)   Fashions

Fashions in clothing changed slowly during the eighteenth
century from plain homespun garments to rich costumes of cotton, linen, silk, and wool. The headdress became more elaborate
and jewelry more commonly worn.

Andrews, C. M. Colonial Folkways, pp. 78-83.
Bartlett, H. R. 18th Cent. Ga. Women, pp. 123-125.
Bruce, A. P. Econ. Hist. Va. Vol. 2: 186-195.
Calhoun, A. Soc. Hist., Amer. Family. Vol. 1: 246.
Chastellux, Marquis de. Travels. Vol. 2: 115.
Dexter, E. A. Colonial Women, pp. 42-43.
Dow, G. F. Arts and Crafts, pp. 60-84, 154-203.
Earle, A. M. Child Life, pp. 34-62.
Earle, A. M. Customs and Fashions, pp. 289-330.
Earle, A. M. Two Cent. Costumes. Vol. 1: 51-96, 99-138,
139-159.
Earle, A. M. Home Life, pp. 207-290.
Holliday, C. Women's Life. See index.
Hollister, G. H. Hist. Conn. Vol. 1: 440-445.
McClellan, E. Hist., Amer. Dress, pp. 1-242.
Morison, S. E. Builders, Bay Colony, pp. 162-164, 180,
239-240.
Ridgely, M. What Them Befell, pp. 191, 244.
Rouchefoucault-Liancourt, F. Travels. Vol. 2: 212.
Rowland, K. M. Elizabeth Diggs, W. M. Quart. Ser. 1,
Vol. 4: 22-23.
Singleton, E. Social Life, N.Y., pp. 171-256.
Stanard, M. M. Colonial Va., pp. 186-212.
Tilden, W. S. Hist. Medfield, Mass., p. 148.
Watson, J. F. Annals, Phila., pp. 175-182.
Weeden, W. B. Hist. New Engl. Vol. 1: 250; Vol. 2:
536-538, 695, 743-744.
Woody, T. Hist. Educ. Woman. Vol. 1: 172-173, 250.

(2)   Restrictions on the Dress of Colonial Dames

In 1634, a court order in Massachusetts restricted the
dress of men, women, and children according to their station
in life. Later laws throughout New England relaxed the restrictions. Certain religious groups, however, continued to restrict
the dress of their members.

Bliss, W. R. Sidelights, Meetinghouse, pp. 136-141.
Drake, F. S. Roxbury, Mass., pp. 54-55.
Earle, A. M. Two Cent. Costume. Vol. 1: 61-69.
Fisher, S. G. Men, Women and Manners, p. 185.
Holliday, C. Women's Life, pp. 152-153.
Judd, S. Hist. Hadley, Mass., pp. 91-92.
Kuhns, O. German-Swiss Settlements, p. 170.
Logan, J. A. Part Taken by Women, p. 35.
Myers, G. Ye Olden Blue Laws, pp. 28-46.
Orcutt, W. D. Old Dorchester, pp. 50-51.
Smith, E. V. Hist., Newburyport, p. 20.
Trumbull, J. R. Hist. Northampton. Vol. 1: 290-292.
Weeden, B. W. Hist. New Engl. Vol. 1: 106-107, 226-229.
Winthrop, J. Hist. New Engl. Vol. 1: 120.
Woody, T. Hist. Educ. Women. Vol. 1: 170-171.

(3)   Fashions and Patriotism

Women expressed their patriotism by wearing homespun
clothes themselves and producing quantities of material to be
used by the military and home defense projects.

Bagnall, W. R. Textile Indust., U. S., p. 110.
Biddle, G. V., & Lowrie, S. D. Notable Women, Pa., pp.
    39-40.
Bishop, J. L. Hist., Amer. Manuf. Vol. 1: 394-395.
Coman, K. Indust. Hist., U.S., p. 114.
Earle, A. M. Colonial Dames, pp. 241-244.
Ellet, E. F. Domestic Hist., Amer. Rev., p. 44.
Essex Antiq. Spinning, Essex Antiq. Vol. 1: 51, 87-92;
    Vol. 4: 38.
Holliday, C. Women's Life, pp. 111-112.
Johnson, R. G. Hist. Acct. Salem, West Jersey, p. 127.
Little, F. Amer. Textiles, pp. 77-78.
Tryon, R. M. Household Manuf., U. S., pp. 53-60, 104-111,
    113-116.

e.   The Making and Caring for Clothing

Women made all types of clothing both for men and women.
They washed, dyed, and repaired clothing; printed patterns on cotton,
linen, and silk cloth; did fine needle work; made lace; and were skilled
milliners as well.

(1) Dress Making and Tailoring, Millinery

    Advertisements of dressmakers, tailors and milliners appear in the newspapers of all the colonies. As side lines, many of the women taught children, cut and dressed hair and made mantuas.

    Bartlett, H. R. 18th Cent. Ga. Women, pp. 73-75.
    Calhoun, A. W. Soc. Hist., Amer. Family. Vol. 1: 281.
    Dexter, E. A. Colonial Women, pp. 41, 45.
    Dow, G. F. Arts and Crafts, pp. 275-276.
    Earle, E. A. Colonial Days, N. Y., p. 36.
    Gottesman, R. S. Arts and Crafts, 1726-1776, pp. 147, 297, 318, 327, 332.
    Manges, F. M. Women Shopkeepers, pp. 106-108.
    Scharf, J. T., & Wescott, T. Hist. Phila. Vol. 1: 194.
    Spruill, J. C. Women's Life, pp. 80-81, 285.
    Woody, T. Hist. Educ. Women. Vol. 1: 163, 194, 250-251, 259.

(2) Mending, Remaking, Knitting Clothes

    Women did the mending and remaking of worn clothing. They reknit heels and toes in silk and woolen stockings and mittens.

    Dexter, E. A. Colonial Women, pp. 40-44.
    Earle, A. M. Home Life, pp. 237-238.
    Earle, A. M. Colonial Days, N. Y., p. 169.
    Gottesman, R. S. The Arts and Crafts, 1726-1776, pp. 275, 325.

(3) Washing, Dyeing, and Cloth Printing

    Frequent advertisements in the colonial newspapers indicate that women did laundering, cleaning, dyeing, and "scowering" of all types of clothing and did stamping of designs on cotton, linen, and silk cloth and fulling of woolen cloth.

    Dexter, E. A. Colonial Women, pp. 44-45, 94.
    Dow, G. F. Arts and Crafts, p. 268.
    Earle, A. M. Colonial Dames, p. 66.
    Gottesman, R. S. Arts and Crafts, 1726-1776, pp. 282, 285.
    Gottesman, R. S. Arts and Crafts, 1777-1799, pp. 297, 298.
    Little, F. Amer. Textiles, pp. 186-205.
    Manges, F. M. Women Shopkeepers, p. 110.
    Spruill, J. C. Women's Life, pp. 286-288.

f. Fine Needlework

Largely as a pastime, women did exquisite embroidery, made delicate laces, sewed elaborate designs into quilts and coverlets, and invented the weaving of grasses into straw hats.

Bolton, E. S., & Coe, E. J. Amer. Samplers.
Earle, E. A. Child Life, pp. 321-341.
Early, E. New Engl. Samplers.
Eberlein, H. C., & McClure, A. Amer. Antiques, pp. 78-101, 321-328.
Finley, R. E. Patchwork Quilts.
Gottesman, R. S. Arts and Crafts, 1726-1776, pp. 275, 276, 279, 280-281.
Gottesman, R. S. Arts and Crafts, 1777-1799, p. 294.
Little, F. Amer. Textiles, pp. 170-185.
Meyer, A. N. Women's Work, pp. 278-279.
Mozan, H. J. Women, Science, p. 344.
Murray, Anne W. "Liberty" Quilts, Antiques. Vol. 51-52: 28-30.
Orcutt, W. D. Old Dorchester, pp. 50-51.
Peto, F. Amer. Quilts and Coverlets.
Peto, F. Historic Quilts.
Tryon, R. M. Household Manuf., U. S., p. 215.
Vanderpoel, E. N. Amer. Lace and Lace Makers, pp. 1-8.
Van Rensselaer, (Mrs.) J. K. Mana-ha-ta, pp. 88-89.

D.   Women Printers and Journalists in Colonial Times

There were at least twenty women who were printers before or during the American Revolution. Mrs. Jose Glover was owner of the first printing press in the Colonies, 1638.

a.   General Statements

Some of the women printers took over the presses after their husbands died or went to war for a short time; others made a career for themselves as publishers of newspapers; and still others ran the presses as one of several enterprises. A number became official state printers.

Brigham, C. S. Journals & Journeymen, pp. 71-79.
Dexter, E. A. Colonial Women, pp. 166-179, 212-214.
Hamill, F. Some Unconventional Women Biblio. Soc. Amer. Vol. 49, 4th Quart.: 300-314,
Heartman, F. Check List of Printers, U. S.
Meyer, A. N. Woman's Work, p. 279.
Oldham, E. M. Early Women Printers, Amer. Boston Publ. Libr. Quart., Jan., pp. 6-26; April, pp. 78-92; July, pp. 141-150.
Thomas, I. Hist. Printing. Vols. 1 & 2: see index.
Woody, T. Hist. Educ. Women. Vol. 1: 249, 260-263.

b. In New England

Anne Franklin, Sarah Goddard, Margaret Draper, Mrs. Russell, and later Mary Crouch became distinguished printers in New England before the end of the eighteenth century.

Bishop, J. L. Hist. Amer. Manuf. Vol. 1: 176-177.
Bridenbaugh, C. Cities Wilderness, pp. 130, 291-292, 462-463, 459.
Chapin, H. M. Ann Franklin, Printer.
Dexter, E. A. Career Women, pp. 108-109.
Dunton, J. Life & Errors, pp. 139-143.
Earle, A. M. Colonial Dames, pp. 57-62, 64-68.
Mason, G. C. Reminicences, Newport, p. 84.
Sanborn (Mrs.), A. H. The Newport Mercury, Newport H. S.
Bull. No. 65: 1-11.
Tapley, H. S. Salem Imprints, pp. 56-59.
Updike, W. Hist. Episcopal Church, Narragansett, pp. 153-155,
(Sarah Goddard.)
Winterich, J. T. Books and Printing, pp. 25-26.

c. In the Middle Atlantic Colonies

In the Middle Atlantic colonies, Anna Zenger, Cornelia Bradford, Elizabeth Holt, Mrs. Reid, Mary Dickson, and Elizabeth Oswald all distinguished themselves in the field of printing and publishing during the period.

Bishop, J. L. Hist. Amer. Manuf. Vol. 1: 176-177.
Bridenbaugh, C. Cities Wilderness, pp. 132, 293-295, 457, 461.
Cooper, Kent. Anna Zenger.
Dexter, E. A. Career Women, pp. 105, 107.
Earle, A. M. Colonial Dames, pp. 65-66, 68.
Hildeburn, C. R. Sketches, Printers, pp. 31-33, 96-98.
Manges, F. M. Women Shopkeepers, p. 113.
Nelson, Wm. Arch., N.J. Ser. 1, Vol. 24: 90, 100.
Scott. Counterfeiting. See index, women's names.
Seidensticker, O. First Cent., German Printing, pp. 168, 253.
Smyth, A. H. Writings, Benjamin Franklin. Vol. 1: 324, 344;
Vol. 3: 378.
Winterich, J. T. Books, Printing, p. 98.

d. In the Southern Colonies

There were at least eight women printers and publishers of distinction in the southern colonies during the eighteenth century. Dinah Nuthead, Anne Green, Elizabeth Timothy, Sarah Hillhouse, Clementina Rind, Mary Goddard, Verlinda Stone, and Mrs. Boden each contributed to the culture of the colonies through their printing efforts.

Bartlett, H. R. 18th Cent. Ga. Women, pp. 68-69.
Bibbens, R. M. Beginnings Md., pp. 76-77.
Calhoun, A. Soc. Hist., Amer. Family. Vol. 1: 277.
Cohen, H. S. C. Gazette, see index Elizabeth Timothy.
Dexter, E. A. Career Women, pp. 102-104.
Earle, A. M. Colonial Dames, pp. 58-60, 62-64.
Elzas, B. Jews, S. C., pp. 37-39, 44-45, 88-89.
Hillhouse, M. P. Hist. Colls., pp. 144-146, 468-470, 477.
Hirsch, A. H. Huguenots, S. C., p. 243.
Knight, L. L. Ga.'s Landmarks. Vol. 1: 1047-1058; Vol. 2: 1039.
Richardson, H. D. Sidelights, Md. Hist. Vol. 1: 147.
Salley, A. S. First Presses, S. C., Biblio Soc. Amer. Proc. Vol. 2: 28-69.
Spruill, J. C. Women's Life, pp. 263-266.
White, G. Hist. Colls., Ga., pp. 687-688.
Wroth, L. C. Hist. Printing, Md., pp. 1-16, 84-89, 119-146.

E.   Colonial Women in Merchandising

a.   Importers

Women entered the field of merchandizing very early in the colonial period and sold a wide variety of articles, some of which were imported either from England and Europe or from other colonies.

Adams, S. W., & Stiles, H. R. Hist. Wethersfield. Vol. 1: 656.
Ames, Azel. Mayflower Log, pp. 58, 63.
Bartlett, H. R. 18th Cent. Ga. Women, pp. 72-73.
Calhoun, A. Soc. Hist., Amer. Family. Vol. 1: 101, 169.
Dexter, E. A. Colonial Women, pp. 10, 21-33, 105-106.
Dexter, E. A. Career Women, pp. 140-142.
Earle, A. M. Colonial Days, N. Y., pp. 162-163.
Earle, A. M. Colonial Dames, pp. 56, 73-4.
Elzas, B. Jews, S. C., p. 44.
McCrady, E. Hist. S. C. Royal Govt., pp. 672-676.
Marcus, A. R. Amer. Jewry. Vol. 2: 13, 401.
P.M.H.B. Free Society of Traders. Vol. II: 175-180.
Spruill , J. C. Women's Life, p. 284.
Tyler, F., & Brown, H. T. Grandmother Tyler's Book, p. 268.
Van Rensselaer, (Mrs.) J. K. Mana-ha-ta, pp. 33, 234-236.
Weeden, W. B. Hist. New Engl. Vol. 2: 633-634.
Wharton, A. H. Colonial Days, pp. 77-78.

b.   Women Owners of General Stores

Many women owned general stores that sold everything from pins to anchors or seeds to flour.

Abbott, E. Women, Indust., p. 14.
Beedy, H. C. Mothers, Maine, pp. 147-156.
Bentley, W. Diary. Vol. 1, see index Abigail Berry, Elizabeth
Greenwood, Hannah Webb, Rebecca Smith and Elizabeth
Welcome.
Biddle, G. B., & Lowrie, S. E. Notable Women, Pa., pp. 31-2.
Colton, J. M. Annals, Manhattan, p. 23.
Crevecoeur, J. H. de. Letters, pp. 146-150.
Dexter, E. A. Colonial Women, pp. 18-37, 209-210.
Earle, E. A. Colonial Days, N. Y., pp. 159-161.
Gottesman, R. S. Arts and Crafts, 1726-1776, pp. 271-272.
Gottesman, R. S. Arts and Crafts, 1777-1799, p. 101.
Green, H. C., & M. W. Pioneer Mothers. Vol. 1: 180.
Lamson, D. F. Hist. Manchester, Mass., pp. 286-287, 337-338.
Lee, F. Arch., N. J. Ser. 2, Vol. 2: 49.
McCrady, E. S. C. Royal Govt., pp. 670-676.
Manges, F. M. Women Shopkeepers, pp. 40-70, 116.
Marcus, J. P. Early Amer. Jewry. Vol. 2: 13-14, 354, 397-401.
Morris, R. B. Hist., Amer. Law, p. 129.
Nelson, W. Arch., N. J. Ser. 1, Vol. 24: 424-426; Ser. 2, Vol.
4: 114.
Poyas, E. Days of Yore.
Scharf, J. T. & Westcott, T. Hist., Phila. Vol. 1: 194.
Spruill, J. C. Women's Life, pp. 276, 278, 283-284.
Van Rensselaer, (Mrs.) J. K. Mana-ha-ta, pp. 26, 236.
Watertown. Records. Vol. 2: 48, 54, 76.
Wharton, A. H. Colonial Days, p. 76.
Woody, T. Hist. Educ. Women. Vol. 1: 259-260.

c. Women Owners of Garden Produce, Grocery Stores

Women owned groceries where all manner of garden produce was
sold. Women not only produced food for their homes but also processed
many food products for sale such as chocolate, mustard, and spices.
They pickled fish, vegetables, and meats. They butchered animals,
bolted flour, preserved vegetables and fruits, and baked many types of
bread and pastry.

Andrews, C. M. & E. W. Journ., Janet Shaw, pp. 178-179.
Corey, D. P. Hist., Malden, Mass., pp. 681-682.
Dexter, E. A. Colonial Women, pp. 19, 25, 27, 52, 114-117, 183-
184.
Dexter, E. A. Career Women, pp. 144-147.
Dow, G. F. Arts and Crafts, pp. 281, 305.
Earle, A. M. Colonial Dames, pp. 56, 87.
Greene, L. J. Negro, Colonial New Engl., pp. 307-308.
Spruill, J. C. Women's Life, pp. 110, 276-277, 287-289.
Tilden, W. S. Hist., Medfield, Mass., p. 197.
Weeden, W. B. Hist., New Engl. Vol. 1: 111, 310.
Woody, T. Hist. Educ. Women. Vol. 1: 194, 259-260.

d. Women Owners of Bakeries, Candy, and Delicatessen Stores

Women often specialized in baked goods, sweetmeats, and jellies
and preserves.

Bartlett, H. R. 18th Cent. Ga. Women, pp. 71-72.
Dexter, E. A. Colonial Women, pp. 46-51.
Gottesman, R. S. Arts and Crafts, 1726-1776, p. 288.
Spruill, J. C. Women's Life, pp. 80-81, 287-288.
Woody, T. Hist. Educ. Women. Vol. 1: 193.

e. Women Tobacconists

Several women specialized in tobacco products with considerable success.

Dexter, E. A. Colonial Women, p. 20.
Gottesman, R. S. Arts and Crafts, 1726-1776, p. 318.
Manges, F. M. Women Shopkeepers, pp. 68, 112.

f. Women Owners of Drug and Cosmetic Stores

Colonial women had considerable knowledge of herbs, ointments,
salves, and cosmetics, which they used in their production and sale
of healing potions.

Dexter, E. A. Colonial Women, pp. 29-30, 51.
Dow, G. F. Arts and Crafts, p. 286.
Lee, F. Arch., N. J. Ser. 2, Vol. 2: 573.
Spruill, J. C. Women's Life, p. 283.
Tapley, H. S. Salem Imprints, pp. 99, 100, 104.

g. Women Owners of Dry Goods and Clothing Stores

Many of the clothing stores in the colonies were owned, or part-
ly owned, by women. Much of their stock was imported, even during
the Revolutionary War days. Each new shipment from abroad was
advertised in the newspapers.

Bridenbaugh, C. Cities in the Wilderness, pp. 338-341.
Dexter, E. A. Colonial Women, pp. 40-45.
Dexter, E. A. Career Women, pp. 142-143.
Dow, G. F. Arts and Crafts, pp. 162, 163, 171, 175, 181, 184.
Gottesman, R. S. Arts and Crafts, 1726-1776, pp. 107, 271, 272,
    324.
Gottesman, R. S. Arts and Crafts, 1777-1799, pp. 147, 297, 318.
Spruill, J. C. Women's Life, pp. 279, 281, 288.
Woody, T. Hist. Educ. Women. Vol. 1: 163, 194, 250-251, 259,
    260, 263.

h. Women Owners of Hardware Stores

Women owners of hardware stores were not uncommon in colonial days. Their stock was diversified and apparently well chosen for their customers.

Dexter, E. A. Colonial Women, pp. 21-32, 51.
Dexter, E. A. Career Women, p. 145.
Dow, G. F. Arts and Crafts, pp. 228-231.
Dow, G. F. Every Day Life, Mass., p. 126.
Gottesman, R. S. Arts and Crafts, 1726-1776, p. 352.
Lee, F. Arch., N. J. Ser. 2, Vol. 2: 60.
Manges, F. M. Women Shopkeepers, p. 102.
Prime, A. C. Arts and Crafts. Vol. 2: 149.

i. Women Owners of Book Stores and Binderies

Mary Katharine Goddard and Cornelia Bradford ran book stores in connection with their printing establishments. A few women were successful in importing books and stationery for sale before 1775. After the Revolution, the market for books rose rapidly.

Dexter, E. A. Colonial Women, pp. 30, 169.
Dexter, E. A. Career Women, p. 145.
Earle, A. M. Colonial Dames, p. 60.
Gottesman, R. S. Arts and Crafts, 1777-1799, pp. 265-266, 363.
Hamill, F. Unconventional Women, Biblio. Soc. Amer. Vol. 49: 300-314.
Manges, F. M. Women Shopkeepers, p. 54.
Nelson, W. Arch., N. J. Ser. 1, Vol. II: 108-109.
Thomas, I. Hist., Printing. Vol. 2: 444, 447, 449.
Woody, T. Hist. Educ. Women. Vol. l: 163, 164-165.

j. Real Estate Saleswomen

A few women dealt in real estate. Sometimes, the land was a part of the family estate or an estate of which a woman was executrix.

Bartlett, H. R. 18th Cent. Ga. Women, pp. 65-66.
Davenport, J. Letters, Mass. H. S. Colls. Ser. 4, Vol. 7: 487-532.
Dexter, E. A. Colonial Women, pp. 100-103, 109-110, 115.
Lee, F. Arch., N. J. Ser. 2, Vol. 2: 498, 512.
Nelson, W. Arch., N. J. Ser. 1, Vols. 12, 24, 25, 26, 27, 28, 29; Ser. 2, Vols. 3, 4. See index women's names.
Stryker, W. Arch., N. J. Ser. 2, Vol. l: 22, 35, 318, 330.
Twitchell. Spanish Arch., N. M. Vol. 1, see index women's names.
Woody, T. Hist. Educ. Women. Vol. l: 257.

F.   Diverse Occupations of Colonial Women

a.   General Listings

The list of occupations in which colonial women were engaged continues to grow as old documents are unearthed and new histories written. It would appear that, at one time or another, they engaged in all the occupations known to the men.

Ames, S. M. Studies, Va., pp. 111-146.
Bridenbaugh, C. Colonial Craftsman, pp. 105-108.
Calhoun, A. W. Soc. Hist., Amer. Family. Vol. 1: 101.
Dexter, E. A. Colonial Women, pp. 53-56.
Gottesman, R. S. Arts and Crafts, 1726-1776 (see index).
Gottesman, R. S. Arts and Crafts, 1777=1799 (see index).
Hart, A. B. Commonwealth Hist., Mass. Vol. 2: 371-373.
Weeden, W. B. Hist., New Engl. Vol. 1: 336, 398, 436; Vol. 2: 731-32, 885.
Woody, T. Hist. Educ. Women. Vol. 1: 160-166.

b.   Women Attorneys, Administrators and Executrixes

Women acted as administrators and executrixes of family estates in all of the colonies. They also had the power of attorney for their husbands in numerous instances, as in the case of Hannah Penn, who transacted much of the legal business related to the colony in Pennsylvania. Margaret Brent was a successful attorney for many people in the courts of Maryland. Rachel Miller was notary for Jemima Wilkinson and her religious settlement, and Bridget Usher and Mary Peacocke were "attorneys" in Massachusetts.

Ames, S. M. Studies, Va., p. 158.
Andrews, M. P. Hist., Md. Vol. 1: 185-187, 201-202, 257, see index Margaret Brent.
Andrews, M. P. Founding Md., pp. 201, 267.
Bartlett, H. R. 18th Cent. Ga. Women, pp. 67-68.
Biddle, G. B., & Lowrie, S. D. Notable Women, Pa., pp. 7-10, 17-19, 26-28.
Bland, S. Power of Attorney, W. M. Quart. Ser. 2, Vol. 4: 202.
Brent, C. H. Descendants, Giles Brent, pp. 42-50.
Brigham, W. Compact, New Plymouth, p. 32.
Browne, W., & Hall, C. Arch., Md. Vols. 1 & 4, see index under Margaret Brent.
Bruce. Econ. Hist., Va. Vol. 1: 412.
Calhoun, A. W. Soc. Hist., Amer. Family. Vol. 1: 277.
Coates, A. Century Legal Ed. N.C. Law Rev. Vol. 24: 307-340.
Cobbledick, M. R. Status of Women, p. 149.
DeForest, E. Walloon Family. Vol. 1: 171-173.
Drinker, S. Hannah Penn.
Holliday, C. Woman's Life, pp. 297-298.

Hull, William I. William Penn, pp. 57-61.
Jenkins, H. M. Family William Penn, pp. 67-106.
Johnson, R. G. Hist., Salem, West Jersey, pp. 46-56.
Lamb, M. J. Hist. N.Y.C. Vol. 1: 279.
Lawrence, T. Hist. Lawrence Family, pp. 145-147.
Lee, F. Arch., N. J. Ser. 2, Vol. 2, see index Settlement &
    Sales, Administrators.
McCrady, E. S. C. Proprietory Govt., pp. 235, 270, 272, 290,
    317, 326, 469, 546.
Mass. Bay Colony. Record, Court Assistants. Vol. 1: 193,
    237, 275, 294, 330.
Meyer, A. N. Woman's Work, pp. 220-221.
Morris, R. Hist., Amer. Law, pp. 130-132.
Nelson, W. Arch., N. J. Ser. 1, Vols. 12, 27, 28, 29; Ser. 2,
    Vols. 3 & 4, see index.
N.Y. Hist. Soc. Colls. Attorneys. Vol. 78: 108-110.
Northampton Co., Va. Records. Vol. 17: 310-311.
Pound, Arthur. The Penns, p. 225 ff.
Prowell, G. F. Hist., Camden Co., N.J., p. 646.
Ramey, M. E. Margaret Brent.
Reeve, T. Baron & Femme, pp. 79-80.
Richardson, H. D. Sidelights, Md. Hist. Vol. 1: 148-150.
Rochfoucault-Liancourt, F. Travels. Vol. 1: 205.
Semmes, R. Captains & Mariners, see index under Margaret
    Brent.
Stryker, W. Arch., N. J. Ser. 2, Vol. 1: 15, 83, 84, 421, 469.
Thomas, J. W. Chronicles Md., pp. 29-50.
Twitchell. Arch., Spanish, N.M. Vol. 1, see index.
Woody, T. Hist. Educ. Women. Vol. 1: 248-249, 257-258.
Worcester Soc. Antiq. Colls. Vol. 3: 23, 48.
Worth, H. B. Nantucket Land & Landowners, Nantucket H.A.
    Proc. Vol. 2: 300-335.

c.   Women Barbers and Beauty Operators

From Maine to Georgia women acted as barbers and beauty
specialists for men and women.

Bentley, W. Diary. Vol. 2: 304, 437; Vol. 4, p. 415.
Duane, W. Diary, Christopher Marshall, pp. 176-177.
Spruill, J. C. Women's Life, p. 121.
Woody, T. Hist. Educ. Women. Vol. 1: 163.

d.   Women Blacksmiths

Where workers were scarce and horses needed to be shod or
tools mended, a few women became blacksmiths, at least until they
married a strong man to carry on the work.

Dexter, E. A. Colonial Women, p. 53.
Earle, A. M. Colonial Life, N.Y., p. 159.

e.   Women Botanists and Naturalists

Jane Colden and Martha Logan became excellent botanists and
florists and described and classified many plants. Hannah English
showed a remarkable knowledge of birds, vipers, and insects.

Dexter, E. A. Colonial Women, pp. 118-119.
Earle, A. M. Colonial Dames, pp. 85-87.
Herbst, J. New Green World, p. 143.
Holman, M. C. Western Neck, p. 13.
Jervey, E. H. Martha Ramsay, S.C.H.G. Mag. Vol. 36: 136-
137.
Prior, M. B. Letters, Martha Logan, S.C.H.G. Mag. Vol. 59:
38-46.
Ramsay, D. Martha Ramsay.
Ravenel, H. Charleston, pp. 124-125, also see index under Eliza
Pinckney.
Spruill, J. C. Women's Life, p. 278.
Van Rensselaer, (Mrs.) J. K. Mana-ha-ta, pp. 258-259.
Wallace, D. D. Hist. S. C. Vol. 1: 408.
Wallace, D. D. Henry Laurens, see index Martha Ramsay.
Woody, T. Hist. Educ. Women. Vol. 1: 249.

f.   Women in Food Processing

Colonial women processed many types of food from grains,
meat, and fish to delicate sweetmeats.

Dexter, E. A. Colonial Women, pp. 47-51.
Gottesman, R. S. Arts and Crafts, 1726-1776, p. 288.
Manges, F. M. Women Shopkeepers, pp. 98-100, 112.
Myers, A. C. Narratives Pa., p. 287.
Ramsay, D. Hist., S. C. Vol. 2: 221.
Scharf, J. T., & Westcott, T. Hist., Phila. Vol. 1: 194.
Spruill, J. C. Women's Life, pp. 287-289.
Weeden, W. B. Hist., New Engl. Vol. 1: 310.
Woody, T. Hist. Educ. Women. Vol. 1: 193.

g.   Women in the Metal, Glass and Wood Crafts

Women ground spectacles and other articles of glass. They
painted houses and did all manner of carpentry work. They were successful tinkers and makers of small metal articles, such as curling
combs.

Dexter, E. A. Colonial Women, p. 51.
Gottesman, R. S. Arts and Crafts, 1726-1776, pp. 96, 352.

Gottesman, R. S. Arts and Crafts, 1777-1799, p. 237.
Manges, F. M. Women Shopkeepers, pp. xvii, 103-104.
Myers, A. C. Narratives Pa., pp. 288-290.
Phillips, U. P. Plantation and Frontier. Vol. 1: 352-353.
Prime, A. C. Arts and Crafts. Ser. 2: 149.
Scott. Counterfeiting, see index, women's names.
Weeden, W. B. Hist., New Engl. Vol. 1: 168.
Woody, T. Hist. Educ. Women. Vol. 1: 193, 261.

h.   Women Owners of Mills

Women are found to have been owners of saw mills, flour mills, cider mills and "horse mills."

Ames, S. M. Studies, Va., pp. 117, 120, 122-125.
Barker, C.R. The Gulph Mill, P.M.H.B. Vol. 53: 168-174.
Biddle, G. B., & Lowrie, S. D. Notable Women, Pa., pp. 60-62.
Green, H. C. & M. W. Pioneer Mothers, pp. 410-420.
Needles, S. H. Governor's Mill & Globe Mills, P.M.H.B. Vol. 8: 285-293.
Nelson, W. Arch., N.J. Ser. 1, Vol. 11: 256, 430; Vol. 27: 40, 289-290, 478-479, 505, 609-610.

i.   Women Morticians

Widows and nurses not infrequently acted as morticians.

Gottesman, R. S. Arts and Crafts, 1726-1776, p. 141.
Manges, F. M. Women Shopkeepers, p. 111.
Wharton, A. H. Colonial Days, pp. 147-148.

j.   Women Sextons

Women acted as sextons for churches and, in one case, Harvard College, a woman acted as sexton for an educational institution.

Dexter, E. A. Colonial Women, p. 97.
Spruill, J. C. Women's Life, p. 304.

k.   Women in the Shipping Business and Ferries

Cornelia De Peyster is said to have brought the first cargo of salt to New Amsterdam. Margaret Philipse is thought to have owned and operated the first packet line between England and the colonies. Several women owned and operated ferries, and others owned and operated wharves as commercial ventures.

Ames, S. M. Studies, Va., pp. 142-144.
Dexter, E. A. Colonial Women, pp. 104, 107, 114.

Green, H. C. & M. W. Pioneer Mothers. Vol. 1: 188-193.
James, B. B., & Jameson, J. F. Journal, Jasper Danckaerts,
    see index Margaret Philipse.
Manges, F. M. Women Shopkeepers, p. 114.
Mason, G. C. Reminiscences, Newport, pp. 358-359.
Mass. Bay Colony. Record. Court of Assistants, Vol. 1: 61.
Nelson, W. Arch., N. J. Ser. 1, Vol. 28: 34, 81.
Spruill, J. C. Women's Life, pp. 32, 241, 304.
Van Rensselaer, (Mrs.) J. K. Mana-ha-ta, pp. 33-35.
Van Wyck, F. Keskachauge, pp. 410-411.
Weeden, W. B. Hist., New Engl. Vol. 1: 366.
Woody, T. Hist. Educ. Women. Vol. 1: 164-165, 260.

l. Women Makers of Soap, Candles, and Wax Works

Women were the chief producers of such necessary commodi-
ties as soap and candles. These were made of by-products of other
home industries such as lye from ashes, fats from meat and fish, and
wax from bayberries and honey combs.

Andrews, C. M., & E. W. Journ. Janet Schaw, pp. 203-204,
Dexter, E. A. Colonial Women, p. 52.
Gottesman, R. S. Arts and Crafts, 1777-1799, p. 405.
Scudder, H. E. Men and Manners, pp. 80-84.

m. Women Upholsterers

Women in all the colonies did the work of upholstering all types
of furniture, caneing chairs, and building special pieces of furniture.

Dexter, E. A. Colonial Women, p. 51.
Dexter, E. A. Career Women, pp. 148-149.
Gottesman, R. S. Arts and Crafts, 1726-1776, pp. 137, 141-142.
Gottesman, R. S. Arts and Crafts, 1777-1799, p. 146.
Manges, F. M. Women Shopkeepers, p. 105.
Prime, A. C. Arts and Crafts. Ser. 1: 205.
Spruill, J. C. Women's Life, p. 288.

n. Women in the Whaling Business

Martha Smith, in 1718, went into the business of catching and
processing whales on a large scale. Her whalers were successful
and produced large quantities of oil for sale. Other women owned
whaling vessels.

Earle, A. M. Colonial Dames, pp. 74-75.
Edwards, E. J., and Rattray, J. E. "Whale Off," pp. 231-234.
Halsey, A. F. Old Southampton, p. 108.
Weeden, W. B. Hist., New Engl. Vol. 1: 436.
Worth, H. B. Nantucket Lands & Landowners, Nantucket H. A.

Proc. Vol. 2: 308, 310, 319.

o.   Leather Workers

Colonial women made all types of leather articles from straps to shoes.

Manges, F. M. Women Shopkeepers, pp. 104-5.
Nelson, W. Arch., N. J. Ser. 1, Vol. 26: 346.

p.   Wall Paper Manufacturers

Prime, A. C. Arts and Crafts. Ser. 2: 279.

q.   Rope and Net Makers

Manges, F. M. Women Shopkeepers, p. 102.

r.   Owners of Iron Foundries

Bining, A. C. Pa. Iron Manuf., Pa. Hist. Commission. Vol. 4,
    see index Anna Nutt.
James (Mrs.), T. P. Thomas Potts, Jr., pp. 29-30, 53-54, 371-
    374.
Pa. Soc. Colonial Dames. Forges & Furnaces, see index Anna
    Nutt.

Colonial Women in the Arts

A.   Colonial Women in the Field of Literature

a.   General Statements

Women contributed some of the earliest literary works in the history of United States in spite of their lack of educational opportunities, their large families, and their heavy work schedules.

Beard, M. Amer. Through Women's Eyes, pp. 54-87.
Benson, M. S. Women 18th Cent. Amer., pp. 188-222.
Dexter, E. A. Colonial Women, pp. 126-142.
Dexter, E. A. Career Women, pp. 90-92, 97-99.
Earle, A. M., & Ford, E. E. Early Prose & Verse.
Meyer, A. N. Women's Work, pp. 108-111.
Mills, W. J. Hist. Houses, N. J., pp. 139-150.
Salley, A. S. Bibliography Women Writers, S. C., Southern
    H.S. Publs. Vol. 6: 143.
Violette, A. G. Economic Feminism, pp. 24-50.

b.   Colonial Women Narrative Writers

Women were among the first narrative writers on the colonies. They wrote of their experiences generally in the form of journals, diaries, or letters.

(1)   Narrative Writers

Mary Rowlandson was the first narrative writer to have her work published. She wrote an account of her capture by the Indians. Her work was followed by similar accounts based on fact or fiction.

Cairns, W. B. Early Amer. Writers, pp. 190-198.
Cotton, A. An Account of Our Late Troubles, Va.
Dexter, E. A. Colonial Women, pp. 130-134, 139-140.
Force, Peter (ed.) Tracts & Other Papers. Vol. 1.
    Mrs. An Cotton.
Graham, I. Life & Writings.
Harrison, F. B. Footnotes, 17th Cent. Va., Va. Hist.
    Mag. Vol. 50: 289-299.
Marvin, A. P. Hist., Lancaster, Mass., pp. 10, 95, 98-114.
Morison, S. E. Intellectual Life, New Engl., pp. 189-191.
Nourse, H. S. Records, Lancaster, Mass., pp. 98-106.
Peckham, H. H. Captured by Indians.
Rowlandson, M. Captivity & Restoration.
Trent, W. P., and Wells, B. W. Colonial Prose and
    Poetry, pp. 193-204.
Winsor, J. Mem. Hist., Boston. Vol. 2: 387-436.
Woody, T. Hist. Educ. Women. Vol. 1: 249.

(2)   Journals, Diaries, Memoirs

A number of colonial women left memoirs, journals, or diaries that have literary as well as historic value.

Adams, H. Memoirs, Hannah Adams.
Ambler, M. Diary, V.M.H.B. Vol. 45: 152-170.
Andrews, C. M., & E. W. Journ., Janet Schaw.
Armes, E. Nancy Shippen, Her Journ. 1777-1800.
Baird, C. W. Hist. Huguenot Emigration. Vol. 2: 112-114,
    182-183, 396-397.
Baldwin, S. Ride Across Conn., New Haven Col. H. S.
    Colls. Vol. 9: 161-169.
Bartlett, E. S. Journ. Great Grandmother Conn. Quart.
    Vol. 1: 265-270.
Beatty, J. M. Susan Assheton's Book, P.M.H.B. Vol. 55:
    174-186.
Biddle, H. D. Journal, Elizabeth Drinker.
Biddle, G. B., & Lowrie, S. D. Notable Women, Pa., pp.
    58-59, 82-84.
Blake, F. E. Hist. Princeton Mass. Vol. 1: 302-322.

Cadbury, S. Diary, Ann Warder, P.M.H.B. Vol. 17: 144-461; Vol. 18: 51-63.
Callender, H. Diary, P.M.H.B. Vol. 12: 432-456.
Carey, H. Diary, Tyler's Quart. Vol. 12: 160-173.
Codman, M. Journ., Katherine Amory.
Cook, M. W. Journ., Friends Intelligencer. Vol. 54, cont'd. in each issue.
Dexter, E. A. Colonial Women, pp. 133-134, 139-140.
Dow, G. F. Holyoke Diaries.
Drinker, E. Journ., P.M.H.B. Vol. 13: 298-308.
Dwight, E. A. Memorials, Mary White.
Earle, A. M., & Winston, A. Diary, Boston School Girl.
Eve, S. Journ., P.M.H.B. Vol. 5: 19-36, 191-205.
Fisher, J. Journ., Esther Burr, New Engl. Quart. Vol. 3: 297-315.
Forbes, H. M. Listing, New Engl. Diaries.
Gilman, A. Diary, Dorothy Dudley.
Greely, M. W. Cambridge, 1776.
Hinckley, R. H. Diary Christiana Leach, P.M.H.B. Vol. 35: 343-349.
Holbrook, H. P. Journ., Eliza Lucas Pinckney.
Hopkins, S. Memoirs, Sarah Osborn.
Hoskins, E. B. Fanny Saltar's Reminiscences, P.M.H.B. Vol. 40: 187-198.
Hubbs, R. Memoirs.
Huntington, A.S. Under Colonial Roof Tree, pp. 26-104.
Jackson, J. W. Margaret Morris, Her Journ.
Knight, S. K. Journ.
Logan, M. S. Part Taken by Women, pp. 159-160.
Matthews, W. Amer. Diaries, see index under women's names.
Maxwell, W. Memoirs, Helen Calvert Read, Lower Norfolk Co. Antiq. Vols. 1, 2 & 3, see index.
Morris, A. W. The Romance of Two Hannahs, Newport H.S. Bull. No. 26.
Myers, A. C. Journ., Sally Wister, pp. 13-17.
Overton, J. Long Island Story, pp. 79-81.
Palmer, E. Journ., Friend's H.S. Journ. Vol. 6: 38-40, 63-71, 133-139.
Post, L. M. Diary, Grace Barclay.
Poyas, E. Days of Yore.
Ramsay, D. Memoirs, Martha Ramsay.
Rawle, Anna. Loyalist's Account, P.M.H.B. Vol. 16: 103-107.
Searle, L. Memoirs, Sarah Atkins, Essex Inst. H. Colls. Vol. 85: 151-180.
Sheahan, H. B. Amer. Memory, pp. 76-78.
Smith, J. J. Letters, Journs., Richard Hill, pp. 209-237, 337-367.
Stone, W. L. Journ., Friederika Riedesel.

Talbot, M. Educ. Women, pp. 7-8.
Thomas, A. L. Journ., Nancy Lloyd.
Titus, A. Madame Knight's Diary, Bostonian Soc. Publ. No. 9: 99-126.
Trent, W., & Wells, B. Colonial Prose & Poetry. Part 2: 327-346.
Vaux, G. Diary, Hannah Callender, P.M.H.B. Vol. 12: 432-456.
Wallace, D. D. Hist., S. C. Vol. 1: 151.
Webber, M. L. Journ., Ann Manigault, S.C.H.G. Mag. Vol. 20: 57-63 ff; Vol. 21: 10-23 ff.
Werner, R. C. Diary, Grace Galloway, P.M.H.B. Vol. 55: 32-94; Vol. 58: 152-189.
Winship, G. P. Journ., Madam Knight.
Wister, S. Journ., P.M.H.B. Vol. 9: 318-333, 463-478; Vol. 10: 51-56.

(3)   Correspondence of Colonial Women

Fortunately, a considerable amount of the correspondence of the colonial women has been preserved. The letters deal with all aspects of colonial life.

Adams, C. F. Letters, Mrs. John Adams.
Adams, C. F. Familiar Letters.
Blair, A. Letter, Martha Braxton, W. M. Quart. Ser. 1, Vol. 16: 174-180.
Bobbe, D. Abigail Adams.
Boggs, J. L. Cornelia Patterson Letters, N.J.H.S. Proc. New Ser, Vol. 15: 508-517; Vol. 16: 56-67, 186-201.
Bradford, G. Portraits, Amer. Women, pp. 1-32.
Brooks, G. Dames & Daughters, pp. 169-214.
Farmar, E. Letters, P.M.H.B. Vol. 40: 199-207.
Franklin, E. Letter, N.J.H.S. Proc. Ser. 2, Vol. 5: 127-128.
Griscom, C. A. Letters, Sarah Tellier, P.M.H.B. Vol. 38: 100-109.
Izard, R. Letter, Mrs. Wm. Lee, V.M.H.B. Vol. 8: 16-28.
Lee, F. B. Arch., N. J. Ser. 2, Vol. 2: 195-196.
Marcus, J. P. Early Amer. Jewry. Vol. 1: 58-63, 68-72.
Mitchell, S. New Letters, Abigail Adams.
Munroe, S. Letter, Mary Mason, Md. H. Mag. Vol. 29: 245-252.
Nelson, W. Arch., N.J. Ser. 2, Vol. 4: 552.
"Rosalinda" Letter.
Richards, L. E. Abigail Adams.
Riley, E. M. Deborah Franklin, Proc. Amer. Philos. Soc. Vol. 95: 239-245.
Sachse, J. Wayside Inns, pp. 60-62.
Scheer, G. F., & Rankin, H. F. Rebels & Redcoats, pp.

224, 319, 321.
Sheahan, H. B. Amer. Memory, pp. 131-132, 191-193.
Sweeney, J. A. Norris-Fisher Correspondence, Del. H.
   Mag. Vol. 6: 187-232.
Thompson, H. F. Letter, Rebecca Franks, P.M.H.B. Vol.
   16: 216.
Thomson, H. Letters, P.M.H.B., Vol. 14: 28-40.
Tyler, Lyon G. (ed.). Letters, County Record Books,
   W. M. Quart. Ser. 1, Vol. 4: 77-78, 169-177.
Van Doren, C. Jane Mecom.
Van Doren, C. Letters, Benj. Franklin & Jane Mecom.
Wheatley, P. Letters, Phillis Wheatley.
Whitney, J. Abigail Adams.
Wm. & M. Quart. Letters. Ser. 1, Vol. 4: 77-78, 169-170,
   171, 173-176.
Williams, H. Letters, S.C.H.G. Mag. Vol. 21: 3-9.

c.   Colonial Women Poets

There were at least twelve colonial "female poets" whose poetry was recognized as a contribution to the literature of the period.
Two of these were Negro women.

(1)   Anne Bradstreet

Anne Bradstreet,who was born in England and came to New
England with her husband in 1630, was the first American poet.
She had eight children and suffered many hardships. Her poems
were published in England by her brother. See also List of 104
Outstanding Women.

   Anderson, J. Memorable Women. Vol. 1: 156-184.
   Berryman, J. Homage, Mist. Bradstreet.
   Bradstreet, A. Poems.
   Cairns, W. P. Early Amer. Writers, pp. 146-164.
   Campbell, H. Anne Bradstreet.
   Dexter, E. A. Colonial Women, pp. 126-130.
   Ellis, J. H. Works, Anne Bradstreet.
   Griswold, R. W. Female Poets, pp. 17-21.
   May, C. Amer. Female Poets, pp. 15-19.
   Morison, S. E. Builders, Bay Colony, pp. 320-336.
   Morison, S. E. Intellectual Life, New Engl., pp. 218-222.
   Pancoast, H. S. Intro. Amer. Literature, pp. 57-63.
   Trent, W. B., & Wells, B. W. Colonial Prose and Poetry,
      pp. 271-287.
   Wharton, A. H. Colonial Days, pp. 101-111.
   White, E. W. Tenth Muse, Anne Bradstreet, W.M. Quart.
      Ser. 3, Vol. 8: 355-377.
   Winsor, J. Mem. Hist., Boston. Vol. 4: 336-337.

(2)   Mercy Warren

Mercy Warren distinguished herself in several literary
fields, one of which was poetry. She was born in Plymouth
Colony in 1728 and died in 1814. See also List of 104 Outstanding
Women.

Anthony, K. First Lady, Rev.
Brown, A. Mercy Warren.
Cairns, W. B. Early Amer. Writers, pp. 384-394.
Crawford, M. C. Old Boston Days, pp. 323-327.
Ellet, E. F. Women, Amer. Rev. Vol. 1: 73-106.
Griswold, R. Female Poets, pp. 21-23.
Holliday, C. Women's Life, pp. 100-101, 145.
Hutcheson, M. M. Mercy Warren, W. M. Quart. Ser. 3,
    Vol. 10: 378-402.
Logan, M. S. Part Taken by Women, pp. 124-128.
Marble, A. R. Mercy Warren, New Engl. Mag. New Ser.,
    Vol. 28: 163-180.
May, C. Amer. Female Poets, pp. 42-45.
Rourke, C. Roots Amer. Culture, pp. 78, 111-114.
Tyler, M. C. Hist., Amer. Literature. Vol. 2: 419.
Warren, M. Poems.
Wharton, A. H. Colonial Days, pp. 111-112.
Winsor, J. Mem. Hist., Boston. Vol. 2: 457.

(3)   Phillis Wheatley

Phillis Wheatley was a Negro who was born in Africa a-
bout 1755 and sold as a slave in Boston in 1761. She was educated
by her mistress, Mrs. Wheatley. Her poems were published in
London in 1773. See also List of 104 Outstanding Women.

Crawford, M. C. Old Boston Days, pp. 314-322.
Dexter, E. A. Colonial Women, pp. 140-142.
Graham, S. Phillis Wheatley.
Greene, L. J. The Negro, Colonial New Engl., pp. 243-
    245.
Griswold, R. Female Poets, pp. 30-33.
Heartman, C. F. Letters, Poems of Phillis Wheatley.
May, C. Amer. Female Poets, pp. 39-41.
Wheatley, P. Memoirs and Poems.
Woody, T. Hist. Educ. Women, pp. 92, 124, 132.

(4)   Jane Turrell

Jane Turrell was born in Boston in 1708 and lived only 27
years. Her husband wrote memoirs of her life and included
many of her poems. See also List of 104 Outstanding Women.

Brooks, C. Hist., Medford, pp. 319-324.
Dexter, E. A. Colonial Women, pp. 137-138.
Holliday, C. Woman's Life, pp. 82, 130, 277.
May, C. Amer. Female Poets, pp. 21-25.
Turrell, E. Jane Turrell.
Winsor, J. Mem. Hist. Boston. Vol. 2: 429-430.

(5)   Other Women Poets

Sarah Morton, Elizabeth Ferguson, Deborah Logan,
Susanna Wright, Hannah Griffetts, Mrs. Stockton, Anne Eliza
Bleecker, Eliza Townsend, Lucy Terry, and others wrote and
had some of their poems published during this period.

Bentley, W. Diary. Vol. 2: 246.
Biddle, G. B., & Lowrie, S. D. Notable Women, Pa., pp.
    24-25, 46-48.
Bill, A. House Called Morven, pp. 21-33.
Boudinot, J. J. Elias Boudinot. Vol. 1: 29-32, 179.
Bridenbaugh, C. & J. Rebels & Gentlemen, pp. 107, 111-115,
    125-126, 152, 285.
Cairns, W. B. Early Amer. Writers, p. 205.
Dexter, E. A. Career Women, pp. 94-95, 97.
Ellet, E. F. Women Amer. Rev. Vol. 1: 189-201: Vol. 3:
    13-34.
Field, V. B. Constantia Univ. Maine Studies. Ser. 2, Vol.
    33.
Gratz, S. Material on Elizabeth Ferguson, P.M.H.B. Vol.
    39: 257-321, 385-409; Vol. 41: 385-398.
Greene, L. J. Negro, Colonial New Engl., pp. 242-248.
Griswold, R. W. Female Poets, pp. 24-29, 33-43.
Hazard, S. Register, Pa. Vol. 8: 177-178.
Heiges, G. L. Benj. Franklin, Lancaster Co. H.S. Journ.
    Vol. 61: 3-6.
Heistand (Mrs.), H. Samuel Blunston, Lancaster Co. H.S.
    Journ. Vol. 26: 193.
Logan, M. S. Part Taken by Women, pp. 179-181, 190-194.
May, C. Amer. Female Poets, pp. 26-38.
Nelson, W. Arch., N.J. Ser. 1, Vol. 20: 169.
Pendleton, E., & Ellis, M. Sarah Wentworth, Univ. Maine
    Bull. No. 34.
Reninger, M. Susanna Wright, Lancaster Co. H.S. Journ 63:
    183-185.
Rowson, Susanna. Misc. Poems.
Starrett, V. All About Mother Goose.
Watson. Annals, Phila. Vol. 1: 535-537, 560-561.
Wharton, A. H. Colonial Days, pp. 112-124.

d.   Early American Women Novelists and Dramatists

Dramatic writings and the sentimental novel became very popular in the last quarter of the eighteenth century. Four women writers

105

were among the authors that were widely read. Susannah Rowson, Charlotte Lennox, and Hannah Foster wrote novels that were very popular. Susannah Rowson and Mercy Warren both wrote two dramas apiece which were well received.

Brown, H. The Sentimental Novel.
Dexter, E. A. Career Women, pp. 82-83, 90.
Dunlap, W. Hist. Amer. Theatre. Vol. 2: 381-387.
Foster, H. The Coquette.
Hornblow, A. Hist. Theatre Amer. Vol. 1: 209-212;
Maynadier, G. H. First Amer. Novelist.
Pancoast, H. S. Intro. Amer. Literature, p. 349.
Rowson, S. Charlotte Temple.
Rowson, S. Charlotte's Daughter.
Warren, M. The Group.
Warren, M. Poems, Dramatic and Miscellaneous.
Watson, J. F. Annals, Phila. Vol. 1: 559.
Wegelin, O. Early Amer. Fiction, pp. 30-31.
Winsor, J. Mem. Hist., Boston. Vol. 3: 637-643.
Wright, L. H. Amer. Fiction, see index.

e.   Early American Women Essayists and Historians

A number of women wrote religious tracts and moral essays, and two women also wrote histories.

(1)   Women Who Wrote Religious Tracts

Mrs. Lloyd and others wrote religious tracts in which heaven and hell vied for the reader's interest. Hannah Adams wrote thoughtful treatises on religion based on her study of the scriptures.

Adams, H. Letters, Gospels.
Adams, H. Truth, Excellence, Christian Religion.
Adams, H. View of Religion.
Dexter, E. A. Colonial Women, pp. 134-137.
Hopkins, S. Susanna Anthony.
Tilden, O. M. Hannah Adams, Dedham H.S. Register.
    Vol. 7: 83-100.
So. Car. Hist. Gen. Mag. Mary Fisher Crosse. Vol. 12:
    106-108.
Wallace, D. D. Hist., S.C. Vol. 1: 411.

(2)   Early Historians

Hannah Adams, born in Massachusetts in 1755 and largely self-educated, wrote not only on the subject of religion but also history. She was the first colonial woman writer to make literature a professional occupation. Mercy Warren wrote a history of the American Revolution.

Adams, H. Alphabetical Compendium, Various Sects.
Adams, H. Hist., Jews.
Adams, H. Narrative of, Controversity.
Adams, H. An Abridgement, Hist., New Engl.
Adams, H. Dictionary, all Religions.
Lutz, Alma. Early Amer. Women Historians, Boston
    Libr. Quart. Vol. 8 (2): 85-99.
Meyer, A. N. Women's Work, p. 108.
Stoney, L. C. (ed.) Day on Cooper River, pp. 60, 83, 104-
    105, 107.
Warren, Charles. E. Gerry, J. Warren & Mercy Warren
    and the Ratification of the Constitution, Mass. H.S.
    Proc. Vol. 64: 143-164, 262.
Warren, M. Hist. Amer. Rev.
Winsor, J. Mem. Hist. Boston. Vol. 4: 341-342.

B.   Colonial Women in Artistic Endeavors

Several colonial women distinguished themselves through their artistic accomplishments. Henrietta Johnston is thought to have been the first woman painter in America. At least eight other women were noted for their artistic work during the colonial period.

Bridenbaugh, C. & J. Rebels & Gentlemen, pp. 166-168, 174.
DeForest, E. Walloon Family. Vol. 1: 205-208.
Flexner, J. T. Amer. Painting, pp. 91-93.
Groce, G., & Wallace, D. Dictionary, Artists.
Keyes, H. E. Coincidence & Henrietta Johnston Antiques. Vol. 16:
    490-494, 1929.
Morgan, J. H. Early Amer. Painters, pp. 8-9, 12, 21.
Prime, A. C. Arts and Crafts. Ser. 1, Vol. 8: 38; Ser. 2: 153, 318.
Rutledge, A. W. Artists, Life, Charleston Amer. Philosophical Soc.
    Transc. New Series, Vol. 39, pt. 2: 122-123, 157, 178.
Rutledge, A. W. Charleston's First Artistic Couple Antiques. Vol.
    52: 101-102.
Spruill, J. C. Women's Life, p. 259.
Wallace, D. D. Hist., S. C. Vol. 1: 409.
Willis, E. First Woman Painter America, Internatl. Studio, 1927,
    July, pp. 13-20, 84.
Willis, E. Henrietta Johnston Antiq. Vol. 11: 46-48.
Wright, L. B. Cultural Life Amer. Colonies, pp. 210, 213.

C.   Colonial Women in the Entertainment Field, Music, and Drama

Women had entered all the fields of entertainment from the earliest colonial days. They owned wax works, they danced the "Corant and Figg upon a Roap," they became famous actresses and musicians of note.

a.   Women in Early Entertainment

Ye Olden Blue Laws in New England and, for a short time in the Southern colonies, forbade or restricted most forms of entertainment. However, Mrs. Briggs' exhibit of wax works gradually gave place to performing groups in the taverns and public squares and, later, to theatrical productions.

Bartlett, H. R. 18th Cent. Ga. Women, pp. 94-99.
Dexter, E. A. Colonial Women, pp. 155-156.
Dow, G. F. Arts and Crafts, p. 287.
Earle, A. M. Home Life, p. 146.
Earle, A. M. Stage Coach and Tavern Days, pp. 200-203.
Fisher. Men, Women, Manners. Vol. 1: 91.
Holliday, C. Woman's Life, p. 113.
Myers, G. Ye Olden Blue Laws, pp. 47-64, 126-164, 201-244.
Oliver, F. Diary W. Pychon, pp. 142, 146.
Spruill, J. C. Women's Life, pp. 95, 110.
Stanard, M. M. Colonial Va., pp. 230-235.
Wharton, A. H. Through Colonial Doorways, pp. 65-96, 197-229.

b. Women in the Early Theatre

The names of actresses appear in the records of the first theatrical performances in the colonies. Mrs. Hallam accompanied her husband and his company to Virginia in 1752 and played the leading lady in many plays. Miss Cheer was the popular leading lady of the Douglas Company. Other women of talent soon became known in the cities where the theatres flourished.

Andrews, C. M. Colonial Folkways, pp. 110-129.
Bartlett, H. R. 18th Cent. Ga. Women, pp. 91-93.
Bentley, W. Diary. Vol. 1: 379, 381, 384; Vol. 2, see index theatre.
Bernard, J. Retrospections of Amer., p. 11.
Bridenbaugh, C. Cities, Wilderness, pp. 279, 437.
Dexter, E. A. Colonial Women, pp. 157-165.
Dexter, E. A. Career Women, pp. 78-83.
Dunlap, W. Hist. Amer. Theatre. Vol. 1: 1-8, 17, 407-410.
Fitzpatrick, J. C. Diaries, George Washington, Vols. 1, 2, 3, 4, see index theatre.
Graydon, A. Memoirs, pp. 202-207, 248, 278-279, 338.
Hornblow, A. H. Hist., Theatre, Amer., pp. 58-61, 69-113, 114-118, 120-169, 197-290.
Ireland, J. N. Records, N.Y. Stage, See index.
McCrady, E. S.C. Royal Govt., pp. 526-529.
Odell, G. C. Annals, N.Y. Stage. Vol. 1: 32 ff.
Parsons, J. C. Diary, J. Hiltzheimer, pp. 201-202, 204-206.
Richardson, H. D. Sidelights, Md. Hist. Vol. 1: pp. 144-146.
Scharf, J. T., & Westcott, T. Hist. Phila. Vol. 2: 965-967.
Seilhamer, G. O. Hist. Amer. Theatre. Vol. 1: 11 ff.
Sonneck, O. G. Concert Life, pp. 16, 72, 168, 170, 173, 179, 215.
Stanard, M. M. Colonial Va., pp. 229-251.

Wm. & M. Quart. Sarah Hallam. Ser. 1, Vol. 12: 236-237.
Willis, E. The Charleston Stage, see index.
Wright, R. Forgotten Ladies, pp. 34-60.

c. Women in the Field of Music

Women have taken part in musical performances from the very
early colonial days when Ann Hutchinson persuaded Reverend John
Cotton to let women join in the church singing. While no outstanding
woman musician appeared, a number of women with pleasant voices
became very popular as concert performers.

Bartlett, H. R. 18th Cent. Ga. Women, pp. 90-91.
Bentley, W. Diary. Vols. 1, 2 see index singing, singing
  schools.
Bliss, W. R. Sidelights Meetinghouse, pp. 221-233.
Bridenbaugh, C. Cities, Wilderness, pp. 133, 290, 294-295,
  446-464.
Covey, C. Puritanism & Music, W. M. Quart., Ser. 3, Vol. 8:
  378-388.
Dexter, E. A. Career Women, p. 71.
Drinker, S. Music & Women, p. 268.
Ellis, F., & Evans, S. Hist., Lancaster Co., Pa., p. 480.
Fitzpatrick, J. Diaries, George Washington. Vol. 4: 253.
Henry, J. Moravian Life, pp. 125, 129.
Gottesman, R. S. Arts and Crafts, 1777-1799, pp. 368, 378, 397.
Kuhns, O. German Swiss Settlements, p. 171.
McCrady, E. S.C. Royal Govt., pp. 491-492, 526, 528-529.
Maurer, M. Moravians, No. Car., W. M. Quart. Ser. 3, Vol. 8:
  214-227.
Miller, E. K. An Ephrata Hymnal, Antiq. Vols. 51-52: 260-262.
Rush, B. Essays, p. 64.
Sachse, J. F. Music, Ephrata Cloister.
Singleton, E. Social Life, N .Y., pp. 259-326, 365.
Sonneck, O. G. Early Concert Life, pp. 11-328.
Sonneck, O. G. Early Concerts, New Music Rev. Vol. 5: 952-
  957.
Stanard, M. M. Colonial Va., pp. 308-313.
Wharton, A. H. Through Colonial Doorways, pp. 23-64.

X

THE CHARITABLE ACTIVITIES OF COLONIAL WOMEN
IN THE COMMUNITIES

Colonial women contributed to the support of the churches and schools of
re colonies. They also initiated, endowed, and supervised orphanages and

109

charity schools. They organized philanthropic societies through which to make their charitable work more effective.

Barnard, E. K. Dorothy Payne, Quakeress.
Bartlett, H. R. 18th Cent. Ga. Women, pp. 103-104.
Baudier, R. Catholic Church La., pp. 122-142.
Biddle, G. B., & Lowrie, S. D. Notable Women, Pa., pp. 4-5, 31.
Bolton, S. K. Successful Women, pp. 110-126.
Clement, J. Noble Deeds Amer. Women, pp. 213-217.
Crowell, R. Hist. Essex, Mass., pp. 107-111.
Dexter, E. A. Colonial Women, pp. 59, 84, 106.
Earle, A. M. Colonial Dames; pp. 75, 258, 275.
Felt, J. B. Annals, Salem, p. 176.
Green, H. C. & M. W. Pioneer Mothers. Vol. 1: 206.
Holliday, C. Women's Life, pp. 111-112, 174-226, 301.
Innes, J. H. New Amsterdam, pp. 78-79.
Lippincott, H. M. Early Phila., p. 326.
McCrady, E. S.C. Royal Govt., pp. 486-490.
Melish, J. Travels. Vol. 1: 121.
Nelson, W. Arch., N.J. Ser. 1, Vol. 26: 524-525; Vol. 27: 288, 606.
Nourse, H. S. Records, Lancaster Co., Mass., p. 138.
Roelker, W. G. Benjamin Franklin, see index.
Scharf, J. T., & Wescott, T. Hist., Phila. Vol. 2: 1469.
Sharp, T. Heavenly Sisters, pp. 117-158.
Shea, J. G. Hist. Catholic Church. Vol. 1: 568-582.
Starbuck, A. Hist., Nantucket, p. 533.
Tyler, L. G. Narratives, Va., p. 339.
Van Rensselaer, (Mrs.) J. K. Mana-ha-ta, pp. 29-32, 161-162, 198, 199, 264, 353-355, 382-3.
Waters, T. F. Ipswich. Vol. 2: 298-300, 393-402.
Watertown. Watertown Records. Vol. 2: see index.
Wharton, A. H. Colonial Days, pp. 15, 76-77.
Wm. & Mary Quart. "Ladies of the Assoc." Vol. 8: 36.
Woody, T. Hist. Educ. Women. Vol. 1: 202.

104 Outstanding Colonial Women

The following listing contains the names of 104 colonial women who contributed to the solution of the problems of their day. Each woman's name is followed by the name of the colony in which she was born, her most significant contribution, dates of her birth and death (when known), names of her husband (or husbands), and specific page references to numbered items in the bibliography which follows.

At the time of colonization, the industrial revolution had barely started. In England, and in Europe generally, agriculture, industry, and trade were family affairs. In the America of the pioneer days, conditions favored the continuance of such a system. Both law and custom made provision for married women to act as their husbands' partners and for widows (or spinsters) to conduct their own affairs.

An effort has been made here to give examples of women of different nationalities, religions, and callings, to show the wide range of their activities and influence in the building of America.

S.H.D.

Adams, Abigail Smith
Massachusetts.   Helpmate.   1744-1818
m. John Adams, President of the United States

6.	328.pp.154-159	479.
65. pp.83,193	339. II,p.550	569.
97.	341. III,p.306 (port)	619. pp.107-115
108. pp.1-32	362. p.84	621. pp.191,229,230
128. pp.169-214	364. pp.40-87	741.
263. II,pp.31-37 (port.)	399.	743. pp.20-38
317. II,pp.19,29,168	438. pp.214-217	744. see index
317.III,pp.32-59,62,149,		749. (port.)
150,331,335,(port)		

Adams, Hannah
Massachusetts.   Historian, essayist.   1755-1831

8.	14.	328. (port.) p.159-160
9.	15.	399.
10.	16.	438. pp.793-794
11.	22.	744. pp.54,55,57,97
12.	71. p.171	749.
13. IV,p.110 (port.)	240. p.269	1020. (port.)

Alexander, Mary (Polly) Spratt Provoost
New York,   Entrepreneur.   1694-1760
m. Samuel Provoost.   m. James Alexander

215. pp.105,106	317. I,p.193	702. see Index
238. p.162	488. p.129	

Austin, Ann
Massachusetts.   Quaker missionary   -1665

17. p.264	266. p.434	643. p.249
112. pp.108-112	405. p.4,26-29,65,266,	760. p.129
215. p.146	358	

Browne, Charlotte (Mrs.)
English Army.   Medical Corps, Nurse.   c.1754

Carter, Frances Ann Tasker
Virginia.   Agronomist.   1737-1797
m. Councillor Robert Carter

Claypole, Elizabeth Griscom Ross Ashburn
Pennsylvania.   Flag-maker.   1752-1836
m. John Ross   m. Joseph Ashburn   m. John Claypole

Coming, Affra Harleston
South Carolina.   Agronomist.   d.1699
m. John Coming

Corbin, Margaret Cochran
Pennsylvania.   Revolutionary heroine.   1751-1800
m. John Corbin

Crosse, Mary Fisher Bayley
Massachusetts.   Quaker missionary.   1624-1690
m. William Bayley, 1662   m. John Crosse, 1678

Dare, Eleanor White.
Virginia.   First English pioneer.   d. c. 1587
m. Ananias Dare

Darragh, Lydia Barrington.
Pennsylvania.   Revolutionary heroine.   1728-1789
m. William Darragh
80. p.38   263. I,pp.199-206   720. II,p327,385
169. p.88   343. I,p.48   720. III,p.265
215. pp.73-76   438. pp.154-156   749.
                                  600. I,p.368   826.

Davenport, Elizabeth Wooley.
Connecticut.   Agent for Governor Winthrop.   d. after 1660
m. Rev. John Davenport.
150. pp.4,131,158   215. pp.111,112   1043.
                                  237. pp.52-55

Digges, Elizabeth
Virginia.   Agronomist.   d. 1699
m. Edward Digges, Governor of Virginia, or Col. William Digges
134. II,see Index   643. pp.21,25,305   974.
215. p.109   673. p.290   1058.

Doughty, Ann Graves Cotton Eaton
Virginia.   Historian.   c. 1625
m. William Cotton.   m. Nathaniel Eaton.   m. Francis Doughty
237. p.24   643. p.234   880.
289. see Index   874. pp.290-299

Douglass, Sarah Hallam.
Charleston and New York.   Actress.   d. 1773
m. Lewis Hallam   m. David Douglass
121. pp.140 ff.   640. see Index   1079. I,p.73
215. pp.158-160 (port.)   643. see Index
609. I,pp.11 ff   749. under Douglass

Drinker, Elizabeth Sandwith
Pennsylvania.   Quaker diarist.   1743-1807
m. Henry Drinker.
79.   121. see Index   730. see Index
80. p. 58   227.   836.

Drummond, Sarah Prescott
Virginia.   Political speaker.   c. 1670
m. William Drummond
39. p.162   749.   838.
643. pp.233,235,236   1056.

Dyer, Mary
Massachusetts   Quaker missionary.   d. 1660
m. William Dyer
17. p.268   237. p.118   399.
22.   266. p.434   405. pp.53,79

26. I,pp.221-242   317. p.237   754. I,pp.313-316
112. p.25   328. p.292   760. p.130
                                339. I,p.479-481

Easty, Mary
Massachusetts.   Witch.   d. 1692
281. IX,pp.176-179,181-183   621. p.73   1075. p.128

Estaugh, Elizabeth Haddon.
New Jersey.   Pioneer.   1680-1762
m. John Estaugh
76. pp.296-312   237. p.49   549. p.646
215. p.100   399.   749.
                                405. p.388   811.

Fages, Dona Eulelia de Callis y
California.   Pioneer.   c. 1783
m. Governor Pedro Fages
54. I,pp.387-393   161. pp.398-400   358. I,p.529-530

Farquher, Jane Colden
New York.   Botanist.   1724-1766
m. William Farquher
215. p.118   238. pp.164-166   702. pp.258-259
237. p.86   350. p.143

Fergusson, Elizabeth Graeme
Pennsylvania.   Poet.   1739-1801
m. Hugh Henry Fergusson
80. p.46   399.   720. II,p.108
121. see Index (port.)   438. p.179-181   730. p.13
263. I,pp.219-232 (port.)   720. I,p.376   744.
343. VIII,p.177   860. (port.)

Franklin, Ann Smith
Rhode Island.   Printer.   1696-1763
m. James Franklin
125. pp.71-79   159. pp.337-344.   215. p.168.
                                                          459. p.84.

Franks, Abigail Levy
Pennsylvania.   Pioneer Jewess.   1696-1756
m. Jacob Franks, 1719
430. p.111   438. p.631.   455. I,pp.58-72
                                                          537. p.200

Gannett, Deborah Sampson
Massachusetts.   Revolutionary heroine.   c. 1776
m. Robert Gannett
195. p.70   328. p.497   708.

263. II,pp.143-158 (port)   341. p.306   744. pp.1,14-16
317. II.pp.207,265-279   438. pp.143-149   763. (port. front)
                              453.

Goddard, Mary Katherine
Maryland.   Editor and publisher.   c. 1775
125. pp.71-79   237. p.57   759. pp.262-263
215. pp. 171-173   643. p.266   764. pp.119-146

Goddard, Sarah
Maryland.   Editor and publisher.   c.1776
125. pp.71-79   237. p.57   694. pp.153-155

Grant, Anne MacVicar
New York.   Writer.   1755-1838
m. Rev. Grant of Laggan
215. pp.115, 116   313.   749 (port.)
241. p.439   328. p.332

Hart, Nancy Morgan
Georgia.   Revolutionary heroine.   c.1776
m. Capt. Benjamin Hart
59. pp.79-88   744. pp.26,27   821.
263. II,pp.263-269   749.

Heck, Barbara Ruckle
New York.   Methodist co-foundress.   1734-1804
m. Paul Heck
215. pp.149-150   438. pp.509-510   650. pp.175-212
399.   643. p.248

Henry, Anne Wood
Pennsylvania.   County treasurer.   1732-1799
m. William Henry
80. p.41   408. pp.19,20-24,28,
                                  52,53

Hillhouse, Sarah Potter
Georgia.   Editor and publisher.   18th century
m. David Hillhouse
59. pp.68-69   355. pp.144-146,468-470   737. pp.687,688
214. pp.102,104   477   759. I,pp.249,262,263
                              419. I,pp.1047,1058

Hinestrosa, Francisca
Florida.   First European pioneer.   d.1534
m. Fernando Baustista
88. p.29   623. p.398   695. pp.83,226
576. II,pp.149,368   632. I,p.105   706. p.403
                              632. II,pp.133-134

Hume, Sophia Wigington
South Carolina.   Quaker preacher.   1702-1774
m. Robert Hume

643. p.252	981.	1045.
712. I,p.411	1002.	

Hutchinson, Anne Marbury
Massachusetts.   Religious leader.   1591-1643
m. William Hutchinson

2. pp.307-340	265.	589.
7. I,pp.371-532	327.	749.
49.	339. I,p.382	759. I,p.163
64. p.48	362. p.41	750. p.125
123. I,pp.220-225	379. pp.18-29	917.
128. pp.1-29	399.	929.
196. p.210	405. pp.4-25	830.
201.	438. pp.37-43	1077
215. pp.60,142-146	482. pp.134-140,147-154	17. p.165

Johnston, Henrietta
South Carolina.   Artist.   d.1729
m. Rev. Gideon Johnston

18. p.146	484. pp.8,9	977.
286. p.91	712. I,p.409	978.
399.	760. p.291	1064
	905. (ports.)	

Knight, Sarah Kemble
Massachusetts.   Writer and educator.   1666-1727
m. Richard Knight.

8. p.78	317. I,pp.442-455	728. pp.36,37,40
28. pp.75-102	339. II,p.224	749.
215. pp.3-6,83,84,133-135	399.	750.
237. pp.135-159	621. pp.76-78	987.
	681. pt.II,pp.327-346	

La Tour, Frances Mary Jacqueline
Maine.   Landowner and negotiator.   d.1645
m. Sieur Charles St. Etienne de la Tour

16. pp.34-36	237. pp.130-134	317. I,pp.311-328
28. pp.31-58	243. pp.296-308	531. pp.157-159

Logan, Deborah Norris
Pennsylvania.   Social and intellectual leader.   1761-1839
m. Dr. George Logan

17. p.75	399.	999.
10. p.80	494.	1012.
28. pp.245-284	720. III,pp.231,447	1068
	756. pp.279-328	720. I,see Index

117

Logan, Martha Daniell
South Carolina. Horticulturist. 1702-1779
m. Capt. George Logan
122. p.12   328. p.393   560. pp.124,125
237. p.86   543.   964.

Ludwell, Lady Frances Culpeper Stephèns Berkeley
Virginia. Helpmate. 17th century
m. Samuel Stephens, Governor of Carolina. m. Sir William Berkeley, Governor
of Virginia. m. Philip Ludwell, Governor of North Carolina.
445. p.270   645. p.204   772.
643. pp.160,235   669. p.474   1076 (port) III,841

McCauley, Mary Ludwig Hays (Moll Pitcher)
Pennsylvania. Revolutionary heroine. 1754-1832
m. John Caspar Hays m. George McCauley.
80. pp.72,73   379. pp.47-54   744. pp.16,17
87. 251   438. pp.162-165,176   1077. p.68
                              601. p.333

Manigault, Judith Giton Royer
South Carolina. Pioneer and agronomist. d.1711
m. Noe Royer. m. Pierre Manigault, 1698
52. II,112-114,182,183,396,397   553. I, pp.5-8   712. I,p.151
357. p.174,229-231   643. p.13   760. p.286
                                                          889.

Masters, Sybilla
Pennsylvania. Inventor. c.1712
m. Thomas Masters.
241. p.260   935. pp.279,285,377   Copy of Patent,
                                                          Franklin Institute,
                                                          Philadelphia, Penna.

Mendoza, Dona Ana de Zaldivar y
New Mexico. Pioneer. 16th century
m. Juan Guerra
335. II, p.89   Villagra, Gaspar Perez   History of New
                              de. trans. Gilberto   Mexico
                              Espinosa. pp. 97-98   Los Angeles, The
                                                          Quivira Society,1933

Montour, Madame Catherine
Pennsylvania. Negotiator. c.1684-1752
m. Roland Montour, Seneca Chief
80. pp.16,17   749.   856.

119

335. II,pp.69,70   Villagra, Gaspar Perez   History of New
                                de. trans. Gilberto   Mexico.
                                Espinosa.pp.91,224   Los Angeles, The
                                                             Quivira Society,1933

Penn, Hannah Callowhill
Pennsylvania. Colonial administratrix. 1671-1726
m. William Penn, Founder of Pennsylvania
228.   396. see Index   720. I, see Index
317. I,p.365   523. see Index   795. pp.76-82
377. pp.57,59,60,105   540. see Index   867.
862.

Phillipse, Margaret Hardenbroek de Vries
New York, Shipowner and merchant. d.1690.
m. Capt. Peter de Vries   m. Frederick Phillipse, 1662
64. p.30   238. pp.156-158   702. see Index
215. pp.107,108   317. I,pp.186-187   703. II,pp.217,226,228
237. p.73   197,222   705. p.411
                                392. see Index   728. p.77

Pinckney, Eliza Lucas
South Carolina   Agronomist. 1723-1793
m. Charles Pinckney, Chief Justice of South Carolina
18. p.213   237. pp.76-84   561.
64. pp.28,67   339. II,p.99   643. see Index
65. pp.33 ff,86 ff   361.   712. I,pp.384-385
128. pp.103-132   362. pp.80,295   744. p.21
215. pp.119-125   438. pp.106-112   760. p.287
                                553. II,pp.209-212,220   985.

Poole, Elizabeth
Massachusetts.   Founder of Taunton. 1599-1654
215. p.103   237. p.51   485. p.26

Provoost, Maria de Peyster Schrick Spratt
New York. Merchant. d. 1700
m. Paulus Schrick. m. John Spratt m. David Provoost
215. pp.104,105   399.   702. see Index

Ramsay, Martha Laurens
South Carolina.   Horticulturist. 1759-1811
m. Dr. David Ramsay
237. p.85   560. p.390   711. see Index
553. II, p.221   643. pp.47,48,55,230-   749.
554.   231   897.

Reed, Esther de Berdt
Pennsylvania. War relief worker. 1746-1780
m. Joseph Reed, President of the Executive Council of Pennsylvania

71. p.252   339. II,p.467   744. p.18
169. p.80   438. pp.105-106   749.
263. I,pp.47-71 (port.) 562.   1081. II,p.106
                         563. II,pp.253-279

Riedesel, Baroness Frederica de
New York. Helpmate. 1746-
m. Col. Baron de Riedesel, British Army
196. p. 130   601. pp. 282-284   916.
263. I, pp.142-166 (port.) 605. pp. 36-40   949.
328. p. 488   657.   996. (port.)
                         749.

Roberts, Mary
South Carolina. Artist. d.1761
m. Bishop Roberts
546. pp.8,38   761. p.213   978.
643. p.259   977.

Rosehill, Lady Margaret Cheer
Pennsylvania. Actress. 18th century
m. Lord Rosehill, 1768
121. pp.140-142,157,182 314. see Index   609. I,pp.11 ff
215. p.160   370. I. see Index   643. p.261
231. I. see Index   510. I, p.32

Rowlandson, Mary White
Massachusetts. Writer. c.1675
m. Rev. Joseph Rowlandson
148. pp.190-198   399.   585.
215. pp.131-133   486. pp.123,138,188-   622. I,p.142
237. pp.23,24   191,194   681. I, pp. 193-204
                         524.   749.

Rowson, Susanna
Massachusetts. Playwright and teacher. c.1762-1824
131. p.9 ff   399.   752. III,p.643
214. see Index   519. p.349   744. p.122
223. p.86   584. pp.75-87   762. see Index
231. I,p.407,410   723. pp.30,31   999.
370. I,pp.209-212   749.   1042.

Schuyler, Catherine Van Rensselaer
New York. Revolutionary heroine. 1733-1804
m. Major-General Philip Schuyler
263. I,pp.71-77 (port.) 380.   749.
317. II,pp.85-94 (port.) 438. pp.115-117,200   756. pp.71-111

Schuyler, Margarita Schuyler
New York. Administratrix. 1701-1782
m. Col. Philip Schuyler
313. see Index   399.   670. pp.187,190-213

Springfield, Laodicea Langston
South Carolina. Revolutionary heroine. 1760-
m. Thomas Springfield
162. pp.135-138   263. I,pp.323-330   317. II,304-316

Standerin, Ann Lee
New York. Religious foundress. 1736-1784
m. Abraham Standerin (Stanley)
32.   316.   606.
33.   328. p.389   618.
71. p.273   399.   689. pp.140-165
215. pp.151-153   438. p.509   789.
269.   465.   1076. (port.)I,p.161

Starbuck, Mary Coffin
Nantucket. Community leader. 1645-1717
m. Nathaniel Starbuck
174. pp. 30, 56, 97   356. see Index (port.)   1071.
270. IV, see Index   448. see Index

Stockton, Annis Boudinot
New Jersey. Poet. 1736-1801
m. Richard Stockton
81. pp.21-33 (port.)   263. II,pp.13-34   670. pp.106-140 (port.)
105. I,pp.28-32,179   431. I,p.381   728. pp.113,116

Stone, Virlinda Cotton Burdett Boughton
Maryland. Journalist. c.1650
m. Thomas Burdett. m. Richard Boughton. m. William Stone.
Governor of Maryland
107. II,p.686   329. p.265   880.
237. pp.49,236   643. p.236

Stoothoff, Saartze Roelof Kierstede von Borsum
New York. Official interpreter. d.1693
m. Dr. Hans Kierstede, 1642 m. Cornelis von Borsum, m. Elbert Elbertson
                                                          Stoothoff, 1683

317. I,see Index   509. II,p.510   703. I,p.479
423. I,p.207   702. p.24   705. p.740

Threrwitz, Emily Geiger.
South Carolina. Revolutionary heroine. b.c.1760
m. Threrwitz
162. pp.135-138   317. II,pp.207, 256-263,   712. II,p.278
263. II,p.341   343   749.

122

438. pp.175-176   1081. II,p.695

Timothy, Ann Donovan
South Carolina. Pioneer journalist. 1727-1792
m. Peter Timothy
125. pp.71-79   347. p.44   674. II,pp.158-255
178. p.247   357. pp.241,243   983.
237. p.64   643. pp.263-265,278

Timothy, Elizabeth
South Carolina. Pioneer journalist. c.1757
m. Louis Timothy
125. pp.71-79   357. pp.241,243   983.
178. see Index   643. pp.263-265,278

Townley, Elizabeth Smith Lawrence Carteret
New Jersey. Helpmate. c.1711
m. William Lawrence.   m. Governor Philip Carteret, 1681.   m. Sir Richard Townley
354. p.79   583. II,pp.207,209   740. see Index
429. pp.29,136-145   739. pp.107-108   801.

Tranchepain, de Saint Augustine, Sister Marie
Louisiana. Religious foundress. d.1733.
62. pp.103-107,136-138   273. pp.9,17   620. I,pp.568-570,
92. pp.20-30   292. pp.242-252   581-582
142. pp.68-79   306. pp.29-32   749.
214. p.18   418. I,pp.686-696   759. I,pp.329-330

Turell, Jane Colman
Massachusetts. Poet. 1708-1735
m. Ebenezer Turell
127. pp.319-324   362. p.92   685.
215. pp.137,138   463. pp.21-25   752. II,pp.429-430

Van Rensselaer, Maria Van Cortlandt
New York. Colonial administrator. 1645-1689
m. Jeremias Van Rensselaer
701.   702. pp.88,95,96,117,145

Warren, Mercy Otis
Massachusetts. Historian and satirist. 1728-1815
m. James Warren
22.   324. pp.21-23   584. pp.78,111-114
40.   328. p.546   692. II,p.419
65. pp.56 ff,77   339. (port.)   709. pp.30-37
129.   362. pp.100,145   714.
148. pp.384-394   399.   715.
192. pp.323-337   438. pp.124-128,200   716.
263. I,pp.91-126 (port.)   463. pp.42-45   728. pp.111-112

744. pp.1,8,9,97   752. II,p.457   919.
749. (port.)   891. (port.)

Washington, Martha Dandridge Custis
Virginia. Helpmate. 1732-1802
m. Col. Daniel Parke Custis. m. George Washington, President of the United States

128. pp.133-168	379. pp. 55-71	744. pp. 6-18, 185
185. (port.)	399.	749. (port.)
212.	438. pp. 207-213	1042.
263. II,pp.9-30 (port.)	643. see Index	1074.
328. pp.549-550	729. (port.)	1077. p. 63
364. pp.1-39	743. pp. 3-19	

Washington, Mary Ball
Virginia. Helpmate. 1708-1789
m. Augustine Washington

263. I,pp.33-47 (port.)	440.	744. pp.3-6
317. I,pp.455-485	550.	749. (port.)
328. pp.547-549	643. pp.60-61,107,351	777.
399.	671.	794.
438. pp.205-206	684.	

Watteville, Benigna Zinzendorf de
Pennsylvania. Moravian educator. 1725-1789
m. John de Watteville, 1746
868.   see also references under Zinzendorf, Anna
                          Caritas Nitschmann

Wheatley, Phyllis
Massachusetts. Negress poet. 1755-1784

192. pp.314-322	324. pp.30-33	749.
215. pp.140-142 (port.)	346.	759. I,pp.92,124,132
312.	463. pp.39-41	1075. p.334 (port.)
320. pp.243-245	732.	

Whitmore, Mrs.
Vermont. Midwife. c.1760
m. Thomas Whitmore
215. p.61   676. pt.3,p.110   759. I,p.163

Wilkinson, Jemima
Rhode Island. Preacher 1752-1819.

10. pp.321-322	522. pp.65-66,145	694. pp.233-236
71. pp.270-272	578. I,pp.205-215	722. II,pp.808-809
237. pp.173-188	584. p.196	749.
376.	689. pp.115-121	980.
		1065.

Williams, Hannah English
South Carolina. Biologist. 1692-1722
m. Matthew English. m. William Williams

| 18. p.123 | 712. I,p.408 | 1061. |
| | | 759. I,p.249 |

Winthrop, Margaret Tyndal
Massachusetts. Helpmate. 1591-1647
m. Governor John Winthrop

243.	317. I,pp.283-299	344. p.5
		482. see Index.
		686.

Wright, Prudence Cummings
Massachusetts and New Hampshire. Revolutionary heroine. c.1775
m. David Wright

| 145. pp.336-337 | 263. II,295-296 | 756. pp.239-240 |

Wright, Susanna
Pennsylvania. Silk promoter and poet. 1697-1784

80. p.29	720. I,p.560	877.
343. p.177	720. II,pp.168,438	971.
437. fig.20	728. p.113	

Yardley, Lady Temperance Flowerdew Yardley West
Virginia. Helpmate. 1593-1636
m. Sir George Yardley, Governor of Virginia. m. Capt. Francis West, Governor
of Virginia, 1627. m. Ralph Yardley of London, 1629

38. pp.148,169,249,299	398. p.27	1003.
39. p.111	765. see Index	1030.
		1033.

Zenger, Anna Catherina Maul
New York. Printer and editor. c.1704-1751
m. John Peter Zenger

| 64. p.67 | 125. pp.71-79 | 215. pp.169-170 |
| 87. p.233 | 187. | 352. pp.31-33 |

Zinzendorf, Anna Caritas Nitschmann
Pennsylvania. Moravian educator. 1715-1760
m. Count Nicolaus Ludwig von Zinzendorf

| 300. (port.) | 349. pp.82,93,131,132,141 | 565. pp.85,91 |

Bibliography

Books

1. Abbot, Edith. Women in Industry: A Study in American Economic History.
    New York, Appleton & Co., 1910.
2. Abramowitz, I. ed. The First Great Prisoners. Anthology of Literature
    Written in Prison. New York, Dutton, 1946.
3. Acrelius, Israel. A History of New Sweden or the Settlements on the River
    Delaware. Stockholm, Harberg & Hassellberg, 1759.
4. Adams, Charles F. ed. Antinomianism in the Colony of Massachusetts
    Bay. Boston, The Prince Society, 1894.
5. Adams, Charles F. Familiar letters of John Adams and his wife, Abigail
    Adams, during the Revolution. New York, Hurd & Houghton Co.,
    1876.
6. Adams, Charles F. Letters of Mrs. Adams, wife of John Adams. Boston,
    Little, Brown & Co., 1840.
7. Adams, Charles F. Three Episodes of Massachusetts History. 2 vols.
    Boston, Houghton Mifflin, 1892.
8. Adams, Hannah. An Abridgement of the History of New England. Boston,
    author, 1805.
9. Adams, Hannah. An Alphabetical Compendium of the Various Sects which
    have appeared in the World from the beginning of the World to the
    present day. Boston, Edes & Son, 1784.
10. Adams, Hannah. Dictionary of all Religions and Religious Denominations.
    New York, Eastburn & Co., 1817.
11. Adams, Hannah. The History of the Jews from the Destruction of
    Jerusalem to the 19th century. Boston, J. Eliot, Jr., 1812.
12. Adams, Hannah. Letters on the Gospels. Cambridge, Hillyard & Metcalf
    Co., 1824.
13. Adams, Hannah. Memoir of Miss Hannah Adams, written by herself.
    Boston, Gray & Bowen, 1832.
14. Adams, Hannah. A Narrative of the Controversity between Rev. Jeddiah
    Moss, D.D., and the Author. Boston, J. Eliot, Jr., 1814.
15. Adams, Hannah. The Truth and Excellence of the Christian Religion,
    Exhibited in Two Parts. Boston, John West, 1804.
16. Adams, Hannah. A view of Religions in Two Parts. Boston, Manning &
    Loring, 1801.
17. Adams, James T. The Founding of New England. Boston, Atlantic
    Monthly Press, 1921.
18. Adams, James T. Provincial Society, 1690-1763. New York, Macmillan
    Co., 1927.
19. Adams, John. Sketches of the History, Genius, Disposition, Accomplish-
    ments, Employments, Customs, and Importance of the Fair Sex, by
    a Friend of the Sex. London, G. Kearsley, 1790.
20. Adams, Sherman W. & Stiles, Henry R. History of Ancient Wethersfield,
    Connecticut. 2 vols. New York, Grafton Press, 1904.
21. Allen, Myron O. History of Wenham (1630-1860) Boston, Bazin &
    Chandler, 1860.
22. Allen, William. American Biographical and Historical Dictionary. Boston,
    W. Hyde & Co., 1857.

. Ames, Azel.   The May-flower and Her Log.   Boston, Houghton Mifflin
    Co., 1901.
⬥. Ames, Susie M.   County Court Records of Accomak, Northampton,
    Virginia, 1632-1640. American Legal Records, No. 7. Washington,
    D.C., American Historical Association, 1954.
⬥. Ames, Susie M.   Studies of the Virginia Eastern Shore in the 17th century.
    Richmond, Va., Dietz Press, 1940.
⬥. Anderson, (Rev.) James.   Memorable Women of the Puritan Times. 2
    vols.   London, Blackie & Son, 1862.
⬥. Andrews, Charles M.   The Beginnings of Connecticut, 1632-1662.   New
    Haven, Conn., Yale University Press, 1934.
8. Andrews, Charles M.   The Colonial Background of the American Revolution.
    New Haven, Conn., Yale University Press, 1924.
9. Andrews, Charles M.   Colonial Folkways: A Chronicle of American Life
    in the Reign of the Georges.   New Haven, Conn., Yale University
    Press, 1919.
0. Andrews, Charles M.   The Colonial Period of American History. 4 vols.
    New Haven, Conn., Yale University Press, 1934-1937.
1. Andrews, Charles M.   Journal of a Lady of Quality, Janet Schaw.   New
    Haven, Conn., Yale University Press, 1921.
2. Andrews, Edward D.   The Gift to be Simple: Songs, Dances, and Rituals
    of the American Shakers.   New York, J. F. Augustin, 1940.
3. Andrews, Edward D.   The People Called Shakers.   New York, Oxford
    University Press, 1953.
4. Andrews, Garnett.   Reminiscences of an Old Georgia Lawyer.   Atlanta,
    Franklin Printing House, 1870.
5. Andrews, Henry F. ed.   List of Freemen, 163 -1691, Massachusetts Bay
    Colony.   Exira, Iowa, Exira Print. Co., 1906.
6. Andrews, Matthew P.   Founding of Maryland.   New York, Appleton-
    Century Co., 1933.
7. Andrews, Matthew P.   Tercentenary History of Maryland. 4 vols. Chicago,
    Clarke Publishing Co., 1925.
8. Andrews, Matthew P.   The Soul of a Nation.   New York, Charles
    Scribners, 1943.
9. Andrews, Matthew P.   Virginia, Old Dominion.   Garden City, Doubleday
    Doran Co., 1937.
0. Anthony, Katharine.   The First Lady of the Revolution, Mercy Warren.
    New York, Doubleday & Company, 1958.
1. Armes, Ethel, ed.   Nancy Shippen: Her Journal Book.   Philadelphia,
    Lippincott Co., 1935.
2. Armstrong, Zella.   Notable Southern Families. 2 vols. Chattanooga, Tenn.,
    Lookout Publishing Co., 1918-1926.
3. Arnold, James N.   The Records of the Proprietors of Narragansett:
    Otherwise Called the Fones Record, Rhode Island Colonial
    Gleanings, Vol. I.   Providence, Narragansett Historical Publishing
    Co., 1894.
4. Arthur, John P.   Western North Carolina: A History from 1730-1913.
    Raleigh, N.C., Daughters of the American Revolution, 1914.
5. Asbury, Francis.   Journal of Bishop Francis Asbury. 3 vols.   New York,
    Bangs & Mason, 1821.

46.   Ashe, Samuel A.   History of North Carolina. 2 vols.   Raleigh, N. C.,
Edwards & Broughton, 1925.
47.   Ashmead, Henry G.   Historical Sketch of Chester on the Delaware.
Chester, Pa., Historical Committee of Chester, 1883.
48.   Atwater, Edward E.   History of the City of New Haven, Connecticut.
Meriden, Conn., Journal Publishing Co., 1902.
49.   Augur, Helen.   An American Jezebel, Life of Anne Hutchinson.   New York,
Brentano Co., 1930.
50.   Baber, Ray E.   Marriage and the Family.   New York, McGraw Hill, 1953.
51.   Bagnall, William R.   The Textile Industry of the United States, 1639-1810.
Cambridge, Riverside Press, 1893.
52.   Baird, Charles W.   History of Huguenot Emigration to America. 2 vols.
New York, Dodd, Mead Co., 1885.
53.   Baker, John W.   History of Hart County, Georgia.   Atlanta, Ga., Foote
& Davies Co., 1933.
54.   Bancroft, Hubert H.   The Works of Hubert H. Bancroft. Vol.XVIII
(History of California, Vol.I)   Vol. XXXIV   San Francisco,
A. L. Bancroft & Co., 1884-1888.
55.   Bancroft, Hubert H.   History of Arizona and New Mexico.   San
Francisco, The History Company, 1889.
56.   Barber, John W., & Howe, Henry.   Historical Collections of New Jersey.
New Haven, Conn., J. Barber, 1868.
57.   Barnard, Ella Kent.   Dorothy Payne, Quakeress.   Philadelphia, Ferris
& Leach Co., 1909.
58.   Barnes, Earl.   Women in Modern Society.   New York, Huebsch Co., 1912.
59.   Bartlett, Helen R.   Eighteenth Century Georgia Women. Baltimore,
University of Maryland, 1939. Ph.D Thesis (Typed)
60.   Bassett, John S., ed.   Writings of Colonel William Byrd of Westover in
Virginia.   New York, Doubleday Page & Co., 1901.
61.   Bates, Samuel A., ed.   Braintree Town Records.   Braintree Mass.,
Randolph, 1886.
62.   Bandier, Roger.   The Catholic Church in Louisiana.   New Orleans, La.,
author, 1939.
63.   Bayer, Henry G.   The Belgians, First Settlers in New York and in the
Middle States.   New York, The Devin-Adair Co., 1925.
64.   Beard, Charles A. & Mary R.   A Basic History of the United States.
New York, Doubleday Doran, 1944.
65.   Beard, Mary R., ed.   America through Women's Eyes.   New York,
Macmillan, 1933.
66.   Beedy, Helen C.   Mothers of Maine.   Portland, Me., Thurston Printing
Co., 1895.
67.   Bemis, Albert F. & Burchard, John.   The Evolving House. 3 vols.
Cambridge, Mass. The Technology Press, 1933-1936.
68.   Bennett, John.   Letters to a Young Lady. 2 vols.   New York, Duyckinck
& Co., 1796.
69.   Bennett, John.   Strictures on Female Education.   London, T. Cadell Co.,
1788.
70.   Benson, Adolph B., & Hedin, Naboth.   Swedes in America, 1638-1938.
New Haven, Conn., Yale University Press, 1938.

71.   Benson, Mary S.   Women in the 18th Century America: A Study of
       Opinions and Social Usage.   New York, Columbia University
       Press, 1935.
72.   Bentley, William.   Diary of Rev. William Bentley, 1759-1819. 4 vols.
       Salem, Mass., The Essex Institute, 1905-1914.
73.   Bernard, John.   Retrospections of America, 1797-1811.   New York,
       Harpers & Bros., 1887.
74.   Bernheim, G. D.   History of the German Settlements and of the Lutheran
       Church in North Carolina.   Philadelphia, Lutheran Bookstore,
       1872.
75.   Berryman, John.   Homage to Mistress Bradstreet.   New York, Farrar,
       Strauss, & Cudahy, 1956.
76.   Best, Mary A.   Rebel Saints.   New York, Harcourt, Brace & Co., 1925.
77.   Beverly, Robert.   History and Present State of Virginia, in Four Parts.
       Richmond, Va., Randolph Co., 1855.
78.   Bibbins, Ruth M.   The Beginnings of Maryland in England and America.
       Baltimore, Remington Co., 1934.
79.   Biddle, Henry D.   Extracts of the Journal of Elizabeth Sandwith Drinker,
       1759-1807.   Philadelphia, Lippincott Co., 1889.
80.   Biddle, Gertrude B. & Lowrie, Sarah D. eds.   Notable Women of
       Pennsylvania.   Philadelphia, University of Pennsylvania Press, 1942.
81.   Bill, Alfred.   A House called Morven.   Princeton, N.J. Princeton
       University Press, 1954
82.   Bingham, Caleb.   American Preceptor.   Boston, author, 1833.
83.   Bingham, Caleb.   The Young Lady's Accidence.   Boston, author, 1794.
84.   Bining, Arthur C.   Pennsylvania Iron Manufacture in the 18th Century.
       Publication of the Pennsylvania Historical Commission. Vol. IV.
       Harrisburg, Pa., The Commission, 1938.
85.   Bishop, Cortlandt F.   History of Elections in the American Colonies.
       New York, Columbia College Press, 1893.
86.   Bishop, John L.   History of American Manufacturers, 1608-1860. 2 vols.
       Philadelphia, E. Young & Co., 1864.
87.   Bittinger, Lucy F.   The Germans in Colonial Times.   Philadelphia,
       Lippincott Co., 1901.
88.   Blackman, Lucy W.   The Women of Florida. (Not given) Southern His-
       torical Publication Association, 1940.
89.   Blake, Francis E.   Annals, Dorchester Neck, Massachusetts.   Boston,
       Clapp & Son, 1899.
90.   Blake, Francis E.   History of the Town of Princeton, Massachusetts.
       2 vols. Princeton, Mass., Princeton, 1915.
91.   Blake, Jonathan.   History of the Town of Warwick, Massachusetts.
       Boston, Noyes, Homes & Co., 1873.
92.   Blandin, Isabella M.   History of Higher Education of Women in the South
       Prior to 1860.   New York, Neale Publishing Co., 1909.
93.   Blanton, Wyndam.   Medicine in Virginia in the 17th Century.   Richmond,
       Va., Wm. Byrd Press, 1930.
94.   Bliss, William R.   The Old Colony Town.   Boston, Houghton Mifflin, 1893.
95.   Bliss, William R.   Side-lights from the Colonial Meeting-House.   Boston,
       Houghton Mifflin, 1894.
96.   Blumenthal, Walter H.   Women Camp Followers of the American Revolu-
       tion.   Philadelphia, George MacManus Co., 1952.

97.   Bobbe, Dorothie.   Life of Abigail Adams. 1744-1818. New York, Minton, Balch & Co., 1929.
98.   Bolton, Charles K.   Scotch-Irish Pioneers. Boston, Bacon & Brown, 1910.
99.   Bolton, Ethel S. & Coe, Eva J.   American Samplers. Boston, Massachusetts Colonial Dames, 1921.
100.   Bolton, Herbert E.   Anza's California Expedition. Vols. I & II. Berkeley, University of California Press, 1930.
101.   Bolton, Herbert E.   Rim of Christendom. New York, Macmillan, 1936.
102.   Bolton, Herbert E.   Spanish Exploration in the Southwest, 1542-1706. New York, Charles Scribners, 1916.
103.   Bolton, Sarah, K.   Successful Women. Boston, Lothrop Co. 1888.
104.   Boorstin, Daniel J.   The Americans: The Colonial Experience. New York, Random House, 1958.
105.   Boudinot, Jane J.   Life of Elias Boudinot. 2 vols. Boston, Houghton Mifflin, 1896.
106.   Bowne, Eliza S.   A Girl's Life Eighty Years Ago; Selections from the Letters of Eliza Southgate Bowne, 1783-1809. New York, Scribners' Sons, 1887.
107.   Bozman, John L.   The History of Maryland from its First Settlement in 1633 to the Restoration in 1660. 2 vols. Baltimore, J. Lucas & E. K. Dawes, 1837.
108.   Bradford, Gamaliel.   Portraits of American Women. Boston, Houghton Mifflin, 1919.
109.   Bradford, Gamaliel.   Wives. New York, Harper & Brothers, 1925.
110.   Bradford, William.   The History of Plymouth Plantation, 1606-1646. New York, Charles Scribners, 1908.
111.   Bradstreet, Anne.   Poems and Prose. New York, (not given) 1897.
112.   Brailsford, Mabel R.   Quaker Women, 1650-1690. London, Duckworth & Co., 1915.
113.   Branagan, Thomas.   Excellency of the Female Character Vindicated. Harrisburg, Pa., author, 1807.
114.   Brandon, Edward J., ed.   The Records of the Town of Cambridge, Massachusetts, 1630-1703. Cambridge, Wilson & Son, 1901.
115.   Brent, Chester H.   The Descendants of Colonel Giles Brent, Captain George Brent, and Robert Brent, Gent. Rutland, Vt., Tuttle Publishing Co., 1946.
116.   Brewer, John M.   List of early Maryland Settlers, 1634-1682. Typewritten, Rare Book Room, U.S. Library of Congress, Washington, D.C., 1901.
117.   Brickell, John.   Natural History of North Carolina. Dublin, author, 1737.
118.   Bridenbaugh, Carl.   Cities in the Wilderness: The First Century of Urban Life in America, 1625-1742. New York, Ronald Press, 1938.
119.   Bridenbaugh, Carl.   The Colonial Craftsman. New York, New York University Press, 1950.
120.   Bridenbaugh, Carl.   Gentleman's Progress: The Itinerarium of Alexander Hamilton, 1744. Chapel Hill, N. C., University of North Carolina Press, 1948.
121.   Bridenbaugh, Carl & Jessica.   Rebels and Gentlemen: Philadelphia in the Age of Franklin. New York, Reynal & Hitchcock, 1942.
122.   Briggs, Loutrel W.   Charleston Gardens. Columbia, S.C., University of South Carolina Press, 1951.

123. Briggs, L. Vernon. History and Genealogy of the Cabot Family, 1475-1927. 2 vols. Boston, author, 1927.

124. Briggs, Martin S. The Homes of the Pilgrim Fathers in England and America, 1620-1685. New York, Oxford University Press, 1932.

125. Brigham, Clarence S. Journals and Journeymen. Philadelphia, University of Pennsylvania Press, 1950.

126. Brigham, William. The Compact with the Charter and Laws of the Colony of New Plymouth. Boston, Dutton & Wentworth 1836.

127. Brooks, Charles. History of the Town of Medford, Massachusetts, 1630-1855. Boston, J. M. Usher, 1855.

128. Brooks, Geraldine. Dames and Daughters of Colonial Days. New York, Thomas Y. Crowell & Co., 1900.

129. Brown, Alice. Mercy Warren. New York, Charles Scribners, 1896.

130. Brown, Alice, et al. Three Heroines of New England Romance. Boston, Little, Brown & Co., 1894.

131. Brown, Herbert R. The Sentimental Novel in America, 1789-1860. Durham, N.C., Duke University Press, 1940.

132. Browne, William H. Maryland: History of a Palatinate. Boston, Houghton Mifflin, 1884.

133. Browne, William H., & Hall, Clayton, C. Archives of Maryland. Vols. I, IV, X, XII, XXXXI, Baltimore, Maryland Historical Society, 1883-1916.

134. Bruce, Philip A. Economic History of Virginia in the 17th Century. 2 vols. New York, Macmillan, & Co., 1895.

135. Bruce, Philip A. Institutional History of Virginia in the 17th Century. 2 vols. New York, Putnam's Sons, 1910.

136. Bruce, Philip A. Social Life of Virginia in the 17th Century. Richmond, Va., author, 1907.

137. Buck, Solon J., & Elizabeth H. Planting of Civilization in Western Pennsylvania. Pittsburgh, Pa., Pittsburgh University Press, 1939.

138. Buckley, James M. History of Methodism in the United States. Vol. I. New York, Christian Literature Co., 1896.

139. Bunce, Oliver B. The Romance of the Revolution. New York, Bunce & Brother, 1854.

140. Buoy, Charles W. Representative Women of Methodism. New York, Hunt & Eaton, 1893.

141. Burnaby, Andrew. Travels through the Middle Settlements in North America, 1759-1760. London, author, 1775.

142. Burns, James A. Catholic School System. New York, Benzinger Bros., 1908.

143. Burns, James A. & Kohlbrenner, B. J. History of Catholic Education in the United States. New York, Benzinger Bros., 1937.

144. Burton, John. Lectures on Female Education and Manners. New York, Samuel Campbell Co., 1794.

145. Butler, Caleb. History of the Town of Groton, Massachusetts. Boston, T. R. Marvin, 1848.

146. Butts, Sarah H. The Mothers of Distinguished Georgians. New York, Little & Co., 1902.

147. Cable, George W. Strange, True Stories of Louisiana. New York, Charles Scribners Sons, 1889.

148. Cairns, William B. Selections from Early American Writers, 1607-1800. New York, Macmillan Co., 1909.

149. Calder, Isabel M. Colonial Captivities, Marches, and Journeys. New York, Macmillan Co., 1935.

150. Calder, Isabel M. The New Haven Colony. New Haven, Conn., Yale University Press, 1934.

151. Calhoun, Arthur W. The Social History of the American Family. 3 vols. New York, Barnes and Noble, 1945.

152. Calvert, Calvert Papers. 1st Selection: Vol. XXVII. 2nd Selection. Vol. XXIV. 3rd Selection. Vol. XXV. Baltimore, Maryland Historical Society, 1889-1899.

153. Cambridge, Massachusetts. Records of the Town of Cambridge 1630-1703. Cambridge, Mass., The City Council, 1901.

154. Campbell, Helen. Anne Bradstreet and Her Time. Boston, Lothrop Co., 1891.

155. Carlisle, Robert. An Account of Bellevue Hospital. New York, Society of the Alumni of Bellevue Hospital, 1893.

156. Carman, Harry J. American Husbandry. 2 vols. New York, Columbia University Press, 1939.

157. Channing, Edward. History of the United States. 6 vols. New York, Macmillan Co., 1905-1925.

158. Chapin, Henry. Address. Unitarian Church, Uxbridge, Mass., 1864. Worcester, Mass. Charles Hamilton, 1881.

159. Chapin, Howard M. Ann Franklin of New Port; Printer. Cambridge, Mass., (not given) 1924.

160. Chapman, Charles E. Founding of Spanish California. New York, Macmillan Co., 1916.

161. Chapman, Charles E. History of California: Spanish Period. New York, Macmillan Co., 1921.

162. Chapman, John A. School History of South Carolina. Richmond, Va., Everett Wadding Co., 1894.

163. Chastellux, Marquis de. Travels in North America in the Years 1780-1782. Translated by George Grieve. New York, White, Gallaher & White. 1827.

164. Chavez, Fray Angelico. Origins of New Mexico Families. Santa Fe., N. M., Historical Society of New Mexico, 1954.

165. Child, Frank S. A Colonial Witch; A Study of the Black Art in Connecticut. New York, Baker & Taylor, 1897.

166. Clark, Alice. Working Life of Women in the 17th Century. London, George Routledge Ltd., 1919.

167. Clark, Victor S. History of Manufacturers in the United States. 3 vols. Washington, Carnegie Institution of Washington, 1916-1928.

168. Clay, John C., Annals of the Swedes on the Delaware. Chicago, John Ericson Memorial Committee, 1938.

169. Clement, Jesse, ed. Noble Deeds of American Women. Buffalo, N.Y., Derby & Co., 1851.

170. Clement, John. Sketches of the First Emigrant Settlers in Newton Township, Old Gloucester County, West New Jersey. Camden, N.J., S. Chew Co., 1877.

171. Clews, Elsie W. Educational Legislation and Administration of the Colonial Governments. New York, Columbia University Press, 1899.

172. Cobbledick, M. Robert. The Status of Women in Puritan New England,

1630-1660. New Haven, Conn., Yale University Press, 1936.
173. Codman, Martha Co., ed.   Journal of Katherine Greene Armory, 1775-
1777. Boston, editor, 1923.
174. Coffin, Allen.   The Coffin Family. Life of Tristam Coffyn, Nantucket,
Massachusetts. Nantucket, Mass., Hussey & Robinson, 1881.
175. Coffin, Charles C.   Old Times in the Colonies. New York, Harper Bros.,
1908.
176. Cogswell, Elliott C.   History of Nottingham, Deerfield, and Northwood,
New Hampshire. Manchester, N.H., (not given) 1878.
177. Cogswell, Leander W.   History of the Town of Henniker, New Hampshire.
Concord, N. H., Republican Press, 1880.
178. Cohen, Hennig.   South Carolina Gazette. Columbia, S.C., University of
South Carolina Press, 1953.
179. Coles, George.   Heroines of Methodism. New York, Carlton & Porter,
1857.
180. Colton, Julia M.   Annals of Old Manhattan, 1609-1664. New York,
Brentano Co., 1901.
181. Coman, Katherine.   Industrial History of the United States. New York,
Macmillan, 1905.
182. Comfort, William W.   The Quakers in Pennsylvania. Gettysburg, Pa.,
Pennsylvania Historical Association, 1948.
183. Commons, John R. et al.   A Documentary History of American Industrial
Society. 10 vols. Cleveland, O., Arthur Clark Co., 1910-1911.
184. Commons, John R.   History of Labor in the United States. 2 vols. New
York, Macmillan Co., 1936
185. Conkling, Margaret C.   Memoirs of the Mother and Wife of Washington.
Auburn, N.Y., Derby, Miller & Co., 1850.
186. Conway, Moncure D.   Life of Thomas Paine. 2 vols. New York, Putnams
Sons, 1892.
187. Cooper, Kent.   Anna Zenger. New York, Farrar, Strauss & Co., 1946.
188. Corey, Deloraine. P.   History of Malden, Massachusetts. Malden, Mass.,
author, 1899.
189. Coulter, Ellis M.   Short History of Georgia.   Chapel Hill, N.C., University of North Carolina Press, 1933.
190. Crawford, Mary C.   Famous Families of Boston, Massachusetts. 2 vols.
Boston, Little Brown & Co., 1930.
191. Crawford, Mary C.   Little Journeys in Old New England. Boston, Page &
Co., 1906.
192. Crawford, Mary C.   Old Boston Days and Ways. Boston, Little, Brown &
Co., 1924.
193. Crawford, Mary C.   Little Pilgrimages among Old New England Inns.
Boston, Page & Co., 1907.
194. Crawford, Mary C.   Romantic Days in the Early Republic . Boston, Little,
Brown & Co., 1912.
195. Crawford, Mary C.   The Romance of Old New England Churches. Boston,
Page & Co., 1904.
196. Crawford, Mary C.   The Romance of Old New England Rooftrees. Boston,
Page & Co., 1903.
197. Crawford, Mary C.   Social Life in old New England. Boston, Little,
Brown & Co., 1914.

198.   Cresson, Caleb.   The Diary of Caleb Cresson, Quaker. Philadelphia,
        author, 1877.
199.   Crevecoeur, J. Hector de.   Letters from an American Farmer. London,
        author, 1782.
200.   Crowell, Robert.   History of the Town of Essex, 1634-1700. Boston,
        C. C. P. Moody, 1853.
201.   Curtis, Edith.   Anne Hutchinson. Cambridge, Mass., Washburn & Thomas,
        1930.
202.   Cutbush, Edward.   Observations on the Means of Preserving the Health of
        the Soldiers and Sailors and on the Duties of the Medical Depart-
        ment of the Army and Navy.   Philadelphia, Thomas Dobson, 1808.
203.   Dalcho, Frederick. Historical Account of the Protestant Church of South
        Carolina. Charleston, S.C., E. Thayer Co., 1820.
204.   Dall, Caroline H.   College, Market and Court: or Woman's Relations to
        Education, Labor, and Law. Boston, Lee & Shepard Co., 1867.
205.   Darwin, Erasmus.   A Plan for the Conduct of Female Education in Board-
        ing Schools, Private Families, and Public Seminaries. Philadelphia,
        Ormond Co., 1798.
206.   Davidson, Elizabeth H.   The Establishment of the English Church in Con-
        tinental American Colonies. Historical Papers of Trinity College
        Historical Society, series XX. Durham, N.C., Duke University Press,
        1938.
207.   Davis, John   Personal adventures and travels of four years and a half in
        the United States of America. London, author, 1817.
208.   Davis, Walter A., ed.   The Old Records of the Town of Fitchburg. 6 vols.
        Fitchburg, Mass., Sentinel Printing Co., 1898.
209.   De Brahm, John G.W.   History of the Three Provinces: South Carolina,
        Georgia, and East Florida. Cambridge, Mass., Wormsloe, Co.,
        1849.
210.   De Forest, Emily J.   A Walloon Family in America. 2 vols. Boston,
        Houghton Mifflin, 1914.
211.   Desmond, Alice C.   Alexander Hamilton's Wife.   New York, Dodd, Mead
        & Co., 1954.
212.   Desmond, Alice C.   Martha Washington.   New York, Dodd, Mead & Ço.,
        1944.
213.   De Windt, Caroline A., ed.   Correspondence of Miss Adams, daughter of
        John Adams. 2 vols. New York, Wiley & Putnam, 1841-2.
214.   Dexter, Elizabeth A.   Career Women of America, 1776-1840. Francestown,
        N.H., Marshall Jones Co., 1950.
215.   Dexter, Elizabeth A.   Colonial Women of Affairs. Boston, Houghton Mifflin
        Co., 1924.
216.   Dexter, Edwin G.   A History of Education. New York, Macmillan Co., 1919.
217.   Dilworth, Thomas.   Schoolmaster's Assistant. A Compendium Arithmetic
        in Five Parts. Philadelphia, R. Aitken Co., 1781.
218.   Doggett, Carita.   Dr. Andrew Turnbull and the New Smyrna Colony. --
        Florida, Drew Press, 1919.
219.   Dow, George F. ¯ The Arts and Crafts in New England, 1704-1775. Topsfield,
        Mass., Wayside Press, 1927.
220.   Dow, George F.   Everyday Life in the Massachusetts Bay Colony. Boston,
        Society for Preserving New England Antiquities, 1935.

21. Dow, George F., ed.   The Holyoke Diaries, 1709-1856. Salem, Mass., Essex Institute, 1911.
22. Dow, George F.   Records of the Salem Commons, 1713-1739. Salem, Mass., Essex Institute, 1903.
23. Drake, Francis S.   Town of Roxbury. Roxbury, Mass., author, 1878.
24. Drake, Samuel G.   Annals of Witchcraft in New England. Boston, Elliot Woodward Co., 1869.
25. Drake, Samuel G., ed.   More Wonders of the Invisible World. Roxbury, Mass., W. E. Woodward, 1866.
26. Drake, Samuel A. & Watkins, K. W.   Old Boston Taverns and Tavern Clubs. Boston, W. A. Butterfield, 1917.
27. Drinker, Cecil K.   Not So Long Ago: A Chronicle of Medicine and Doctors in Colonial Philadelphia. New York, Oxford University Press, 1937.
28. Drinker, Sophie H.   Hannah Penn and the Proprietorship of Pennsylvania. Philadelphia, National Society of Colonial Dames of America in Penna., 1958.
29. Drinker, Sophie H.   Music and Women. New York, Coward-McCann Inc., 1948.
30. Duane, William ed.   Passages from the Diary of Christopher Marshall. Philadelphia, Hazard & Mitchell, 1849.
31. Dunlap, William.   History of the American Theatre. 2 vols. New York, Harpers, 1832.
32. Dunton, John.   Life & Errors. London, S. Malthus, 1705.
33. Duxbury, Mass.   Copy of the Old Records, 1642-1770. Plymouth, Mass., Avery Doten, 1893.
34. Dwight, Elizabeth A.   Memorials of Mary Wilder White. Boston, Everett Press, 1903.
35. Earle, Alice M.   Child Life in Colonial Days. New York, Macmillan Co., 1899.
36. Earle, Alice M.   China Collecting in America. New York, Empire State Book Co., 1892.
37. Earle, Alice M.   Colonial Dames and Good Wives. Boston, Houghton Mifflin Co., 1895.
38. Earle, Alice M.   Colonial Days in old New York. New York, Charles Scribners, 1896.
39. Earle, Alice M.   Curious Punishments of Bygone Days. Chicago, Herbert Stone Co., 1896.
40. Earle, Alice M.   Customs and Fashions in Old New England. London, David Mutt Co., 1893.
41. Earle, Alice M.   Home Life in Colonial Days. New York, Macmillan Co., 1899.
42. Earle, Alice M.   In Old Narragansett. New York, Charles Scribners, 1898.
43. Earle, Alice M.   Margaret Winthrop, 1591-1647. New York, Charles Scribners, 1895.
44. Earle, Alice M.   Old Time Gardens. New York, Macmillan, 1901.
45. Earle, Alice M.   A Sabbath in Puritan New England. New York, Charles Scribners, 1893.
46. Earle, Alice M.   Stage Coach and Tavern Days. New York, Macmillan Co., 1900.

247. Earle, Alice M. Sun Dials and Roses of Yesterday. New York, Macmillan Co., 1922.
248. Earle, Alice M. Two Centuries of Costumes in America. 2 vols, New York, Macmillan Co., 1903.
249. Earle, Alice M., & Ford, Emily E., eds. Early Prose and Verse. New York, Harpers & Bros., 1893.
250. Earle, Alice M. & Winston, Anna G. Anna Green Winslow: A Boston school girl of 1771. Boston, Houghton Mifflin Co., 1894.
251. Early, Eleanor. New England samplers. Boston, Waverly House, 1940.
252. Early, Ruth H. By-ways of Virginia history. Richmond, Va., Everett Waddy, 1907.
253. East, Robert A. Business Enterprise in the American Revolutionary Era. New York, Columbia University Press, 1938.
254. Eberlein, Harold D. The Architecture of Colonial America. Boston, Little, Brown & Co., 1951.
255. Eberlein, Harold D. Colonial Interiors. New York, Helburn Co., 1938.
256. Eberlein, Harold D., & McClives, Abbot. A practical book of early American antiques. (Arts and Crafts) Garden City, N.Y., Garden City Publishers, 1936.
257. Edwards, Everett J., & Rattray, Jeannette E. "Whale off": The Story of American Shore Whaling. New York, Frederick Stokes Co., 1932.
258. Edwards, George W. New York as an 18th Century Municipality, Part II, 1731-1776. Studies in History, Economics and Public Law, Vol. LXXV, No. 2. New York, Columbia University Press, 1917.
259. Eggleston, Edward. The Beginners of a Nation. New York, Appleton Co., 1896.
260. Egle, William H. Some Pennsylvania Women during the War of the Revolution. Harrisburg, Pa., Harrisburg Publishing Co., 1898.
261. Ellet, Elizabeth F. Court Circles of the Republic. Philadelphia, Philadelphia Publishing Co., 1872.
262. Ellet, Elizabeth F. Domestic History of the American Revolution. New York, Lippincott Co., 1850.
263. Ellet, Elizabeth, F. The Women of the American Revolution. 3 vols. New York, Baker & Scribner, 1948-1950.
264. Ellis, Franklin, & Evans, Samuel. History of Lancaster County, Pennsylvania. Philadelphia, Everts & Peck, 1883.
265. Ellis, George E. Life of Anne Hutchinson. Boston, Library of American Biography, 1847.
266. Ellis, George E. The Puritan Age and Rule in Massachusetts, 1629-1685. Boston, Houghton Mifflin, 1888.
267. Ellis, John H., ed. The Works of Anne Bradstreet in Prose and Verse. New York, Peter Smith, 1932.
268. Elzas, Barnett A. The Jews of South Carolina. Philadelphia, Lippincott Co., 1905.
269. Evans, Frederick, W. Ann Lee, the Founder of the Shakers. Mt. Lebanon, N. Y. author, 1858.
270. Evans, William & Thomas, eds. Friend's Library, Vols. I, II, IV, V, VI, VII, X, XI, XII, XIII, XIV. Philadelphia, J. Rakestraw Co., 1837-1848.
271. Fairbanks, George R. Spaniards in Florida. Jacksonville, Fla., Columbus Drew, 1868.

72. Faust, Albert, B.   The German Element in the United States. 2 vols.
    Boston, Houghton Mifflin, 1909.

73. Fay, Edwin W.   History of Education in Louisiana. Bureau of Education.
    Circular of Information, No. 1, Washington, U.S. Govt. Print. Off.,
    1899.

74. Felt, Joseph B.   Annals of Salem. Salem, Mass., W. & S. B. Ives Co.,
    1827.

75. Fernow, Berthold, ed.   Documents Relating to the History of the Early
    Colonial Settlements, Principally on Long Island. Documents Re-
    lating to Colonial History of the State of New York, Vol. XIV
    (New series, vol. III). Albany, N.Y., Weed Parsons Co., 1883.

76. Fernow, Berthold, Ed.   Records of New Amsterdam. 7 vols. New York,
    Knickerbocker Press, 1897.

77. Finley, Ruth E.   Old Patchwork Quilts and the Women who made Them.
    Philadelphia, Lippincott, 1929.

78. Fisher, Sydney G.   Men, Women and Manners in Colonial Times,
    Philadelphia, Lippincott Co., 1898.

79. Fiske, John.   The Beginnings of New England or the Puritan Theocracy
    in its Relations to Civil and Religious Liberty Boston, Houghton
    Mifflin, 1889.

80. Fiske, John.   Dutch and Quaker Colonies in America. 2 vols. Boston,
    Houghton Mifflin Co., 1899.

81. Fiske, John.   New France and New England. Boston, Houghton Mifflin,
    1902.

82. Fiske, John.   Old Virginia and her neighbors. 2 vols. Boston, Houghton
    Mifflin, 1897.

83. Fithian, Philip V.   Journal and Letters, 1747-1776. Vineland, N.J.,
    Smith Printing House, 1932.

84. Fitzpatrick, John C., ed.   Diaries of George Washington, 4 vols. Boston,
    Houghton Mifflin, 1925.

85. Fleet, Beverly, ed.   Virginia Colonial Abstracts. Vols. X, XII. Richmond,
    Va., author mimeo, 1941.

86. Flexner, James T.   American Painting; First Flowers of Our Wilderness.
    Boston, Houghton Mifflin, 1947.

87. Flint, Martha B.   Early Long Island: A Colonial Study. New York,
    Putnam's Sons, 1896.

88. Forbes, Harriette, ed.   New England Diaries, 1602-1800. Topsfield,
    Mass., privately printed, 1923.

89. Force, Peter, ed.   Tracts and Other Papers Relating to the Colonies in
    North America. Vol. I, III Washington, author, 1836, 1844.

90. Ford, Worthington, C.   The Boston Book Market. Boston, The Club of Odd
    Volumes, 1917.

91. Fordyce, James.   Sermons to Young Women. London, Cadwell Co., 1778.

92. Fortier, Alcee.   Louisiana Studies: Literature, Customs, and Dialects,
    History and Education. New Orleans, La., Hansell & Bros., 1894.

93. Fosdick, Lucien J.   French Blood in America. New York, Flemming
    Revell Co., 1906.

94. Foster, Hannah W.   The Boarding-school: or Lessons, of a Preceptress
    to her Pupils. Boston, Thomas & Andrews, 1798.

95. Foster, Hannah.   The Coquette. Charlestown, Mass., Etheridge & Larkin
    Co., 1802.

296. Fowler, William W. Woman on the American Frontier. Hartford, Conn., Scranton Co., 1877.
297. Freeze, John G. History of Columbia County, Pennsylvania, Bloomsburg, Pa., Elwell & Bittenbender, 1883.
298. Friends, Society of. Memorials Concerning Deceased Friends from Yearly Meetings, 1788-1819. Philadelphia, Solomon Conrad, 1821.
299. Fries, Adelaide L. Records of the Moravians of North Carolina. 2 vols. Raleigh, N.C., North Carolina History Commission, 1922-1926.
300. Fries, Adelaide L. The Road to Salem. Chapel Hill, N.C., University of North Carolina Press, 1944.
301. Garden, Alexander. Anecdotes of the Revolutionary War. 3 vols. Brooklyn, N.Y., author, (reprint) 1865.
302. Gardiner, Dorothy. English Girlhood at School. London, Oxford University Press, 1929.
303. Gerard, James W. Lady Deborah Moody; a discourse delivered before the New York Historical Society, May, 1880. New York, Patterson Co., 1880.
304. Gilman, Arthur, ed., Theatrum Majorum: The Cambridge of 1776, with the Diary of Dorothy Dudley. Cambridge, Mass., Lockwood, Brooks Co., 1876.
305. Gloucester County Historical Society. Organization and Minutes of the Gloucester County Court, 1686-1687. Woodbury, N.J., Gloucester County Historical Society, 1930.
306. Goebel, Edmund J. A Study of Catholic Secondary Education during the Colonial Period. Washington, Catholic University of America Press, 1936.
307. Good, Harry G. Benjamin Rush and His Services to American Education. Berne, Ind., Witness Press, 1918.
308. Goodwin, Maude W. The Colonial Cavalier, or Southern Life before the Revolution. Boston, Lovell, Coryell & Co., 1894.
309. Gottesman, Rita S. The Arts and Crafts in New York, 1726-1776. New York, New York Historical Society, 1938.
310. Gottesman, Rita S. The Arts and Crafts in New York, 1777-1799. New York, New York Historical Society, 1954.
311. Graham, Isabella. Life and Writings of Mrs. Isabella Graham. New York, Seymour Co., 1816.
312. Graham, Shirley. The Story of Philis Wheatley. New York, Julian Messner, 1949.
313. Grant, Anne M. Memoirs of an American Lady. 2 vols. New York, Appleton Co., 1846.
314. Graydon, Alexander. Memoirs of a Life Chiefly Passed within Pennsylvania. London, T. Cadell, 1822.
315. Greely, Mary W. ed. Cambridge of 1776, with Diary of Dorothy Dudley. Cambridge, Mass., Ladies Centennial Committee, 1875.
316. Green, Calvin, & Wells, Seth Y. (preface) A Summary View of the Millennial Church (commonly called Shakers) Albany, N.Y., Packard & Van Benthuysen, 1823.
317. Green, Harry C. & Mary W. Pioneer Mothers in America. 3 vols. New York, Putnams, 1912.
318. Green, Samuel A. Journal of Sergeant David Holden (1760) of Groton, Massachusetts. Cambridge, Mass., Wilson & Son, 1889.

319.	Greene, Evarts B. & Harrington, Virginia.	American Population before
	the Federal Census of 1790. New York, Columbia University
	Press, 1932.
320.	Greene, Lorenzo J.	The Negro in Colonial New England, 1620-1776.
	New York, Columbia University Press, 1942.
321.	Gregory, Samuel.	A Letter to the Ladies in Favor of Female Physicians
	for Their Own Sex. Boston, privately printed, 1850.
322.	Griffin, Augustus.	Griffin's Journal: First Settlers of Southold. Orient,
	N.Y., author, 1857.
323.	Grimes, J. Bryan.	North Carolina Wills and Inventories. Raleigh, N.C.,
	Edwards & Broughton, 1912.
324.	Griswold, Rufus W.	The Female Poets of America. New York, James
	Miller, 1874.
325.	Griswold, Rufus W.	Republican Court: American society in the Days of
	Washington, New York, Appleton & Co., 1864.
326.	Groce, George C., & Wallace, David H.	Dictionary of Artists in America,
	1564-1860. New Haven, Conn., Yale University Press, 1957.
327.	Hadaway, William S.	Anne Hutchinson and other papers. White Plains,
	N.Y., Westchester Historical Society, 1929.
328.	Hale, Sarah J.	Distinguished Women.	New York, Harper Bros., 1853.
329.	Hall, Clayton C.	Narratives of Early Maryland, 1653-1684. New York,
	Charles Scribners, 1910.
330.	Hall, Edward H.	Margaret Corbin. New York, American Scenic and
	Historical Preservation Society, 1932.
331.	Hallowell, Richard P.	The Quaker Invasion of Massachusetts. Boston,
	Houghton Mifflin, 1883.
332.	Halsey, Abigail F.	In Old Southampton. New York, Columbia University
	Press, 1940.
333.	Halsey, Rosalie V.	Forgotten Books of the American Nursery. Boston,
	C. E. Goodspeed & Co., 1911.
334.	Hamilton, Peter J.	History of North America. Vol. III, The Coloniza-
	tion of the South. Philadelphia, George Barrie's Sons, 1904.
335.	Hammond, George P.	Don Juan de Onate and the Founding of New
	Mexico. Santa Fe, N.M., Historical Society of New Mexico, 1927.
336.	Hanaford, Phoebe A.C.	Daughters of America. Augusta, Me., True &
	Co., 1882.
337.	Hanscom, Elizabeth D.	The Heart of the Puritan. New York, Macmillan
	Co., 1917.
338.	Hanson, John W.	History of Gardiner, Pittstown, and West Gardiner,
	Maine. Gardiner, Me., Wm. Palmer, 1852.
339.	Hart, Albert B.	American History as told by Contemporaries. 5 vols.
	New York, Macmillan Co., 1897-1929.
340.	Hart, Albert B.	Colonial Children. New York, Macmillan Co., 1902.
341.	Hart, Albert B.	Commonwealth History of Massachusetts. 5 vols.
	New York, States History Co., 1928.
342.	Hazard, Samuel.	Annals of Pennsylvania, 1609-1682. Philadelphia,
	Hazard & Mitchell, 1850.
343.	Hazard, Samuel, ed.	Register of Pennsylvania. Vols. I,VIII.
	Philadelphia, W.F. Geddes Co., 1828-1832.
344.	Hazen, Henry A.	History of Bellerica, Massachusetts. Boston, Williams
	& Co., 1883.

345. Heard, John J.   John Wheelwright, 1592-1679. Boston, Houghton Mifflin, 1930.

346. Heartman, Charles F., ed.   Letters and Poems by Phillis Wheatley. New York, editor, 1915.

347. Heartman, Fred.   Checklist of Printers in the United States till 1783. New York, author, 1915.

348. Hening, William W., ed.   Statutes at Large: Laws of Virginia. 13 vols. New York, Bartow & others, 1823.

349. Henry, James.   Sketches of Moravian Life. Philadelphia, Lippincott, 1859.

350. Herbst, Josephine.   New Green World. New York, Hastings House, 1954.

351. Herrick, Cheesman A.   White Servitude in Pennsylvania. Philadelphia, J.J. McVey, 1926.

352. Hildeburn, Charles S.R. Sketches of Printers and Printing in Colonial New York. New York, Dodd, Mead & Co., 1895.

353. Hill, Don G.   Early Records of the Town of Dedham, Massachusetts. 1636-1659. Vols. III, IV. Dedham, Mass., Dedham Transcript, 1894.

354. Hill, Frank A.   The Mystery Solved: Facts Relating to the "Lawrence-Townley", Chase-Townley Marriage and Estate Question. Boston, Rand Avery Co., 1888.

355. Hillhouse, Margaret P.   Historical and Genealogical Collections relating to the Descendants of the Rev. James Hillhouse. New York, T.A. Wright, 1924.

356. Hinchman, Lydia S.   Early Settlers of Nantucket. Philadelphia Lippincott Co., 1896.

357. Hirsch, Arthur H.   The Huguenots of the Colony of South Carolina. Durham, N.C., Duke University Press, 1928.

358. Hittell, Theodore H.   History of California. 4 vols. San Francisco, Pacific Press Publishing House, 1885.

359. Hodge, Frederick W. et al., eds.   Revised Memorial of 1634 by Fray Alonso de Benavides. Albuquerque, N.M., University of New Mexico Press, 1945.

360. Hodgman, Edwin R.   History of the Town of Westford (Massachusetts) 1659-1883. Lowell, Mass., Morning Mail Co., 1883.

361. Holbrook, Harriott. R.   Journal and Letters of Eliza Lucas Pickney. Wormsloe, Ga., author, 1850.

362. Holliday, Carl.   Woman's life in Colonial Days. Boston, Cornhill Publishing Co., 1922.

363. Hollister, G ideon H.   History of Connecticut. 2 vols. New Haven, Conn., Durie & Peck, 1855.

364. Hollaway, Laura C.   Ladies of the White House. Philadelphia, Bradley & Co., 1882.

365. Holman, Mabel C.   The Western Neck. Hartford, Conn., privately printed, 1930.

366. Holtz, Adrian A.   A Study of the Moral and Religious Elements in American Secondary Education up to 1800. Chicago, Chicago University Press, 1917.

367. Honeyman, A. Van Doren, ed.   Archives of New Jersey, 1730-1750. Series I, Vol. XXX. Somerville, N.J., Unionist Gazette, 1918.

68. Hopkins, Samuel. The Life and Character of Miss Susanna Anthony. Worcester, Mass., Leonard Worcester, 1796.

69. Hopkins, Samuel. Memoirs of the Life of Sarah Osborn. Worcester, Mass., Leonard Worcester, 1799.

70. Hornblow, Arthur H. History of the Theatre in America. 2 vols. Philadelphia, Lippincott Co., 1919.

71. Hotten, John C. The Original List of Persons of Quality Who Went from Great Britain to the American Plantations, 1600-1700. London, Chatto & Windus, 1874.

72. Hubbs, Rebecca. A Memoir of ... A Minister of the Gospel in the Society of Friends, Late of Woodstown, New Jersey, Philadelphia, Friend's Book Store, n.d.

73. Hudson, Alfred S. Annals of Sudbury, Wayland, and Maynard, Middlesex County, Massachusetts. Sudbury, Mass., author, 1891.

74. Hudson, Alfred S. History of Sudbury. Boston, Town of Sudbury, 1889.

75. Hudson, Charles. History of the Town of Lexington. Boston, Marvin & Son, 1876.

76. Hudson, David. History of Jemima Wilkinson, a Preacheress of the 18th century. Geneva, N.Y., author, 1821.

77. Hull, William D. William Penn: A Topical Biography. New York, Oxford University Press, 1937.

78. Hulton, Annie. Letters of a Loyalist Lady, 1767-1776. Cambridge, Mass., Harvard Univesity Press, 1927.

79. Humphrey, Grace. Women in American History. Indianapolis, Ind., Bobbs-Merrill Co., 1919.

80. Humphreys, Mary G. Catherine Schuyler. New York, Charles Scribners, 1897.

81. Hunt, Gaillord, ed. Journals of the Continental Congress, 1774-1789. Vol. II. Washington, U.S. Govt. Print Off., 1912.

82. Huntington, Arria S. Under a Colonial Roof-Tree. Boston, Houghton Mifflin, 1891.

83. Hurd, Duane H. History of Essex County, Massachusetts. 2 vols. Philadelphia, Lewis Co., 1888.

84. Hurd-Mead, Kate C. History of Women in Medicine. Haddam, Conn., Haddam Press, 1938.

85. Iconophiles, Society of. Washington's Reception by the Ladies of Trenton. New York, The Society, 1903.

86. Innes, John H. New Amsterdam and Its People. New York, Charles Scribner's, 1902.

87. Ireland, Joseph N. Records of the New York Stage, 1750-1860. 2 vols. New York, Morell Co., 1866-1867.

88. Jackson, Francis. History of the Early Settlement of Newton, 1639-1800. Boston, Stacy & Richardson, 1854.

89. Jackson, John W., ed. Margaret Morris: Her Journal with a Biographical Sketch and Notes. Philadelphia, MacManus Co., 1949.

90. Jackson, Shirley. The Witchcraft of Salem Village. New York, Farrar, Strauss, & Young, 1956.

91. James, Bartlett B. History of North America. Vol. V: Colonization of New England. Philadelphia, George Barrie's Sons, 1904.

92. James, Bartlett B. & Jameson, J. Franklin, eds. Journal of Jasper Dankaerts, 1679-1680. New York, Charles Scribner's 1913.

393.   James, George W.   In and Out of the Old Missions of California. Boston, Little, Brown & Co., 1905.

394.   James, (Mrs.) Thos. Potts.   Memorial of Thomas Potts, Jr. Cambridge, Mass., author, 1874.

395.   Jameson, J. Franklin.   Narratives of the New Netherlands, 1609-1664. New York, Charles Scribners Sons, 1909.

396.   Jenkins, Howard M.   The Family of William Penn. Philadelphia, author, 1899.

397.   Jernegan, Marcus W.   Laboring and Dependent Classes in Colonial America, 1607-1883. Chicago, University of Chicago Press, 1931.

398.   Jester, Annie L. & Hiden, Martha W.   Adventures of Purse and Person Virginia (1607-1625). Princeton, N.J., Princeton University Press, 1956.

399.   Johnson, Allen & Malone, Dumas. eds.   Dictionary of American Biography. 20 vols. New York, Charles Scribners, 1936.

400.   Johnson, Amandus.   The Swedes on the Delaware, 1638-1664. Philadelphia, International Printing Co., 1927.

401.   Johnson, Clifton,   Old Time Schools and School Books. New York, Macmillan Co., 1904.

402.   Johnson, Robert G.   An Historical Account of the First Settlement of Salem in West Jersey, by John Fenwick, esq. Chief Proprietor of the Same. Philadelphia, Orin Rogers, 1839.

403.   Jones, Frederick R.   History of North America. Vol. IV: Colonization of the Middle States and Maryland. Philadelphia, George Barrie & Sons, 1904.

404.   Jones, Hugh.   The Present State of Virginia. London, J. Clarke, 1724.

405.   Jones, Rufus M.   The Quakers in the American Colonies. London, Macmillan, 1911.

406.   Jones, Rufus M.   The Later Periods of Quakerism. 2 vols. London, Macmillan, 1921.

407.   Jones, William H.   The History of Catholic Education in the State of Colorado. Washington, Catholic University of America Press, 1955.

408.   Jordan, Francis J.   Life of William Henry. Lancaster, Pa., New Era Press, 1910.

409.   Josselyn, John.   New England Rarities Discovered. London, G. Widdowes, 1672.

410.   Judd, Sylvester.   History of Hadley, Massachusetts. Springfield, Mass., Huntting Co., 1905.

411.   Kemp. William W.   The Support of Schools in Colonial New York by the Society for the Propagation of the Gospel. Columbia University Contributions, no.16. New York, T.C. Columbia University, 1913.

412.   Kercheval, Samuel.   History of the Valley of Virginia. Strasburg, Va., Shenandoah Publishers, 1925.

413.   Kilpatrick, William H.   The Dutch Schools of New Netherlands and Colonial New York. Washington, U.S. Govt. Print. Off., 1912.

414.   King, Grace E.   New Orleans: The Place and the People. New York, Macmillan, 1895.

415.   Kittredge, George L.   Witchcraft in Old and New England. Cambridge, Mass., Harvard University Press, 1929.

16. Klain, Zora.   Educational Activities of New England Quakers.
      Philadelphia, Westbrook Printing Co., 1928.
17. Klain, Zora.   Quaker Contributions to Education in North Carolina.
      Philadelphia, Westbrook Printing Co., 1925.
18. Knight, Edgar W.   Documentary History of Education in the South before
      1800. 5 vols. Chapel Hill, N.C., University of North Carolina
      Press, 1949.
19. Knight, Lucien L.   Georgia's Landmarks, Memorials, and Legends. 2
      vols. Atlanta, Ga., author, 1913.
20. Knight, Sarah K.   The Journal of Madame Knight, 1666-1727. New York,
      Peter Smith, 1935.
21. Kohn, Augustus.   Cotton Mills of South Carolina. Charleston, S.C.,
      author, 1907.
22. Kuhns, Oscar.   German and Swiss settlements of Pennsylvania. New
      York, Henry Holt Co., 1901.
23. Lamb, Martha J.   History of the City of New York. 2 vols. New York,
      A.S. Barnes., 1877.
24. Lamson, Darius F.   History of the Town of Manchester, Massachusetts.
      Manchester, Mass., The Town, 1895.
25. Langdon, William C.   Everyday Things in American Life, 1607-1706.
      New York, Charles Scribner's Sons, 1937.
26. Lapham, Alice G.   The Old Planters of Beverly in Massachusetts and
      the Thousand Acre Grant of 1635. Cambridge, Mass., The
      Riverside Press, 1930.
27. Lathrop, Elise L.   Early American Inns and Taverns. New York, R. M.
      McBride Co., 1936.
28. Lathrop, G. P. & Lathrop, R. H.   A Story of Courage. Cambridge, Mass.,
      Riverside Press, 1894.
29. Lawrence, Thomas.   Historical Genealogy of the Lawrence Family. New
      York, E.O. Jenkins Co., 1858.
30. Lebeson, Anita L.   Jewish Pioneers in America, 1492-1847. New York,
      Brentano Co., 1931.
31. Lee, Francis B.   Archives of New Jersey.   Series 2, Vol. II. Trenton,
      N.J., John L. Murphy, 1903.
32. Lee, Francis B.   New Jersey as a Colony and as a State. New York,
      Publishing Society of New Jersey, 1902.
33. Lee, F. D. & Agnew, J. L.   Historical Record of the City of Savannah.
      Savannah, Ga., J.H. Estill, 1869.
34. Leonard, Eugenie A.   Origins of Personnel Services in American Higher
      Education. Minneapolis, Minn., University of Minnesota Press,
      1956.
35. Lewis, Alonzo.   The History of Lynn, Massachusetts. Boston, J.H.
      Eastburn Co., 1829.
36. Lippincott, Horace M.   Early Philadelphia. Philadelphia, Lippincott Co.,
      1917.
37. Little, Frances.   Early American Textiles. New York, Century Co., 1931.
38. Logan, Mary S.   The Part Taken by Women in American History.
      Wilmington, Del., Perry-Nalle Publishing Co., 1912.
39. Lord, Robert H. et al.   History of the Archidiocese of Boston, 1604-1943.
      3 vols. New York, Sheed & Ward, 1944.

440. Lossing, Benson J. Mary and Martha, Mother and Wife of George Washington. New York, Harper & Bros., 1886.
441. Lovell, Albert A. Worcester in the Revolution. Worcester, Mass., Tyler & Seagrave Co., 1876.
442. McClellan, Elizabeth. Historic Dress in America, 1607-1800. New York, Tudor Publishing Co., 1942.
443. McCormac, Eugene I. White Servitude in Maryland. 1634-1820, Johns Hopkins University Studies, series 22, No. 3, 4. Baltimore, Johns Hopkins University Press, 1904.
444. McCormick, Richard P. The History of Voting in New Jersey, 1664-1911. New Brunswick, N.J., Rutgers University Press, 1953.
445. McCrady, Edward. History of South Carolina under Proprietory Government, 1670-1719. New York, Macmillan Co., 1897-1901.
446. McCrady, Edward. History of South Carolina under Royal Government, 1719-1776. New York, Macmillan Co., 1899.
447. McKinley, Albert E. The Suffrage Franchise in the Thirteen English Colonies in America. Philadelphia, University of Pennsylvania Press, 1905.
448. Macy, Obed. History of Nantucket. Boston, Hilliard Gray & Co., 1835.
149. Macy, William F. The Nantucket Scrap Basket. Boston, Houghton Mifflin, 1930.
450. Maddox, William A. The Free School Idea in Virginia before the Civil War. New York, T.C., Columbia University, 1918.
451. Manchester, Mass. Town Records. Salem, Mass., The Town, 1889.
452. Manges, Frances M. Women Shopkeepers, Tavern-Keepers, and Artisans in Colonial Philadelphia. Ph. D. Thesis. typed. Philadelphia, University of Pennsylvania, 1958.
453. Mann, Herman. The Female Review: or Memoirs of an American Young Lady. Dedham, Mass., author, 1797.
454. Marble, Anne R. The Women Who Came in the Mayflower. Boston, The Pilgrim Press, 1920.
455. Marcus, Jacob R. Early American Jewry, 1649-1794. 2 vols. Philadelphia, Jewish Publishing Society, 1951-1955.
456. Martyn, Benjamin. An Account Showing Progress of the Colony of Georgia in America from its First Establishment. Savannah, Ga., Georgia Historical Society, 1842.
457. Marvin, Abijah P. History of the Town of Lancaster, Massachusetts. Boston, Jewett Co., 1859.
458. Mason, E. V. ed. Journal of a Young Lady of Virginia. Baltimore, John Murphy & Co., 1871.
459. Mason, George C. Reminiscences of Newport. Newport, R.I., Charles E. Hammett, 1884.
460. Mason, Sister Mary Paul. Church-State Relationships in Education in Connecticut, 1633-1953. Washington, Catholic University of America Press, 1953.
461. Massachusetts Bay Colony. Record Court Assistants. 3 vols. Boston, County of Suffolk, 1901.
462. Matthews, William. American Diaries: An Annotated Bibliography of American Diaries Written Prior to the Year 1861. Berkeley, Calif., University of California Press, 1945.

3. May, Caroline, ed.   The American Female Poets. Philadelphia, Lindsay & Blakiston, 1848.
4. Maynadier, Gustavius H.   The First American Novelist, Charlotte Lennox. Cambridge, Mass., Harvard University Press, 1940.
5. Melcher, Marguerite F.   The Shaker Adventure. Princeton, Princeton University of Princeton Press, 1941.
6. Melish, John.   Travels in the United States of America in the Years 1806-1811. 2 vols. Philadelphia, author, 1815.
7. Mellick, Andrew D.   Story of an Old Farm. Somerville, N.J. Unionist Gazette, 1889.
8. Meriwether, Colyer.   Our Colonial Curriculum, 1607-1776. Washington, Capitol Publishing Co., 1907.
9. Merrill, Joseph.   History of Amesbury and Merrimac. Haverhill, Mass., Franklin Stiles, 1880.
0. Messler, Abram.   Centennial History of Somerset County, New Jersey. Somerville, N.J., C.M. Jameson, 1878.
1. Metcalf, John G.   Annals of the Town of Mendon, 1659-1880. Providence, R.I., E.L. Freeman, Inc., 1880.
2. Meyer, Annie N.   Woman's Work in America. New York, Henry Holt Co., 1891.
3. Meyer, Gerald D.   The Scientific Lady in England, 1650-1760. Berkeley, Calif., University of California Press, 1955.
4. Mickle, Isaac.   Reminiscences of Old Gloucester, New Jersey. Philadelphia, Townsend Ward, 1845.
5. Miller, Perry.   The New England Mind. Cambridge, Mass., Harvard University Press, 1954.
6. Mills, Weymer J.   Historic Houses of New Jersey. Philadelphia, Lippincott, 1902.
7. Mitchell, Broadus.   William Gregg, Factory Master of the Old South. Chapel Hill, N.C., University of North Carolina Press, 1928.
8. Mitchell, Edwin V.   The American Village. New York, Stackpole Sons, 1938.
9. Mitchell, Stewart.   Abigail Adams, New Letters of, 1788-1801. Boston, Houghton Mifflin, 1947.
0. Montgomery, James.   Cotton Manufacture in the United States. New York, Appleton Co., 1860.
1. Moore, Charles. The Family Life of George Washington. Boston, Houghton Mifflin, 1926.
2. Morgan, Edmund S.   The Puritan Dilemma: The Story of John Winthrop. Boston, Little, Brown, 1958.
3. Morgan, Edmund S.   The Puritan Family: Essays on Religion and Domestic Relations in 17th Century New England. Boston, Boston Public Library, 1944.
4. Morgan, John H.   Early American Painters. New York, New York Historical Society, 1921.
5. Morison, Samuel E.   Builders of the Bay Colony. Boston, Houghton Mifflin, 1930.
6. Morison, Samuel E.   The Intellectual Life of Colonial New England. New York, New York University Press, 1956.
7. Morison, Samuel E.   The Story of the "Old Colony" of New Plymouth. New York, Alfred A. Knopf, 1956.

488. Morris, Richard B.   Studies in the History of American Law. New York, Columbia University Press, 1930.
489. Morton, Louis.   Robert Carter of Nomini Hall. Princeton, Princeton University Press, 1941.
490. Moschzisker, Ann von.   The Emergency Aid of 1776. Philadelphia, Town Printing Co., 1917.
491. Mozans, J.H.   Women in Science. New York, Appleton's 1913.
492. Myers, Albert C.   Hannah Logan's Courtship. Philadelphia, Ferris & Leach, 1904.
493. Myers, Albert C.   Narratives of Early Pennsylvania, New Jersey and Delaware. New York, Charles Scribners, 1912.
494. Myers, Albert C.   Sally Wister's Journal. Philadelphia, Ferris & Leach, 1902.
495. Myers, Elizabeth L.   A Century of Moravian Sisters. New York, F.H. Revell Co., 1918.
496. Myers, Gustavius.   Ye Olden Blue Laws. New York, The Century Co., 1921.
497. Neal, J. Armstrong.   An Essay on the Education and Genius of the Female Sex. Philadelphia, J. Johnson Co., 1795.
498. Neill, Edward D.   Virginia Carolorum: The Colony, 1625-1685. Albany, Joel Munsell's Sons, 1886.
499. Nelson, Charles A.   Waltham, Past and Present. Cambridge, Mass., Thos. Lewis Co., 1879.
500. Nelson, William, ed.   Archives of New Jersey. Series 1: Vols. XI, XII, XIX, XXI, XXIV, XXV, XXVI, XXVII, XXVIII, XXIX. Series 2: Vols. II, III, IV. Paterson, New Jersey, Press Print Co., et al., 1894-1914.
501. Nevins, Allan, ed.   American Social History as Recorded by British Travellers. New York, Henry Holt & Co., 1923.
502. Nevins, Winfield S.   Witchcraft in Salem Village in 1692. Salem, Mass., Salem Press Co., 1916.
503. Northampton County, Virginia.   Records, 1689-1698. Orders. Wills. Northampton.
504. Nourse, Henry S.   Early Records of Lancaster, Massachusetts. Lancaster, Mass., W. J. Coulter, 1884.
505. Noyes, Ethel J. R.   The Women of the Mayflower and the Women of Plymouth Colony. Plymouth, Mass., Memorial Press, 1921.
506. Nugent, Nell M.   Cavaliers and Pioneers. Abstracts of Virginia Land Patents and Grants, 1623-1800. Richmond, Va., Dietz Co., 1934.
507. Nutting, Mary A. & Dock, Lavinia L.   History of Nursing. 2 vols. New York, Putnams Co., 1907-1912.
508. Oberholtzer, Ellis P.   Philadelphia: A History of the City and its People. 4 vols. Philadelphia, S.J.Clarke Co., 1912.
509. O'Callaghan, Edmund B.   History of New Netherlands. 2 vols. New York, Appleton Co., 1846.
510. Odell, George C.D.   Annals of the New York Stage. 2 vols. New York, Columbia University Press, 1927.
511. Oliver, Fitch E.   Diary of William Pychon. Boston, Houghton Mifflin, 1890.
512. Opdyke, Charles W.   Opdyke Genealogy. Albany, New York, Weed Parsons & Co., 1899.

13. Orcutt, William D. Good Old Dorchester. Cambridge, Mass. The University Press, 1908.
14. Osterweis, Rollin G. Three Centuries of New Haven, 1638-1938. New Haven, Conn., Yale University Press, 1953.
15. Overton, Jacqueline. Long Island's Story. New York, Doubleday Doran, 1932.
16. Packard, Francis Randolph. History of Medicine in the United States. 2 vols. New York, P.B. Hoeber Inc., 1931.
17. Paige, Lucius R. History of Cambridge, Mass., 1630-1877. Boston, Houghton Mifflin, 1877.
18. Palmer, W. P., ed. Calendar of Virginia State Papers. Vol. III, VIII. Richmond, Va., J. E. Goode, 1883.
19. Pancoast, H.S. Introduction to American Literature. New York, Henry Holt Co., 1898.
20. Parran, A.N. Register of Maryland's Heraldic Families. Baltimore, H.G. Roebuck & Son., 1935.
21. Parry, Edwin S. Betsy Ross, Quaker Rebel. Philadelphia, Winston, Co., 1932.
22. Parsons, Jacob C. ed. Diary of Jacob Hiltzheimer. Philadelphia, editor, 1893.
23. Peare, Catherine O. William Penn. Philadelphia, Lippincott Co., 1957.
24. Peckham, Howard H. Captured by the Indians. New Brunswick, N.J. Rutgers University Press, 1954.
25. Pennypacker, Samuel W. Pennsylvania Colonial Cases. (prior to 1700). Philadelphia, Rees Welch & Co., 1892.
26. Pennypacker, Samuel W. Settlement of Germantown. Philadelphia, W.J. Campbell, 1899.
27. Pennsylvania Society of Colonial Dames. Forges and Furnaces in the Province of Pennsylvania. Philadelphia, The Society, 1914.
28. Peterson, Arthur A. New York as an 18th Century Municipality: Part I. Columbia University. Studies in History, Economics, and Public Law. Vol. 75, Nos. 1, 2. New York, Longmans, Green, 1917.
29. Peto, Florence. American Quilts and Coverlets. New York, Chanticleer Press, 1949.
30. Peto, Florence. Historic Quilts. New York, American Historical Co., 1939.
31. Phillips, James D. Salem in the 18th Century. Boston, Houghton Mifflin, 1937.
32. Phillips, Ulrich B. Life and Labor in the Old South. Boston, Little, Brown & Co., 1941.
33. Phillips, Ulrich B. Plantation and Frontier. 2 vols. (Documentary History of American Industrial Society, Vol. I, II. John R. Commons ed.) Cleveland, Ohio, Arthur Clark Co., 1910.
34. Pierce, Mary F., comp. Weston Tax Lists, 1757-1827. Boston, A. Mudge & Son, 1897.
35. Pinchbeck, Ivy. Women Workers and the Industrial Revolution. 1750-1850. London, George Routledge & Sons, 1930.
36. Pomfret, John E. The Province of West New Jersey, 1609-1702. Princeton, Princeton University Press, 1956.
37. Pool, David de Sola. Portraits Etched in Stone. New York, Columbia University Press, 1952.

538.   Porter, Kirk H.   History of Suffrage in the United States. Chicago,
        University of Chicago Press, 1918.
539.   Post, Lydia M., ed.   Diary or Personal Recollections of the American
        Revolution. New York, Anson Randolph, 1866.
540.   Pound, Arthur.   The Penns of Pennsylvania and England. New York,
        Macmillan, 1932.
541.   Powell, Lyman P.   History of Education in Delaware. Washington,
        U.S. Govt. Print. Off., 1893.
542.   Powers,Grant.   Historical Sketches of the Discovery, Settlement, and
        Progress of Events in the Coos County and Vicinity, 1754-1785.
        Haverhill, N.H., F. J. Hayes, 1841.
543.   Poyas, Elizabeth A.   Days of Yore, or Shadows of the Past. Charleston,
        S.C. Wm. G. Mazyck, 1870.
544.   Pratt, Daniel J.   The Annals of Public Education in the State of New York
        from 1626 to 1746. Albany, N.Y., Argus Co., 1872.
545.   Price, James, H.   Virginia: A Guide to the Old Dominion. New York,
        Oxford University Press, 1940.
546.   Prime, Alfred C.   The Arts and Crafts in Philadelphia, Maryland, and
        South Carolina, 1721-1785. Series 1. Philadelphia, Walpole Society,
        1929.
547.   Prime, Alfred C.   The Arts and Crafts in Philadelphia, Maryland, and
        South Carolina, 1786-1800. Series 2. Philadelphia, Walpole Society,
        1932.
548.   Pringle, James P.   History of the Town of Gloucester, Massachusetts.
        Gloucester, Mass., author, 1892.
549.   Prowell, George.   History of Camden County, New Jersey. Philadelphia,
        L. J. Richards, 1886.
550.   Pryor, Sara C.   The Mother of Washington and Her Times. New York,
        Macmillan, 1903.
551.   Putnam, Emily J.   The Lady: Studies of Certain Significant Phases of
        Her History. New York, Putnam's Sons, 1910.
552.   Ramey, Mary E.W.   Chronicles of Mistress Margaret Brent. author, 1915.
553.   Ramsay, David.   History of South Carolina. 2 vols. Charleston, S.C.,
        Longworth Co., 1809.
554.   Ramsay, David.   Memoirs of the Life of Martha Laurens Ramsay. London,
        Burton & Briggs, 1815.
555.   Randall, Samuel S.   History of the Common School System of the State of
        New York. New York, Ivison, Blakeman, Taylor & Co., 1871.
556.   Randolph, Sarah N.   The Domestic Life of Thomas Jefferson. Charlotte,
        Va., Thos. Jefferson Memorial Foundation, 1947.
557.   Raper, Charles L.   Church and Private Schools. Greensboro, N.C., J.J.
        Stone, 1898.
558.   Raum, John O.   History of New Jersey. 2 vols. Philadelphia, J.E.
        Potter, 1877.
559.   Ravenel, Harriott H. (Beatrice St. J.)   Architects of Charleston.
        Charleston, N.C. Carolina Art Assoc., 1945.
560.   Ravenel, Harriott H.   Charleston, the Place and the People New York,
        Macmillan Co., 1906.
561.   Ravenel, Harriott H.   Eliza Lucas Pickney. New York, Charles Scribners
        Sons, 1896.

.   Reed, William B.   Life of Esther de Berdt Reed. Philadelphia, C. Sherman, 1853.

3.   Reed, William B.   Life and Correspondence of Joseph Reed. 2 vols. Philadelphia, Lindsay & Blakiston, 1847.

4.   Reeve, Tapping.   Law of Baron and Femme; of Parent and Child; Guardian and Ward; Master and Servant. New Haven, Conn., Oliver Steele, 1816.

5.   Reichel, Levin J.   The Early History of the Church of the United Brethern. (Moravians, 1734-1748) Nazareth, Pa., Moravian Historical Society, 1888.

3.   Reichel, William C.   History of Bethlehem Female Seminary. Philadelphia, Lippincott Co., 1858.

7.   Reynard, Elizabeth.   The Narrow Land. Boston, Houghton Mifflin, 1934.

3.   Reynolds, Myra.   The Learned Lady in England, 1650-1760. Boston, Houghton Mifflin, 1920.

9.   Richards, Laura E.   Abigail Adams and Her Times. New York, Appleton Co., 1917.

).   Richardson, Hester D.   Sidelights on Maryland History. 2 vols. Baltimore, Md., Williams and Wilkins, 1913.

.   Ricord, Frederick W. & Nelson, William, eds.   Archives of New Jersey. Series 1, Vols. IX, X, XIII, XIV. Newark, N.J. Daily Advertiser, 1885-1890.

2.   Ridgely, Mabel L.   What Them Befell. The Ridgelys of Delaware and Their Circle. Portland, Me., The Anthoensen Press, 1949.

3.   Rightor, Henry, ed.   Standard History of New Orleans, Louisiana. Chicago, Lewis Publ. Co., 1900.

4.   Riley, Arthur J.   Catholicism in New England to 1788. Washington, D.C. Catholic University of America Press, 1936.

5.   Riley, Henry T, trans.   Liber Albus. The White Book of the City of London, compiled by John Carpenter, common clerk, 1419. London, Griffin & Co., 1861.

3.   Robertson, James A.   True Relation of the Hardships Suffered by Governor Fernando De Soto and Certain Portuguese Gentlemen during the Discovery of the Province of Florida by a Gentleman of Elvas. 2 vols. Florida State Historical Society. Publication No. 11, 1933.

7.   Robinson, William W.   Ranchos Become Cities. Pasadena, Calif., San Pasqual Press, 1939.

3.   Rochefoucault-Liancourt, Francois de la.   Travels through the United States of North America. 2 vols. London, R. Phillips, 1800.

9.   Roelker, William G., ed.   Benjamin Franklin and Catherine Ray Greene - Their Correspondence. Philadelphia, American Philosophical Society, 1949.

).   Rogers, Albert A.   Family Life in 18th Century Virginia. Ph.D. Thesis. University of Virginia. 1939 (typed).

4.   Rogers, Lou.   Tar Heel Women. Raleigh, N.C., Warren Publ. Co., 1949.

2.   Roof, Katherine M.   Colonel William Smith and Lady. Boston, Houghton Mifflin, 1929.

3.   Ross, Peter.   History of Long Island. 3 vols. New York, Lewis Publ. Co., 1905.

584. Rourke, Constance. The Roots of American Culture. New York, Harcourt, Brace Co., 1942.

585. Rowlandson, Mary. Narrative of her Captivity and Restoration, 1682. Cambridge, Mass., J. Williamson & Son., 1903.

586. Rowson, Susanna. Miscellaneous Poems. Boston, W.&L. Blake, 1804.

587. Rowson, Susanna. Charlotte Temple: A Tale of Truth. Harrisburg, Pa., John Wyeth, 1802.

588. Rowson, Susanna. Charlotte's Daughter, with Memoir by S.L. Knapp. New York, Funk & Wagnall Co., 1828.

589. Rugg, Winifred K. Ann Marbury Hutchinson, 1590-1643. Unafraid; Life of Ann Hutchinson. Boston, Houghton Mifflin, 1930.

590. Rupp, I. Daniel. History of Lancaster County, Pennsylvania. Lancaster, Pa., G. Hill., 1844.

591. Rush, Benjamin. Account of the German Inhabitants of Pennsylvania. Philadelphia, Samuel Town, 1875.

592. Rush, Benjamin. Essays, Literary, Moral and Philosophical. Philadelphia, Thos. & Wm. Bradford., 1806.

593. Sachse, Julius F. The German Pietists of Provincial Pennsylvania. Philadelphia, author, 1895.

594. Sachse, Julius F. Music of the Ephrata Cloister. Lancaster, Pa., author, 1903.

595. Sachse, Julius F. The Wayside Inns of the Lancaster Roadside. Lancaster, Pa., author, 1912.

596. Sale, Edith T. Old Time Belles and Cavaliers. Philadelphia, Lippincott Co., 1912.

597. Salley, Alexander S., ed. Narratives of Early Carolina, 1650-1708. New York, Charles Scribners, 1911.

598. Salmon, Lucy M. Domestic Service. New York, Macmillan Co., 1897.

599. Sargent, Daniel. Our Land and Our Lady. New York, Longmans, Green & Co., 1940.

600. Scharf, John T., & Westcott, Thomson. History of Philadelphia. 3 vols. Philadelphia, Everts & Co., 1884.

601. Scheer, George F. & Rankin, Hugh F. Rebels and Redcoats. New York, World Publ. Co., 1957.

602. Schlesinger, Arthur M. Learning How to Behave. New York. Macmillan Co., 1946.

603. Schlesinger, Arthur M. New Viewpoints in American History. New York, Macmillan Co., 1926.

604. Scott, Kenneth. Counterfeiting in Colonial Pennsylvania. Numismatic Monograph No. 132. New York, American Numismatic Society, 1955.

605. Scudder, Horace E., ed. Men and Manners in America One Hundred Years Ago. New York, Scribner Armstrong, 1876.

606. Sears, Clara E., ed. Gleanings from Old Shaker Journals. Boston, Houghton Mifflin Co., 1916.

607. Seaver, James E. Narrative of the Life of Mary Jemison. Batavia, N.Y., Wm. Seaver & Son, 1842.

608. Seidensticker, Oswald. The First Century of German Printing in America, 1728-1830. Philadelphia, German Pioneer-Verein of Philadelphia, 1893.

609. Seilhamer, George O. History of the American Theatre. 2 vols. Phila., Globe Printing House, 1888.

0. Semmes, Raphael. Captains and Mariners of Early Maryland. Baltimore, Md., Johns Hopkins University Press, 1937.
1. Sewall, Samuel. History of Woburn, Massachusetts. Boston, Wiggin Lunt., 1868.
2. Sewall Samuel E. The Legal Condition of Women in Massachusetts. Boston, C.K. W hipple, 1869.
3. Sewel, Willem. History of the Rise, Increase, and Progress of the Christian People called Quakers 2 vols. Philadelphia, Uriah Hunt, 1832.
4. Seybolt, Robert F. Apprenticeship and Apprenticeship Education in New England and New York. New York, T.C. Columbia University Press, 1917.
5. Seybolt, Robert F. The Private Schools of Colonial Boston. Cambridge, Mass., Harvard University Press, 1935.
6. Seybolt, Robert F. Public Schools of Colonial Boston., 1635-1775. Cambridge, Mass., Harvard University Press, 1935.
7. Seybolt, Robert F. The Town Officials of Colonial Boston, 1634-1775. Cambridge, Mass., Harvard University Press, 1939.
8. Shakers, Elder of the. Testimonies of the Life, Character, Revelations, and Doctrines of Mother Ann Lee. Albany, N.Y., Weed Parsons, 1888.
9. Sharp, T. The Heavenly Sisters. New York, Henry Durell & Co., 1822.
0. Shea, John G. History of the Catholic Church in the United States. 4 vols. New York, author, 1886-1892.
1. Sheahan, Henry B. American Memory. New York, Farrar and Rinehart, 1937.
2. Sheldon, George. A History of Deerfield, Massachusetts. 2 vols. Greenfield, Mass., E.A. Hall Co., 1895.
3. Shipp, Barnard. History of Hernando De Soto and Florida, 1512-1568. Philadelphia, author, 1881.
4. Shurtleff, H arold R. The Log Cabin Myth. Cambridge, Mass., Harvard University Press, 1939.
5. Sickler, Joseph S. History of Salem County, New Jersey. Salem, N.J. Sunbeam Publ. Co., 1937.
6. Simonhoff, Harry. Jewish Notables in America, 1776-1865. New York, Greenberg Co., 1956.
7. Singleton, Esther. Social New York under the Georges, 1714-1776. New York, Appleton Co., 1902.
8. Sioussat, Anna M. Colonial Women of Maryland. Baltimore, Md., Friedenwald Co., 1891.
9. Sioussat, Anna M. Old Manors in the Colony of Maryland. Baltimore, Md., The Lord Baltimore Press, 1911.
0. Small, Walter H. Early New England Schools. Boston, Ginn & Co., 1914.
1. Smith, Abbott E. Colonists in Bondage. Chapel Hill, N.C., University of North Carolina Press, 1947.
2. Smith, Buckingham. Narratives of the Career of Hernando De Soto in the Conquest of Florida. New York, A.S. Barnes, 1904.
3. Smith, Euphemia V. History of Newburyport. Boston, Damrell & Moore, 1854.
4. Smith, Florence M. Mary Astell. New York, Columbia University Press, 1916.

635. Smith, George G.   The Story of Georgia and the Georgia People, 1732-1860. 1732-1860. Atlanta, Ga., Franklin Publ. Co., 1900.
636. Smith, Helen E.   Colonial Days and Ways. New York, Century Co., 1900.
637. Smith, John J., ed.   Letters of Dr. Richard Hill and His Children. Philadelphia, privately printed, 1854.
638. Smith, Preserved.   History of Modern Culture. 2 vols. New York, Henry Holt & Co., 1930-1939.
639. Smyth, Albert H., ed.   Writings of Benjamin Franklin. 10 Vols. New York, Macmillan Co., 1905-1907.
640. Sonneck, Oscar G. T.   Early Concert Life in America, 1731-1800. New York, Musurgia Co., 1949.
641. Spaulding, Melville C.   Historical Handbook of New Jersey. Columbus, O., author, 1895.
642. Springer, Mary E.   Elizabeth Schuyler. New York, Blanchard Co., 1903.
643. Spruill, Julia C.   Women's Life and Work in the Southern Colonies. Chapel Hill, N.C., University of North Carolina Press, 1938.
644. Stanard, Mary M.   Colonial Virginia: its People and Customs, Philadelphia, Lippincott Co., 1917.
645. Stanard, Mary M.   Story of Virginia's First Century. Philadelphia, Lippincott Co., 1928.
646. Starbuck, Alexander.   History of Nantucket. Boston, C.E. Goodspeed, 1924.
647. Starrett, Vincent.   All About Mother Goose. Boston, Apellicon Press, 1930.
648. Stearns, Charles.   The Ladies' Philosophy of Love ... Leominster, Mass., author, 1797.
649. Stenton, Doris M.   The English Woman in History. New York, Macmillan Co., 1957.
650. Stevens, Abel.   The Women in Methodism: Its Three Foundresses. New York, Carlton & Porter, 1866.
651. Stewart, Frank H.   Notes on Old Gloucester. Camden, N.J., New Jersey Society of Penna., 1917.
652. Stewart, George.   A History of Religious Education in Connecticut to the Middle of the 19th Century. New Haven, Conn., Yale University Press, 1924.
653. Stifler, James M.   My Dear Girl ... Letters of Benjamin Franklin and Polly Stevenson. New York, Doran Co., 1927.
654. Stiles, Henry R.   Bundling: Its Origin, Progress and Decline in America. Albany, N.Y. Munsell, 1869.
655. Stockton, Frank, R.   New Jersey from Discovery to Recent Times. New York, Appleton Co., 1896.
656. Stone, Edwin M.   History of Beverly, Massachusetts. Boston, James Munroe Co., 1843.
657. Stone, William L., ed. trans.   Riedesel, Baroness Friederika von Massow. Letters and Journal Relating to the War of the American Revolution and the Capture of the German troops at Saratoga. Albany, N.Y., Joel Munsell, 1867.
658. Stoney, Louisa C., ed.   A Day on the Cooper River, by John B. Irving. Columbia, S.C., R.L. Bryan Co., 1932.
659. Stopes, Charlotte C.   British Freewomen: Their Historical Privilege. London, S. Sonnenschein, 1894.
660. Streeter, Sebastian F.   Papers relating to early history. Baltimore, Md. Historical Society Fund Publication IX. 1876.

661. Stryker, William S. New Jersey Archives. Series 2, Vol. I, 1776-1777. Trenton, N.J., J.L. Murphy Co., 1901.

662. Stryker, William S. Battles of Trenton and Princeton. Boston, Houghton Mifflin, 1898.

663. Sutherland, Stella H. Population Distribution in Colonial America. New York, Columbia University Press, 1936.

664. Symmes, Frank R. History of Old Tennent Church. Cranbury, N.J., G.W. Burroughs, 1904.

665. Talbot, Marion. The Education of Women. Chicago, University of Chicago Press, 1910.

666. Tapley, Harriet S. Salem Imprints; History of the First Fifty Years of Printing in Salem, Massachusetts, 1768-1825. Salem, Mass., The Essex Institute, 1927.

667. Teggart, Frederick J. ed. The Anza Expedition of 1775-1776 Diary of Pedro Font. Vol. III, No. 1. Berkeley, Calif., Academy of Pacific Coast History, University of California Press, 1913.

668. Temple, Josiah H. & Sheldon, George. History of the Town of Northfield, Massachusetts. Albany, N.Y., Joel Munsell, 1875.

669. Terhune, Mary V. Some Colonial Homesteads and their Stories. New York, Putnam's Sons, 1897.

670. Terhune, Mary V. More Colonial Homesteads. New York, Putnam's Sons, 1899.

671. Terhune, Mary V. The Story of Mary Washington. Boston, Houghton Mifflin, 1892.

672. Thomas, Anna L.B. Nancy Lloyd. Journal of a Quaker Pioneer. New York, Frank Maurice Inc., 1927.

673. Thomas, James W. Chronicles of Colonial Maryland. Baltimore, Md., Cushing Co., 1900.

674. Thomas, Isaiah. History of Printing in America, with a Biography of Printers and an Account of Newspapers. 2 vols. Worcester, Mass., author, 1810.

675. Thompson, Benjamin. History of Long Island, New York. New York, E. French, 1839.

676. Thompson, Zadock. History of Vermont. Burlington, Vt., Edward Smith, 1833.

677. Tilden, William S., ed. History of the Town of Medfield, Massachusetts. Boston, George E. Ellis, 1887.

678. Tilton, George H. History of Rehobeth, Massachusetts. Boston, author, 1918.

679. Tittle, Walter, Ed. Colonial Holidays. New York, Doubleday, Page & Co., 1910.

680. Torbert, Alice C. Eleanor Calvert and Her Circle. New York, Willeam-Fredrick Press, 1950.

681. Trent, William P. & Wells, Berry W., eds. Readings from Colonial Prose and Poetry. New York, Thos. Crowell Co., 1903.

682. Trumbull, James R. History of Northampton, Massachusetts. 2 vols. Northampton, Mass., Gazette Printing Co., 1898.

683. Tryon, Rolla M. Household Manufactures in the United States 1640-1860: A Study of Industrial History. Chicago, University of Chicago Press, 1917.

684. Turner, Nancy B. The Mother of Washington. New York, Dodd, Mead & Co., 1930.

685. Turrell, Ebenezer. Memoirs of the Life and Death of that Pious and
      Ingenious Gentlewoman, Mrs. Jane Turrell. Boston, author, 1735.
686. Twichell, Joseph H. Some Old Puritan Love Letters; John and Margaret
      Winthrop, 1618-1638. New York, Dodd, Mead & Co., 1894.
687. Twitchell, Ralph E. The Spanish Archives of New Mexico. 2 vols. Cedar
      Rapids, Iowa., The Torch Press, 1914.
688. Twitchell, Ralph E. Leading Facts of New Mexican History. 5 vols.
      Cedar Rapids, Iowa, The Torch Press, 1911-1917.
689. Tyler, Alice F. Freedom's Ferment. Minneapolis, Minn., University of
      Minnesota Press, 1944.
690. Tyler, Frederick & Helen, eds. Grandmother Tyler's Book, 1775-1866.
      New York, Putnam's Sons, 1925.
691. Tyler, Lyon G. Narratives of Early Virginians, 1606-1625. New York,
      Charles Scribner, 1907.
692. Tyler, Moses C. History of American Literature. New York, Putnam's
      Sons, 1878.
693. Updegraff, Harlan. Origin of the Moving School in Massachusetts. New
      York, T. C. Columbia University Contribution No. 17, 1907.
694. Updike, Wilkins. History of the Episcopal Church in Narragansett.
      Boston, author, 1907.
695. United States. De Soto Expedition Commission. 76th Congress. 1st Ses-
      sion. House Document 71. Final report of the U.S. De Soto
      Expedition Commission. Washington, U.S. Govt. Print. Off., 1939.
696. Valentine, David., T., ed. Manual of the Corporation of the City of New
      York. New York, author, 1860.
697. Vanderpoel, Emily N. American Lace and Lace-makers. New Haven,
      Conn., Yale University Press, 1924.
698. Vanderpoel, Emily N. Litchfield School; Chronicles of a Pioneer School
      from 1792-1823. Cambridge, Mass., Harvard University Press, 1903.
699. Van Doren, Carl, ed. Letters of Benjamin Franklin and Jane Mecom.
      Princeton, N .J., Princeton University Press, 1950.
700. Van Doren, Carl. Jane Mecom. New York, Viking Press, 1950.
701. Van Laer, Arnold J.E., ed. Correspondence of Maria Van Rensselaer,
      1669-1689. Albany, N.Y., University of the State of New York Press,
      1935.
702. Van Rensselaer, Mrs. John K. The Goede Vrouw of Mana-ha-ta. New
      York, Charles Scribner's, 1898.
703. Van Rensselaer, Mariana G. History of the City of New York in the 17th
      Century. 2 vols. New York, Macmillan Co., 1909.
704. Van Winkle, Daniel. Old Bergen. Jersey City, N.J., J.W. Harrison, 1902.
705. Van Wyck, Frederick. Keskachauge, or the First White Settlement on
      Long Island. New York, Putnam's Sons, 1924.
706. Varner, John G. & Jeanette J. Garcilaso de la Vega's Florida of the Inca.
      Austin, Tex., University of Texas Press, 1951.
707. Vermont Society of Colonial Dames. Dedication of a Monument to Ann Story.
      Salisbury, Vt., Colonial Dames, 1905.
708. Vinton, John A. Life of Deborah Sampson. Boston, Wiggin & Parson Lunt,
      1866.
709. Violette, Augusta G. Economic Femminism in American Literature Prior to
      1848. Orono, Me., University of Maine Press, 1925.

710. Wakeley, J. B.   Lost Chapters from the Early History of American Methodism. New York, author, 1858.
711. Wallace, David D.   Life of Henry Laurens. New York, Putnam's Sons, 1915.
712. Wallace, David D.   History of South Carolina. 4 vols. New York, American Historical Society, 1934.
713. Wallas, Ada.   Before the Blue Stockings. New York, Macmillan Co., 1930.
714. Warren, Mercy.   Poems, Dramatic and Miscellaneous. Boston, Thomas & Andrews, 1790.
715. Warren, Mercy.   History.of the Rise, Progress and Termination of the American Revolution. 3 vols. Boston, E. Larkin, 1805.
716. Warren, Mercy.   The Group: 1775. A Drama. Ann Arbor, Mich., University of Michigan Press, 1953.
717. Washburn, Emory.   History of Lancaster Academy. Boston, Phillip, Sampson & Co., 1855.
718. Waters, Thomas F.   Ipswich in the Massachusetts Bay Colony, 1700-1917. 2 vols. Ipswich, Mass., Historical Society, 1917.
719. Watertown.   Watertown Records. 5 vols. Watertown, Mass., Watertown Historical Society, 1894.
720. Watson, John F.   Annals of Philadelphia and Pennsylvania in the Olden Times. 2 vols. Philadelphia, author, 1844.
721. Weber, Samuel.   The Charity School Movement in Colonial Pennsylvania, 1754-1763. Philadelphia, author, 1905.
722. Weeden, William B.   Economic and Social History of New England, 1620-1789. 2 vols. Boston, Houghton Mifflin, 1890.
723. Wegelin, Oscar.   Early American Fiction, 1774-1830. New York, Peter Smith, 1929.
724. Wenham Historical Society.   Wenham (Massachusetts) Town Records, 1642-1706. Wenham, Mass., Historical Society, 1930.
725. Wertenbaker, Thomas J.   The First Americans. New York, Macmillan Co., 1929.
726. Wertenbaker, Thomas J.   Virginia Under The Stuarts, 1607-1688. Princeton, N.J., Princeton University Press, 1914.
727. Wertenbaker, Thomas J.   Patrician and Plebian in Virginia. Charlottesville, Va., author, 1910.
728. Wharton, Anne H.   Colonial Days and Dames. Philadelphia, Lippincott Co., 1908.
729. Wharton, Anne H.   Martha Washington. New York, Charles Scribners, 1897.
730. Wharton, Anne H.   Salons: Colonial and Republican Philadelphia. Philadelphia, Lippincott Co. 1900.
731. Wharton, Anne H.   Through Colonial Doorways. Philadelphia, Lippincott Co., 1893.
732. Wheatley, Phillis.   Phillis Wheatley with Memoirs Poems. Boston, Isaac Knapp, 1838.
733. Wheatley, Phillis.   Letters of Phillis Wheatley. Boston, privately printed, 1864.
734. Wheeler, Ethel R.   Famous Blue-stockings. New York, John Lane Co., 1910.
735. White, Alain C.   The History of the Town of Litchfield, Connecticut, 1720-1920. Litchfield, Conn., Litchfield Historical Society, 1920.

736. White, Elizabeth N.   Mary Browne: The True Life and Times of the
      Daughter of Mr. John Browne, Gent., - Wife of the first English
      Mayor of New York. Providence, R.I., Roger Williams Press,
      1935.
737. White, Rev. George.   Historical Collections of Georgia. New York,
      Pridney & Russell Publ. 1854.
738. White, George S.   Memoir of Samuel Slater. Philadelphia, author, 1836.
739. Whitehead, William A.   East Jersey under the Proprietary Government.
      New York, New Jersey Historical Society, 1846.
740. Whitehead, William, ed.   Archives of New Jersey. Series 1, Vols. II, VII.
      Newark, N.J., Daily Advertiser, 1880-1883.
741. Whitney, Janet.   Abigail Adams. Boston, Little, Brown & Co., 1947.
742. Whiton, John M.   Sketches of the History of New Hampshire from its
      settlement, 1623, to 1833. Concord, N.H. Marsh, Capen & Lyon,
      1834.
743. Whitton, Mary O.   The First First Ladies, 1789-1865. New York,
      Hastings House, 1948.
744. Whitton, Mary O.   These were the Women, 1776-1860. New York,
      Hastings House, 1954.
745. Wickersham, James P.   History of Education in Pennsylvania.
      Lancaster, Pa., author, 1886.
746. Williams, John R.   Philip Vickers Fithian Journal and Letters, 1767-
      1774. Princeton, N.J. Princeton University Press, 1900.
747. Willis, Eola.   The Charleston Stage in the 18th Century. Columbia, S.C.,
      The State Co., 1924.
748. Willison, George F.   Saints and Strangers. New York, Reynal &
      Hitchcock, 1945.
749. Wilson, James G. & Fiske, John   Cyclopaedia of American Biography.
      12 vols. New York, D. Appleton Co., 1900.
750. Winship, George P., ed.   The Journal of Madame Knight. New York,
      Peter Smith Publ. Co., 1935.
751. Winslow, Ola E.   Meetinghouse Hill, 1630-1783. New York, Macmillan
      Co., 1952.
752. Winsor, Justine, ed.,   Memorial History of Boston, 4 vols. Boston,
      Osgood & Co., 1881.
753. Winterich, John T.   Early American Books and Printing. Boston,
      Houghton Mifflin, 1935.
754. Winthrop, John.   The History of New England, 1630-1649. 2 vols.
      Boston, Little, Brown & Co., 1853.
755. Wise, Jennings C.   Ye Kingdome of Accawmacke or the Eastern Shore of
      Virginia in the 17th Century. Richmond, Va., Bell Book Co., 1911.
756. Wister, (Mrs.) Owen J. & Irwin, Agnes.   Worthy Women of Our First
      Century. Philadelphia, Lippincott & Co., 1877.
757. Woody, Thomas.   Early Quaker Education in Pennsylvania. New York,
      T. C. Columbia University Press, 1920.
758. Woody, Thomas.   Quaker Education in the Colony and State of New
      Jersey. Philadelphia, author, 1923.
759. Woody, Thomas.   A History of Women's Education in the United States.
      2 vols. New York, The Science Press, 1929.
760. Wright, Louis B.   The Atlantic Frontier. Colonial American Civilization,
      1607-1763. New York, Alfred A. Knopf, 1947.

761. Wright, Louis B.   Cultural Life of the American Colonies, 1607-1763.
      New York, Harpers Bros., 1957.
762. Wright, Lyle, American Fiction, 1770-1850. San Marino, Calif., Huntington
      Library and Art Gallery, 1948.
763. Wright, Richardson.   Forgotten Ladies. Philadelphia, Lippincott Co.,
      1928.
764. Wroth, Lawrence C.   History of Printing in Colonial Maryland. Baltimore,
      Md., Typolhetae, 1922.
765. Yardley, John H.   Before the Mayflower. London, W. Heinemann Ltd.,
      1931.

MAGAZINE ARTICLES

766. Adams, Charles F.   "Church Discipline in New England". Mass. H.S.
      Proc. ser. 2, 6:477-516, (1891).
767. Adams, Herbert B.   "Allotments of Land in Salem to Men, Women and
      Maids." Essex Inst. H. Colls. 19:167-175, (1882).
768. Ambler, Mary.   "Diary, 1770." V.M.H.B.   45:152-170, (1937).
769. Ames, Susie.   "Law in Action: Court Records of Virginia Eastern
      Shore." W.M. Quart. ser. 3,4:177-191 (1947).
770. Armory, Martha.   "Will".   S.C.H.G. Mag. 12:73-74, (1911).
771. Andrews, Charles M.   "The River Towns of Connecticut: Wethersfield,
      Hartford, and Windsor." Baltimore, Johns Hopkins Studies. 7th
      Series. Vols. 7,8,9 (1889).
772. Bacon, Elizabeth.   "Mrs. E. Bacon's Letter to Her Sister". W.M. Quart.
      ser. 1, 9:4-6, (1901).
773. Baldwin, Simeon.   "Ride Across Connecticut" New Haven Col. H.S.
      Colls. 9:161-169, (1918).
774. Ballagh, James C.   "White Servitude in the Colony of Virginia."
      Baltimore, Johns Hopkins Univ. Studies. ser. 13, vols. 6,7. (1895).
775. Barker, Charles R.   "The Gulph Mill." P.M.H.B. 53:168-174, (1929).
776. Bartlett, Ellen S.   "Bits from Great Grandmother's Journal." Conn.
      Quart. 1:265-270, (1895).
777. Beale, G. W.   "An unwritten chapter in the early life of Mary Washing-
      ton." V.M.H.B.   8:283-287, (1900).
778. Bean, (Mrs.) Robert B.   "The Colonial Church in Virginia." V.M.H.B.
      55:78-84, (1947).
779. Beatty, Joseph M., jr.   "Susan Assheton's Book" P.M.H.B. 55:174-186,
      (1931).
780. Blair, Anne.   "Letter to Martha Braxton." W.M. Quart. ser. 1, 16:174-
      180, (1908).
781. Bland, Sarah.   "Petition." Tyler's Quart. 1:40-41, (1919).
782. Bland, Sarah.   "Sarah Bland." W.M. Quart. ser. 2, 4:202-203, (1924).
783. Boatwright, Eleanor M.   "The Political and Civil Status of Women in
      Georgia, 1783-1860." Ga. H. Quart. 25:301-305, (1941).
784. Boggs, J. Lawrence.   "The Cornelia (Bell) Patterson Letters."
      N.J.H.S. Proc. new series. 15:508-517, (1930), 16:56-67, 186-201
      (1931).
785. Booghers, William F.   "The American Repository." (1883).
786. Booker, Martha.   "Will." Tyler's Quart. 18:171-172 (1937).
787. Bradley, Asa M.   "Hannah Bradley." Granite Monthly 43:315-317 (1911).

788. Bradstreet, Anne. "Will of Anne Bradstreet". Essex Inst. H. Colls. 4:185-190 (1862).
789. Brainard, Jessie M. "Mother Ann's Children in Connecticut. The Enfield Shakers." Conn. Mag. 3:461-474 (1897).
790. Brett, Catharyna. "Letters to Sir Wm. Johnson, 1762." N.Y.H.S. Colls. 6:190-192 (1922).
791. Bronner, Edwin B. "An Early Example of Political Action by Women." Friends H.A. Bull. 43:29-32 (1954).
792. Brown, Margaret L. "Mr. and Mrs. Bingham of Philadelphia." P.M.H.B. 61:286-324 (1937).
793. Browne, Charlotte. "Mrs. Browne's Diary when with Braddock's Army, 1754-1757." V.M.H.B. 32:305-320 (1924).
794. Browning, Charles H. "The Mother of Mary, the Mother of Washington." P.M.H.B. 36:217-221 (1912).
795. Cadbury, Henry J. "Hannah Callowhill and Penn's Second Marriage." P.M.H.B. 81:76-82 (1957).
796. Cadbury, Sarah, ed. "Extracts from the Diary of Mrs. Ann Warder." P.M.H.B. 17:144-461 (1893) 18:51-63 (1894).
797. Callender, Hannah. "Diary." P.M.H.B. 12:432-456 (1888).
798. Calvert, Mary. "Will." Lower Norfolk Co. Antiq. 1:115-116, 119-120 (1895).
799. Camden Co. H.S. Mag. "Manumission of Slaves by Friends." 1:5-6 (1921).
800. Campbell, Amelia D. "Women of New York State in the Revolution." N.Y. State H.A. Quart. 3:155-168 (1922).
801. Carey, Mary "Will." W.M. Quart. ser. 1, 20:289-290 (1912).
802. Carroll, Kenneth L. "Maryland Quakers in the 17th Century." Md. H. Mag. 47:297-312 (1952).
803. Carter, Robert. "Letter." V.M.H.B. 6:88-90 (1898).
804. Carteret, Elizabeth. "Petition." N.J.H.S. Proc. ser. 2 1:33-36 (1867).
805. Cartwright, Elizabeth E. "Will." 1640 Essex Antiq. 1:30-31 (1897).
806. Cary, Harriet. "Diary." Tyler's Quart. 12:160-173 (1931).
807. Chever, George F. "Prosecution of Philip English and his Wife for Witchcraft." Essex Inst. H. Colls. 1:157-181 (1859) 2: see Index (1860) 3:17-29, 67-79, 111-120 (1861).
808. Chever, George F. "Prosecution of Ann Pudeater for Witchcraft, 1692." Essex Inst. H. Colls. 4:37-42, 49-54, (1862).
809. Clapp, Thomas. "Womanhood in Early America." Conn. Mag. 12:233-239 (1908).
810. Clark, David Lee "Brockden Brown and the Rights of Women." Comparative Literature Series, no. 2. Univ. of Texas Bull no. 2212, (1922).
811. Clement, John. "Elizabeth Estaugh and some of her Contemporaries." N.J.H.S. Proc. ser. 3, 7:103-105 (1912).
812. Coates, Albert. "A Century of Legal Education." N.C. Law Rev. 24: 307-401 (1946).
813. Cometti, Elizabeth. "Women in the American Revolution." New Engl. Quart. 20:329-346 (1947).
814. Cook, (Mrs.) Henry L. "Maids for Wives." V.M.H.B. 50:330-332 (1942) 51:71-86 (1943).
815. Cook, Margaret W. "Journal, 1778-1801." Friends Intell. 54, (1897).
816. Corry, J. P. "Some New Light on the Bosomworth Claims." Ga. H. Quart. 25:196-224 (1941).

817. Corry, John P. "The Houses of Colonial Georgia." Ga. H. Quart. 14: 181-201 (1930).

818. Cotton, Ann "An Account of Our Late Troubles in Virginia, 1676." Amer. Col. Tracts Mthly. 1: (no.9, 1898).

819. Cotton, Jane B. "Notes from Early Records of Maryland." Md. H. Mag. 16:279-298,369-385 (1921) 17:60-74,292-308 (1922).

820. Coulter, Ellis M. "A List of the First Shipload of Georgia Settlers." Ga. H. Quart. 31:282-288 (1947).

821. Coulter, Ellis M. "Nancy Hart, Georgia Heroine of the Revolution." Ga. H. Quart 39:118-151 (1955).

822. Coulter, Ellis M. "Mary Musgrove, Queen of the Creeks." Ga. H. Quart. 9:1-30 (1927).

823. Covey, Cyclone. "Puritanism and Music in Colonial America." W.M. Quart. ser. 3, 8:378-388 (1951).

824. Cummings, Joanna "Will, 1644." Essex Antiq. 1:187-188 (1897).

825. Custis, John & Frances. "A Marriage Agreement, 1714." V.M.H.B. 4:64 (1896).

826. Darrach, Henry. "Lydia Darragh of the Revolution." P.M.H.B. 23:86-91 (1899).

827. Davis, Clifton, F. "Cicely Jordan Farrar and Temperance Baley." W. M. Quart. ser. 2, 21:180-183 (1941).

828. Desmond, Alice C. "Mary Philipse: Heiress." N.Y. State H.A. Proc. 45:22-32 (1947).

829. Desmond, Mary E. "The Story of Hannah Dustin." Granite Monthly 31: 287-293 (1901).

830. Dexter, Franklin B. "A Report of the Trial of Ann Hutchinson, 1638." Mass. H.S. Proc. ser. 2, 4:158-192 (1888).

831. Dexter, Franklin B. "Selection from the Correspondence and Miscellaneous Papers of Jared Ingersoll." New Haven Col. H.S. Colls. 9:202-203 (1918).

832. Dexter, Franklin B. "The Removal of Yale College to New Haven in October, 1716." New Haven Col. H.S. Colls. 9:80 (1918).

833. Dillingham, Sarah. "Will, 1636." Essex Antiq. 1:13 (1897).

834. Dole, E. P. "Legal Rights of Married Women in New Hampshire." Granite Monthly 3:264-268 (1880).

835. Downing, Fairfax. "The Governor goes a-wooing." V.M.H.B. 55:6-19 (1947).

836. Drinker, Elizabeth. "Journal of Elizabeth Drinker, 1777-1778." P.M. H.B. 13:298-308 (1889).

837. Drinker, Sophie. "The Two Elizabeth Carterets." N.J.H. Proc. 79 (No. 2) 95-110 (1961).

838. Drummond, Sarah. "Petition for land confiscated after Bacon's Rebellion." V.M.H.B. 22:234-235 (1914).

839. Eckman, Jeannette. "Life among the Early Dutch at New Castle." Del. Hist. 4:246-302 (1950).

840. Edmunds, Alber J. "First Books Imported by America's First Great Library, 1732." (Philadelphia) P.M.H.B. 30:300-308 (1906).

841. Edwards, Mrs. Henry W. "Lady Deborah Moody." Essex Inst. H. Colls. 31:96-102 (1894).

842. Elmer, Lucius Q. "The Constitution and Government of the Province of New Jersey." N.J.H.S. Colls. 7:47-49 (1872).

843. Essex Antiquarian. "Old Norfolk County Records." Essex Antiq. 1:19-24 (1897).

844. Essex Antiquarian. "Spinning in Olden Times." Essex Antiq. 1:51, 87-92, (1897) 4:38 (1900).

845. Essex Institute. "Grants of Land at Salem, Massachusetts." Essex Inst. H. Colls. 4:95-96 (1862).

846. Essex Institute. "Marriage Contract, 1714, between William Moody of Newbury and Abigail Fryer of Berwick." Essex Inst. H. Colls. 81:385-387 (1945).

847. Essex Institute. "Wills, 1640-1645." Essex Inst. H. Colls. 1;3-4 (1859).

848. Eve, Sarah. "Extracts from Journal, 1772." P.M.H.B. 5:19-36, 191-205 (1881).

849. Farmar, Eliza. "Letters to her Nephew, 1774-1783." P.M.H.B. 40:199-207 (1916).

850. Field, Vena B. "Constantia: A Study of the Life and Works of Judith Sargent Murray, 1751-1820." Univ. of Maine Studies. ser. 2, no. 17. 33 (1931).

851. Fisher, J. "Journal of Esther Burr, 1754-1757." New Engl. Quart. 3:297-315 (1930).

852. Flick, Alex C. "Lady Deborah Moody: Grande Dame of Gravesend." Long Is.H.S. Quart. 1:69-75 (1939).

853. Folsom, Joseph F. "Witches in New Jersey." N.J.H.S. Proc. new ser. 7:293-305 (1922).

854. Fowler, S.P. "Records of the Overseers of the Poor, Danvers, 1767-1768." Essex Inst. H. Colls. 2:85-92 (1860).

855. Franklin, Elizabeth. "Letter." N.J.H.S. Proc. ser. 2, 5:127-128 (1877).

856. Freeze, J. G. "Madame Montour." P.M.H.B. 3:79-87 (1879).

857. Goodell, A.C. "Dorothy Lalbie." Essex Inst. H. Colls. 7:129 (1865).

858. Gordon, Ann Isham. "Will." W. M. Quart ser. 1, 14:211-213 (1906).

859. Gould, Elizabeth P. "The Home of Rebecca Nurse." Essex Antiq. 4:135-137 (1900).

860. Gratz, Simon. "Material for a Biography of Mrs. Elizabeth (Graeme) Fergusson." P.M.H.B. 39:257-321,385-409 (1915) 41:385-398 (1917).

861. Gray, Francis C. "Early Laws of Massachusetts." Mass. H.S. Colls. ser. 3, 8:191-237 (1843).

862. Green, Joseph J. "Hannah Penn, Letter." Friends H.S. Journal. 4:133-139 (1907).

863. Green, Samuel A. "Journal, Sargent Holden of Groton. (List of scholars at Townsend School, 1772)." Mass. H.S. Colls. ser. 2, 4:386 (1889).

864. Green, Samuel A. "Trial of Ann Hibbins." Mass. H.S. Colls. ser. 2, 4:313-316 (1889).

865. Gregory, George C. "Nicolas and Jane Martian." V.M.H.B. 42:145-148 (1934).

866. Griscom, (Mrs.) Clement A. "Extracts from Letters of Randolph and Sarah Biddle Tellier, 1789." P.M.H.B. 38:100-109 (1914).

867. Gummere, Amelia M. "Hannah Penn." The Friend. 100:353, 362, 379-380 (1927).

868. Haller, Mabel. "Early Moravian Education in Pennsylvania." Moravian H.S. Trans. 15:1-397 (1953).

869. Hamer, Marguerite B. "Century before Manumission: Sidelights on Slavery in the Mid-18th Century, South Carolina." N.C.H. Rev. 17:

232-236 (1940).
70. Hamer, Marguerite B. "The Foundation and Failure of the Silk Industry in Provincial Georgia." N.C.H. Rev. 12:125-148 (1935).
71. Hamill, Frances. "Some Unconventional Women before 1800: Printers, Booksellers and Collectors." Biblio. S. Papers 49:300-314. (4th quarter, 1955)
72. Harriman, Walter "Mary Woodwell." Granite Monthly, 4:233-239 (1881).
73. Harris, Ralph B. "Philip English." Essex Inst. H. Colls. 66:282-284 (1930).
74. Harrison, Francis B. "Footnotes Upon Some 17th Century Virginians." V.M.H.B. 50:289-299 (1942).
75. Harrison, Sarah. "Will." Tyler's Quart. 9:132 (1927).
76. Hayward, Martha W. "Will." Tyler's Quart. 28:165-166 (1947).
77. Heiges, George L. "Benjamin Franklin in Lancaster County." Lancaster Co. H.S. Journ. 61:3-6 (1957).
78. Heistead, (Mrs.) Henry. "Samuel Blunston, the Man and the Family." Lancaster Co., H .S. Journ. 26:193 (1922).
79. Henry, Mrs. John. "Will." W. M. Quart. ser. 2, 8:117-119 (1928).
80. Hiden, (Mrs.) P. W. "Three Rectors of Hangar's Parish and Their Wife." W. M. Quart. ser. 2, 9:34-41, 299-301 (1939).
81. Hinckley, Robert H. ed. "Selections from the Diary of Christiana Leach, 1765-1796." P.M.H.B. 35:343-349 (1911).
82. Hirsh, Monroe B. "Early Jewish Colony in Lancaster County." Lancaster Co. H.S. Papers 5:91-105 (1901).
83. Hoadly, Charles J. "A Case of Witchcraft in Hartford." Conn. Mag. 5: 557-561 (1899).
84. Holden, James A. "Influence of the Death of Jane McCrea on the Burgoyne Campaign." N.Y. State H. A. Proc. 12:249-294 (1913).
85. Holder, Edward M. "Social Life of the Early Moravians in North Carolina." N.C.H.S. Rev. 11:167-184 (1934).
86. Holman, Mabel C. "Story of Early American Womanhood." Conn. Mag. 11:251-254 (1907).
87. Hoppin, Charles A. "The Bride of Wakefield." Tyler's Quart. 9:224-230 (1928).
88. Hoskins, E. B. ed. "Fanny Salter's Reminicences." P.M.H.B. 40:187-198 (1916).
89. Huguenot Society of South Carolina. re: Judith Manigault Huguenot S.S.C. Trans. 4:48-56 (1897).
90. Hurd-Mead, Kate C. "Medical Women of America." Med. Rev. Rev. 39:101-105 (1933).
91. Hutcheson, Maud M. "Mercy Warren." W. M. Quart. ser. 3, 10:378-402 (1953).
92. Izard, (Mrs.) Ralph. "Letters to Mrs. Wm. Lee." V.M.H.B. 8:16-28 (1900).
93. James, Edward. "Notes on Illiteracy." W. M. Quart. ser. 1, 3:98 (1894).
94. James, Edward W. "The Norfolk Academy, 1785." W. M. Quart. ser. 1, 3:3-8 (1894).
95. James, Edward W. "Grace Sherwood: The Virginia Witch." W. M. Quart. ser. 1, 3:96-101,190-192,242-245 (1894) 4:18-23 (1895).
96. James, Edward W. "Witchcraft in Virginia." W. M. Quart. ser. 1, 1:127-

129 (1891) 2:58-60 (1893).

897. Jervey, Elizabeth H. "Martha Laurens Ramsay. Eulogy." S.C.H.G. Mag. 36:136-137 (1935).

898. Jervey, Th. T. "The Harlestons." S.C.H.G. Mag. 3:154 (1902).

899. Jervey, Th. T. "The White Indentured Servant." S.C.H.G. 12:163-171 (1911).

900. Jervey, Th. T. "Will. Affra Coming." S.C.H.G. Mag. 12:75 (1911).

901. Johnson, Fred C. "Pioneer Physicians of Wyoming Valley (Pennsylvania)." Wyoming H. G. S. Mag. 55-58 (May 11, 1888).

902. Keidel, George C. "Catonsville Biographies: Mrs. Richard Caton, nee Mary Carroll." Md. H. Mag. 17: 74-88, (1922).

903. Keith, Charles P. "The Wife and Children of Sir William Keith." P.M.H.B. 56:1-8 (1932).

904. Kelker, Luther R. ed. "List of Patients, Marine Hospital, Philadelphia, 1784." P.M.H.B. 26:92-100 (1902).

905. Keyes, Homer Eaton. "Coincidence and Henrietta Johnston." Antiques. 16:490-494 (1929).

906. Kiefer, Sr. Monica. "Early American Childhood in the Middle Atlantic Area." P.M.H.B. 68:3-37 (1944).

907. Le Noble, Catherine. "Will of Catherine Le Noble." Huguenot S.S.C. Trans. 13:25-31 (1906).

908. London, City of. "Order to Bring Children." V.M.H.B. 6:232 (1899).

909. Lower Norfolk County (Va.) Antiquary "Witchcraft." Lower Norfolk Co. Antiq. 1:20-21, 56 (1895) 3:34-38, 52-57 (1899).

910. Lowle, Elizabeth. "Will." Essex Antiq. 4:154 (1900).

911. Ludwell, Phill. "Boundary Line Proceedings, 1710." V.M.H.B. 5:9-10 (1897).

912. Lutz, Alma. "Early American Women Historians." Boston, Publ. Libr. Quart 8:85-99 (1956).

913. Lyman, Susan E. "Three New York Women of the Revolution." N. Y. H. S. Quart. 29:77-82 (1945).

914. McArthur, (Mrs.) J. L. "Women of the Revolution." N.Y. State H.A. Proc. 5:153-161 (1905).

915. McKinstry, Mary T. "Silk Culture in the Colony of Georgia." Ga. H. Quart. 14:225-235 (1930).

916. McLean, (Mrs.) Donald. "The Baroness de Riedesel." N.Y. State H.A. Proc. 3:39-44 (1903).

917. McVickar, Estelle R. "Anne Hutchinson: Her Life in New York." N.Y. State H. A. Proc. 9:256-266 (1910).

918. Macon, Elizabeth. "Will." W. M. Quart. ser. 1, 14:265-267 (1906).

919. Marble, Annie Russel. "Mistress Mercy Warren." New Engl. Mag. new ser. 28:163-180 (1903).

920. Maryland Historical Magazine. "First Grants of Land in Maryland." Md. H. Mag. 3:158-169 (1908).

921. Maryland Historical Magazine. "Land Office Records, 1634-1655." Md. H. Mag. 5:166-167, 170, 172, 193, 263, 264, 369, (1910).

922. Mather, Cotton. "Diary, 1687-1708." 2 vols. Mass. H. S. Colls. ser. 7, 8 (1911-1912).

923. Maurer, Maurer. "Music in Wachovia." W. M. Quart. ser. 3, 8:214-227 (1951).

24. Maxwell, William, ed. "My Mother: Helen Calvert Maxwell Read." Lower Norfolk Co. Antiq. Vol.1: 60-62, 96-102, 109-121; Vol. 2: 24-33, 56-61, 79-81, 132-138; Vol. 3: 24-29, 46-50, (1895-1900).

25. Meloon, Everett Scott. "A New Hampshire Heroine." Granite Monthly 60:22-25 (1928).

26. Miller, Elizabeth K. "An Ephrata Hymnal." Antiques 51:260-262 (1947).

27. Mills, Emma L. "How Molly Saved the Fort." Granite Monthly 14:276-281 (1892).

28. Moller, Herbert. "Sex Composition and Correlated Culture Patterns of Colonial America." W. M. Quart. ser. 3, 2:113-153 (1945).

29. Morgan, Edmund S. "The Case against Anne Hutchinson." New Engl. Quart. 10:635-649 (1937).

30. Morgan, Edmund S. "The Puritans and Sex." New Engl. Quart. 15:591-607 (1942).

31. Morris, Anna W. "The Romance of Two Hannahs." Newport H. S. Bull 46: (1923).

32. Mowatt, Charles S. "St. Augustine under the British Flag." Fla. Hist. Soc. Quart. 20:131-150 (1941).

33. Munroe, Sarah. "Letter." Md. H. Mag. 29:245-252 (1934).

34. Murray, Anne W. "The Attitude of the Eagle as Portrayed on an Outstanding Group of 'Liberty' Quilts." Antiques, 51:28-30 (1947).

35. Needles, S. H. "The Governor's Mill and Globe Mills." P.M.H.B. 8: 285-293 (1884).

36. Neible, George W. "Servants and Apprentices Bound and Assigned before James Hamilton, Mayor of Philadelphia, 1745." P.M.H.B. 30: 31: 32. See contents in each volume. (1906-1908).

37. New Jersey Historical Society. "Morris Academy." N.J.H.S. Proc. ser. 1 8:18-31 (1856).

38. New Jersey Historical Society. "Copy of a Minute Book of Nottingham Township, 1692-1710." N.J.H.S. Proc. 58:24, 129, 189-190 (1940).

39. Newsome, A. R. Ed. "Records of Emigrants from England and Scotland to North Carolina, 1774-1775." N.C.H. Rev. 11:39-54, 129-142 (1934).

40. New York Historical Society. re. "Attorneys." N.Y.H.S. Colls. 78:108-110 (1945).

41. New York Historical Society. "Tax list of persons in New Amsterdam who had 1000 guilders or more, 1674." N. Y. H. S. Colls. ser. 2 1:387-388 (1841).

42. New York Historical Society. "Burghers and Freemen." N. Y. H. S. Publ. Fund No. 18. see Index (1885).

43. Nicklin, John B. C. "Benjamin Strother and his Wives." Tyler's Quart. 19:224-225 (1938).

44. Norton, Milo L. "A Mistery Solved." Conn. Quart. 2:59-65 (1896).

45. Oldham, Ellen M. "Early Women Printers of America." Boston Publ. Libr. Quart. Jan:6-26, Apr.:78-92 Jly:141-150 (1958).

46. Palmer, Esther. "Journal, 1704-1705." Friends H. S. Journ. 6:38-40, 63-71, 133-139 (1909).

47. Panagopoulos, E. P. "The Background of the Greek Settlers in the New Smyrna Colony." Fla. H.Q.Rev. 35:95-115 (1956).

48. Parke, Francis N. "Witchcraft in Maryland." Md. H. Mag. 31:271-298 (1936).

949. Parker, Amelia C. "Baroness Riedesel and Other Women in Burgoyne's Army." N. Y. State H.A. Proc. 26:109-119 (1928).
950. Pendleton, Emily & Ellis, Milton. "Philenia, Life and Works of Sarah Wentworth Morton." Univ. of Maine Bull. 34 (1931) Studies, ser. 2, No. 20 (1931).
951. Peniston, Elizabeth. "Will." V.M.H.B. 48:104-105 (1940).
952. Pennsylvania Magazine of History and Biography. "Free Society of Traders, 1682." P.M.H.B. 11:175-180 (1887).
953. Pennsylvania Magazine of History and Biography. "Narrative of Marie Le Roy and Barbara Leininger." P.M.H.B. 29:407-420 (1905).
954. Pennsylvania Magazine of History and Biography. "Sentiments of an American Woman, 1776." P.M.H.B. 18:361-366 (1894).
955. Perley, Sidney. "Methods of Heating in Olden Times." Essex Antiq. 1:183-186 (1897).
956. Perley, Sidney. "Moll Pitcher." Essex Antiq. 3:33-35 (1899).
957. Perley, Sidney. "Persecution of Quakers in Essex County." Essex Antiq. 1:135-140 (1897).
958. Pew, William A. "The Right Honorable Lady Arbella and Her Friends." Essex Inst. H. Colls. 66:395-410 (1930).
959. Philbrick, Eliza. "Spinning in the Olden Times." Essex Antiq. 1:87-92 (1897).
960. Philbrook, Mary. "Woman's Suffrage in New Jersey Prior to 1807." N.J.H.S. Proc. 57:87-98 (1939).
961. Porter, Helen C. ed. "Will of Mary Washington, 1788." Conn. Mag. 11: 216 (1907).
962. Powell, Chilton L. "Marriage in Early New England." New Engl. Quart. 1:323-334 (1928).
963. Powers, Grant. "A Frontier Heroine: Mrs. Richard Wallace." Granite State Mag. 6:55-56 (1910-11).
964. Prior, Mary B. "Letters of Martha Logan, 1760-1763." S.C.H.G. Mag. 59:38-46 (1958).
965. Putnam, Eben. "Danvers Tax List, 1775." Essex Inst. H. Colls. 29: 181-183 (1892).
966. Putnam, Ruth. "Annetje Jan's Farm." Half Moon Series 1:61-98 (1897).
967. Quynn, Dorothy M. "Flora MacDonald in History." N.C.H. Rev. 18:236-258 (1941).
968. Rawle, Anna. "Diary Extracts: A Loyalist's Account of Certain Occurances in Philadelphia after Cornwallis' Surrender at Yorktown." P.M.H.B. 16:103-107 (1892).
969. Rawle, William B. "First Tax List, Philadelphia." P.M.H.B. 8:82-105 (1884).
970. Redman, Alice. "Petition of a Nurse of the Revolution." Md. H. Mag. 17:379 (1922).
971. Reninger, Marion. "Susanna Wright." Lancaster Co. H.S. Journ. 63: 183-189 (1959).
972. Riley, Edward M. "Deborah Franklin Correspondence." Amer. Philosophical Soc. Proc. 95:239-245 (1951).
973. Robbins, Fred G. "Witchcraft." Essex Inst. H. Colls. 65:209-239 (1929).
974. Rowland, Kate M. "The Experience of Mrs. Elizabeth Diggs." W. M. Quart. ser. 1, 4:22-23 (1896).

975. Rubincam, Milton. "Lydia Wright and Her Sisters." N. J. H. S. Proc. 58:103-118 (1940).
976. Rutherford, John. "Notes on the State of New Jersey, written in 1776." N. J. H. S. Proc. ser. 2, 1:85-86 (1867).
977. Rutledge, Anna W. "Artists in the Life of Charleston." Amer. Philosophical Soc. Trans. new ser. 39, pt. 2 (1949).
978. Rutledge, Anna W. "Charleston's First Artistic Couple." Antiques. 52:101-102 (1947).
979. Sachse, Julius F. "The Registers of the Ephrata Community." P. M. H. B. 14:394-402 (1890).
980. St. John, Robert P. "Jemima Wilkinson." N. Y. State H. A. Quart. 11: 158-175. (1930).
981. Salley, Alexander S. "Bibliography of Women Writers in South Carolina." S.H.A. Publ. 6 (1902).
982. Salley, Alexander S. "Col. Miles Bruton." S.C.H.G. Mag. 2:148-151 (1901).
983. Salley, Alexander S. "The First Presses of South Carolina." Biblio. Soc. Proc. 2:28-69 (1908).
984. Sanborn, (Mrs.) Alvah H. "The Newport Mercury." Newport H. S. Bull. 65:1-11 (1929).
985. Sass, Herbert R. "Love and Miss Lucas." Ga. Rev. 10:312-320 (1956).
986. Sawyer, William. "Governor Printz's Daughter." Pa. H. Mag. 25: 109-114 (1958).
987. Sayles, Lucy B. "A Brave Knight of the 17th Century." Conn. Mag. 7: 334-338 (1902).
988. Scarlet, Anne. "Will, 1643." Essex Antiq. 1:100-101 (1897).
989. Schlesinger, Elizabeth B. "Cotton Mather and His Children." W. M. Quart. ser. 3, 10:181-189 (1953).
990. Scisco, Louis Dow. "People of Early Charles County." Md. H. Mag. 23:44-363 (1928).
991. Searle, Lucy. "Memoirs of Mrs. Sarah Atkins." Essex Inst. H. Colls. 85:151-180 (1949).
992. Sellards, E. H. "The Indian Captivity of Jennie Wiley." Tyler's Quart. 31:256-262 (1950).
993. Sewall, Samuel. "Diary." 3 vols. Mass. H. S. Colls. 5, 6, 7, (1878-1882).
994. Shinn, Henry C. "An Early New Jersey Poll List." P.M.H.B. 44:77-81 (1920).
995. Shipton, Clifford K. "Secondary Education in the Puritan Colonies." New Engl. Quart. 7:646-661 (1934).
996. Sinnickson, Leora. "Frederika, Baroness Riedesel." P.M.H.B. 30: 385-408 (1906).
997. Sioussat, Anna "Colonial Women of Maryland." Md. H. Mag. 2:214-226 (1907).
998. Smith, H. A. "Charleston - Original Plan, Early Settlers." S.C.H.G. Mag. 9:12-27, 85-101, 152-160 (1908).
999. Smith, Thelma M. "Feminism in Philadelphia." P.M.H.B. 68:243-268 (1944).
1000. Sonneck, O. G. "Early Concerts in America (before 1750)." New Music Rev. 5:952-957 (1906).

1001. South Carolina Historical and Geneological Magazine. "Emily Geiger." S. C. H. G. Mag. 2:90-91 (1901).

1002. South Carolina Historical and Geneological Magazine. "Mary Fisher Crosse and S. Hume." S. C. H. G. Mag. 12:106-108 (1911).

1003. Southall, James P. "Lady Yardley and Cicely Farrar." V. M. H. B. 50: 74-80 (1942) 51:83, 381-382 (1943) 55:259-266 (1947).

1004. Spalletta, Matteo. "Divorce in Colonial New York." N. Y.H.S. Quart. 39:422-440 (1955).

1005. Spruill, Julia C. "Mistress Margaret Brent, Spinster." Md. H. Mag. 29:259-268 (1934).

1006. Spruill, Julia C. "Southern Housewives before the Revolution." N. C. H. Rev. 13:25-46 (1936).

1007. Spruill, Julia C. "Virginia and Carolina Homes before the Revolution." N. C. H. Rev. 12:320-340 (1935).

1008. Spruill, Julia C. "Women in the Founding of the Southern Colonies." N. C. H. Rev. 13:202-218 (1936).

1009. Stafford, Sarah S. "The Flag of the 'Bon Homme Richard'." N. J. H. S. Proc. ser. 2, 2:193-194 (1871).

1010. Stearns, Bertha M. "Early Philadelphia Magazines for Ladies." P. M. H. B. 64:479-482 (1940).

1011. Stith, Elizabeth. "Will." W. M. Quart. ser. 1, 5:113-117 (1896).

1012. Sweeney, John A. H., ed. "The Norris-Fisher Correspondence -- A Circle of Friends." Del. H. Mag., 6:187-232 (1955).

1013. Sweeny, William M. "A Virginian Pre-nuptial Agreement of 1678." Tyler's Quart. 22:139-141 (1941).

1014. Tandy, Elizabeth. "Our Colonial Heritage of Community Medicine." N. Y. State H. A. Quart. 4:49-54 (1923).

1015. Taylor, E. W. "Hannah Dustin." Granite Monthly 43:177-183 (1911) 46: 207-214 (1914).

1016. Temple, Anne. "Will." W. M. Quart. ser. 1, 13:140 (1904).

1017. Terry, Roderick. "Experiences of a Minister's Wife in the American Revolution; the Sufferings of Rebecca Foote of Branford, Connecticut." Conn. Mag. 11:523-532 (1907).

1018. Thompson, Henry F., ed. "Letters of Rebecca Franks." P. M. H. B. 16:216 (1892).

1019. Thomson, Hannah. "Letters, 1785-88." P. M. H. B. 14:28-40 (1890).

1020. Tilden, Olive M. "Hannah Adams." Dedham H. S. Register 7:83-100 (1896).

1021. Titus, Anson, ed. "Madame Knight: Her Diary and Times." Boston, Soc. Publ. 9:99-126, (1912).

1022. Torrence, Clayton. "A Virginia Lady of Quality and Her Possessions." V. M. H. B. 56:42-56 (1948).

1023. Tucker, Jona. "Old Schools and School Teachers." Essex Inst. H. Colls. 7:241-243 (1865).

1024. Turner, Edward R. "Women's Suffrage in New Jersey." Smith College Studies in History." 1 (July, 1916).

1025. Tyler, Lyon G. "Grammar and Mattey Practice: Model School Founded by Mrs. Mary Whaley in 1706." W. M. Quart. ser. 1, 4:1-14 (1895).

1026. Tyler, Lyon G., ed. "Letters Extracted from County Record Books." W. M. Quart. ser. 1,4:77-78, 169-177 (1896).

27. Tyler, Lyon G. "Education in Colonial Virginia Free Schools." W. M. Quart. ser. 1, 5:219-223 (1897) 6:1-6, 71-85 (1898).

28. Tyler, Lyon G. "Lady Virginia Murray and Her Alleged Claim Against the State of Virginia." W. M. Quart. ser. 1, 24:85-101 (1915).

29. Tyler, Lyon G. "School Teachers in Virginia." W. M. Quart. ser. 1, 7: 178 (1899).

30. Tyler's Quarterly. "Lady Flowerdew Yardley." Tyler's Quart. 2:115-129 (1921).

31. Vaux, George. "Callender, Hannah; Extracts from Her Diary." P. M. H. B. 12:432-456 (1888).

32. Vaux, George. "Rees Thomas and Martha Aubrey; Early Settlers in Merion." P. M. H. B. 13:292-297 (1889).

33. Vawter, Mary H. M. "A Few Virginia Ancestors and Their Doings." Tyler's Quart. 31:82-99, 187-200 (1949-50).

34. Virginia Gazette. 1769. "Ladies of the Association: A Notice." W. M. Quart. ser. 1, 8:36 (1899).

35. Virginia Magazine of History and Biography. "Nurses in the Army, 1778." V. M. H. B. 14:186-187 (1907).

36. Virginia Magazine of History and Biography. "A Marriage Agreement, 1714." V. M. H. B. 4:64-66 (1896).

37. Virginia Magazine of History and Biography. "The Trapanned Maiden." V. M. H. B. 4:218-220 (1896).

38. Wainwright, Nicholas B. "Plan of Philadelphia." P. M. H. B. 80:164-176 (1956).

39. Walker, Lewis B. "Life of Margaret Shippen." P. M. H. B. 24, 25, 26, see index (1900).

40. Waring, Martha G. "Savannah's Earliest Private Schools." Ga. H. Quart. 14:324, 334 (1930).

41. Warren, Charles. "Elbridge Gerry, James Warren and Mercy Warren and the Ratification of the Constitution." Mass. H. S. Proc. 64: 143-164 (1932).

42. Washington, George. "Account Book." P. M. H. B. 29:385-406 (1905) 30:30-56, 159-186, 309-331, 459-478(1906) 31:53-82, 176-194, 320-350, (1907).

43. Waters, T. F. "Sketch of J. Winthrop." Mass. H. S. Colls. ser. 4, 7: see Index (1865).

44. Webber, Mabel L. "Extracts from the Journal of Mrs. Ann Manigault, 1754-1781." S. C. H. G. Mag. 20:57-63, 128-141, 204-212, 256-259 (1919) 21:10-23, 59-72, 112-120 (1920).

45. Webber, Mabel L. "Records of the Quakers." S. C. H. G. Mag. 28:24, 98, 105, 106, 178 (1927).

46. Wells, Mary B. "Some New Hampshire Witches." Granite State Mag. 5: 293-296 (1908).

47. Wendell, Barrett. "Were the Salem Witches Guiltless?" Essex Inst. H. Colls. 29:129-147 (1892).

48. Werner, Raymond C. ed. "Diary of Grace G. Galloway." P. M. H. B. 58: 152-189 (1934).

49. Whaley, Mary. "Will." W. M. Quart. ser. 1, 4:13-14 (1895).

50. Whipple, Sherman L. & Waters, Thomas F. "Puritan Homes." Ipswich H. S. Publs. 27:1-86 (1929).

1051. White, Elizabeth W. "The Tenth Muse - a Tercentenary Appraisal of Anne Bradstreet." W. M. Quart. ser. 3, 8:355-377 (1951).

1052. Whitehead, W. A. "A Brief Statement of the Facts Connected with the Origin, Practices, and Prohibition of Female Suffrage in New Jersey." N. J. H. S. Proc. ser. 1, 8:101-105 (1856).

1053. William and Mary Quarterly. "Mary Brough, Innkeeper." W. M. Quart. ser. 1, 12:82 (1904).

1054. William and Mary Quarterly. "Census of Tithables." W. M. Quart. ser. 1, 8:161-164 (1899).

1055. William and Mary Quarterly. "Sarah Hallam." W. M. Quart. ser. 1, 12: 236-237 (1904).

1056. William and Mary Quarterly. "Heroines, Virginia." W. M. Quart. ser. 1, 15:39-41 (1906).

1057. William and Mary Quarterly. "Libraries in Colonial Virginia." W. M. Quart. ser. 1, 3:246-248 (1894).

1058. William and Mary Quarterly. "Midwifery." W. M. Quart. ser. 2, 2:204 (1922).

1059. William and Mary Quarterly. "Nurse at College." W. M. Quart. ser. 1, 3:131 (1894).

1060. William and Mary Quarterly. "Virginia, Several Early Physicians." W. M. Quart. ser. 1, 14:96-100 (1905).

1061. Williams, Hannah, E. "Early Letters from South Carolina upon Natural History." S. C. H. G. Mag. 21:3-9 (1920).

1062. Willis, Eola. "The First Woman Painter in America." International Studio. pp. 13-20 (July, 1927).

1063. Willis, Eola. "Henrietta Johnston." Antiquarian. 11:46-48 (1929).

1064. Winsley, Ann. "Estate of Ann Winsley." Essex Inst. H. Colls. 7:71-72 (1865).

1065. Wisbey, Herbert A. "Portrait of a Prophetress (Jemima Wilkinson)." N. Y. State H. A. Quart. 38:387-396 (1957).

1066. Wister, Sally. "Journal Extracts." P. M. H. B. 9:318-333, 463-478 (1885) 10:51-56 (1886).

1067. Withington, Lathrop. "Virginia Gleanings in England." V. M. H. B. 18: 83 (1910).

1068. Woodruff, Mary R., ed. "Marriage Contract." Conn. Mag. 1:110.(1907).

1069. Worcester Society of Antiquity. Colls. 2(1800) 3(1881) 4(1882).

1070. Worcester Society of Antiquity. Bulletins. Bull. 16 (1898).

1071. Worth, H enry B. "Nantucket Lands and Landowners." Nantucket H. A. Bull. 2:75-76, 306 (1901).

1072. Worthen, Samuel C. "Witches in New Jersey and Elsewhere." N. J. H. S. Proc. new ser. 8:139-143 (1923).

1073. Worthington, Erastus. "Widow Mary Draper." Dedham H. S. Register. 7:1-6 (1896).

1074. Wylie, J.C. "Mrs. Washington's Book of Cookery." P.M.H.B. 27:436-440 (1903).

PICTORIAL PUBLICATIONS

075. Adams, James T.   Album of American History. New York, Charles
        Scribner's Sons, 1944.
076. Bolton, Charles K.   Portraits of the Founders. Boston, The Boston
        Atheneum, 1919.
077. Bonte, G. W.   America Marches Past. New York, D. Appleton Century
        Co., 1936.
078. Collins, Alan C.   The Story of America in Pictures. New York, Doubleday
        & Co., 1953.
079. Davidson, Marshall B.   Life in America. 2 vols. Houghton Mifflin Co.,
        1951.
080. Frost, John.   Pictorial History of the United States. 4 vols. Philadelphia,
        E. H. Butler, 1843.
081. Lossing, B. J.   Pictorial Field Book of the American Revolution. 2 vols.
        New York, Harper Bros., 1860.
082. Pageant of America: A Pictorial History of the United States. New Haven,
        Conn., Yale University Press, 1927.

ADDENDA

Drinker, Sophie H.   "Votes for Women in 18th Century New Jersey. Proc.
    N.J.H.S. Vol. 80 (Jan., 1962).

Drinker, Sophie H.   "Women Attorneys of Colonial Times." Md. H. Mag.
    Vol. 56:335-351 (1961).